NARROW GAUGE MODELLING IN 009 SCALE

NARROW GAUGE MODELLING IN 009 SCALE

BOB BARNARD

THE CROWOOD PRESS

First published in 2019 by
The Crowood Press Ltd
Ramsbury, Marlborough
Wiltshire SN8 2HR

www.crowood.com

© Bob Barnard 2019

All rights reserved. No part of this publication may be reproduced or transmitted in any form or by any means, electronic or mechanical, including photocopy, recording, or any information storage and retrieval system, without permission in writing from the publishers.

British Library Cataloguing-in-Publication Data
A catalogue record for this book is available from the British Library.

ISBN 978 1 78500 525 1

Dedication
This book is dedicated to Sue, who tolerates a house full of narrow gauge layouts with good grace.

Acknowledgements
Challenges from John de Frayssinet made me aim for higher modelling standards. In preparing this book I have been helped by Mike Bayly, David Prime, Paul Titmuss, Mick Thornton and Garry Whiting. Information about the Raleigh Weir worksite came from Tony Nicholson and Keith Vingoe of the Lynton & Barnstaple Railway Trust. Sue gave me editorial advice and made many cups of tea.

Photographs are by the author unless otherwise credited.

Typeset by Jean Cussons Typesetting, Diss, Norfolk

Printed and bound in India by Replika Press Pvt Ltd

CONTENTS

	PREFACE	6
1	**INTRODUCTION**	9
2	**MAKING A START IN 009**	19
3	**PLANNING A LAYOUT**	36
4	**LAYOUT CONSTRUCTION**	58
5	**LOCOMOTIVES**	74
6	**EXAMPLE LOCOMOTIVE PROJECTS**	96
7	**ROLLING STOCK**	127
8	**OPERATION, CONTROL AND SIGNALLING**	142
9	**MAKING THE MOST OF A 009 LAYOUT**	160
10	**EXHIBITING AND PHOTOGRAPHING A 009 LAYOUT**	174
	APPENDIX: SUPPLIERS OF 009 PRODUCTS	187
	INDEX	191

PREFACE

Railways, and model railways, have always been part of my life. My father began his career working for the Southern Railway (SR), so he made sure that we paused to watch trains whenever possible during family outings.

Aged seven or so, I was given a Tri-Ang 00 scale train set, and my father used this as an excuse to begin (or resume) making models himself – tinplate (and later nickel silver) 00 scale SR engines. I read the model railway magazines, where my inspiration came principally from Peter Denny's descriptions of his magnificent Buckingham branch layout, but also from other fine modellers of the period.

As I entered my teens, I began building SR locos for the 00 scale layout that my father and I had built together. Having gained some basic engineering

My first scratchbuilt locomotive, an ex-SER O1 0-6-0 dating from the early 1960s.

Holidaying in Devon in 1962, we spent a showery day following the course of the long-closed Lynton & Barnstaple Railway. We drove along a section that had since become a road, admired the impressive Chelfham viaduct, and found the former stations, such as Lynton (pictured here).

Returning from Devon, I found my father's first edition of L.T. Catchpole's book **The Lynton & Barnstaple Railway***, and began to consider, aged twelve, how I could make models of the narrow gauge engines pictured within.* L.T. CATCHPOLE

PREFACE

Our 1963 family holiday was to North Wales, staying near the Ffestiniog Railway (FR). I was now completely 'hooked' on narrow gauge steam trains, and a few years later joined the Ffestiniog Railway Society. This FR train was later photographed arriving at Porthmadog Harbour station.

I have modelled other railways, including the Glyn Valley Tramway, whose short locomotives and rolling stock allowed me to squeeze a tiny layout into a cupboard in a small flat.

skills from Meccano and other construction toys, I began assembling whitemetal kits, later progressing to scratchbuilding.

Alongside other hobbies, my engineering studies at university, and then work, marriage and family, my interest in narrow gauge in general, and the Lynton & Barnstaple in particular, never left me.

My liking for unusual locomotives led to other projects, including American geared logging locomotives (after visiting Cass, West Virginia, and having had a cab ride in Oregon).

I steadily developed a set of simple, reasonably time-efficient techniques for making robust 009 layouts and rolling stock. The model railway hobby has moved on a long way in fifty years, but I find that my well-tried techniques usually suit me best – supplemented by modern products and techniques.

For many years I was a solitary modeller. I sometimes bought modelling magazines, but did not belong to a model railway club or participate in modelling projects with others. However, I did join

I modelled some War Department Light Railways (WDLR) locomotives, such as this Alco 2-6-2T seen on the Haute Somme railway in Northern France.

My interest in Beyer Garratts was awakened by the arrival of NGG16s on the Welsh Highland Railway.

the 009 Society. I also joined one or two narrow gauge railway societies, and began to participate (from a distance) with the Lynton & Barnstaple Railway Trust. I still modelled alone, but received great assistance with the details of my L&B models from various knowledgeable L&B Trust members, via email and also in face-to-face discussions. With the advent of on-line discussion groups, I finally became more 'social', enjoying the interaction with others and admiring their skills, which often surpassed or complemented my own abilities.

In retirement, I began attending local 009 Society group meetings, enjoying the modelling discussions that took place there. As a result, I have friends around the world. I value their knowledge and opinions, and I enjoy trying to help them.

The wide range of 009 modellers' interests: the part-complete Backwoods Lyn, described later in this book, dwarfs a small industrial diesel on Paul Titmuss's Melton Market layout at a local 009 Society meeting.

CHAPTER ONE

INTRODUCTION

This book gives a personal impression of the subject of narrow gauge railway modelling in 009 scale. There is room for alternative opinions and techniques, but it describes a set of tried-and-tested methods. It discusses the complex questions of scale and gauge for narrow gauge model railways, and arrives at a working definition of what is covered by 009 scale, and outlines the origins and history of 009 modelling. It highlights the work of a few influential pioneers who encouraged the adoption of the scale among modellers, and identifies the range of skills needed to create a scale model railway, along with any particular skills needed by the 009 modeller.

The range of prototype narrow gauge railways is then considered, along with some of the different traditions and practices adopted by such railways in different parts of the world. Some thoughts are presented on how a modeller may select a subject for a model in the light of available commercial products, and the different levels of challenge that particular prototypes may present. The book then covers the construction of a 009 layout, locomotives and rolling stock, the control of layouts, and their maintenance and improvement.

Throughout, the book considers the challenges involved in representing an actual historical prototype. Other options give the modeller licence to deviate from historical accuracy to a greater or lesser extent, and this may simplify their task. The example projects draw lessons from some existing models, as well as giving step-by-step descriptions of projects undertaken in the course of preparing the book.

Finally the book touches on the challenges of exhibiting models, and suggests how help can be obtained from other modellers.

SCALE AND GAUGE

It would be good if the subject of scale and gauge were simple to explain, but for historical reasons it is quite complex.

SCALE

The scale of a model is quite simple: it is the ratio of the model size to that of the original. So, for example, a scale of 1 to 4 or 1:4 would represent a quarter-scale model. If the original were 1m long, the model would be 0.25m long.

The 1ft 11½in gauge track with 40lb/yard rail, near Parracombe, Devon. W. W. DUNNING

GAUGE

The gauge of railway track is the nominal distance between the inner edges of the running rails. What is commonly called 'standard gauge', used widely on full-size railways around the world, is 4ft 8½in (1,435mm). Certain counties have adopted slightly different gauges for their national networks, including 5ft (1,520mm), 5ft 3in (1,600mm) and 5ft 6in (1,667mm). These are referred to generically as 'broad gauge'.

In Britain, specialist suppliers and amateur model engineers, seeking interoperability, had long built their live-steam engines to run on one of a series of standardized track gauges, which originally included Gauge 5 (5in, 127mm), Gauge 3 (3½in, 89mm), Gauge 2 (2½in, 64mm), Gauge 1 (1¾in, 45mm) and Gauge 0 (1¼in, 32mm).

There was a practice amongst model engineers of providing their live-steam engines with somewhat oversized boilers, to ensure reliable steaming. So from the earliest days the scale of a locomotive model might not be strictly correct for the gauge of track it runs on.

Between World Wars I and II, the tradition of model railways spread from the well-off to a wider section of the population. These new modellers had more modest homes than their wealthier predecessors, so Gauge 0 models became more popular than the larger sizes, as they required less space and were inherently less expensive. Gauge 0, with its 1¼in (32mm) gauge track, is understood in Britain to be built to 1:43.5 scale.

Between the wars, some skilled modellers without sufficient space for a Gauge 0 railway in their homes began to adopt a smaller, H0 (presumably Half-0) scale of 1:87 on 16.5mm gauge track. With this scale, the larger continental and British main-line locomotives could be built quite feasibly, but the smaller dimensions of older British prototypes (with small boilers) presented challenges because of the size of the electric motors available at the time.

00 scale was the less-than-ideal solution, retaining the 16.5mm track gauge of H0, but increasing the size of the rolling stock to permit electric motors to be accommodated. This process was somewhat analogous to the provision of oversized boilers on live-steam models.

Once a scale/gauge combination is widely adopted, familiarity leads to the terms 'scale' and 'gauge' being used interchangeably – so 00 scale becomes 00 gauge.

00 gauge, because it originated as the next logical scale in a series including Gauges 3, 2, 1 and 0, is correctly written as 00 (that is, zero zero). In speech it is usually called 'O-O' or 'Double-O' (that is, with the letter 'O').

IMPERIAL VERSUS METRIC

Steam locomotives in Britain were generally built to imperial measurements (feet, inches and fractions of an inch). However, few modellers nowadays would find it easy to work in fractions of an inch – who can easily say what $^{17}/_{32}$in + $^{3}/_{16}$in is? – so metric dimensions (metres and decimal sub-divisions of a metre) are universal for modelling.

As the scale for our models we need a value in millimetres that corresponds to a round figure in imperial measurements. The originators of 00 scale probably thought 'H0 scale (3.5mm = 1ft, 1:87) is a bit small and will be difficult to convert, so let's make 4mm = 1ft.'

4mm = 1ft (4mm/1ft, 1:76.2) turns out to be quite convenient to work with, as 1mm = 3in, 2mm = 6in, and so on. So, 2ft 9in diameter wheels can easily be converted to 11mm (2ft = 8mm, 9in = 3mm, 8+3 = 11). Those who possess imperial micrometers, which measure accurately in thousandths of an inch (thou), also find that conversion is straightforward, as 1mm is quite close to 40-thou.

Thus the scale adopted for 00 gauge models became 1:76.2 (often approximated to 1:76).

MODELLING STANDARD GAUGE

A so-called 'standard gauge' railway, with a nominal 4ft 8½in (1,435mm) track gauge, should theoretically convert to 4ft 8½in in the model scale. In 4mm/1ft scale, the track gauge should be 18.83mm gauge, and different groups of finescale modellers have adopted various closer approximations to this

INTRODUCTION | 11

value than the 16.5mm gauge of 00, the commonest historically being EM (18mm). Now, there is a significant following for 'Protofour' or 'P4' standards, using the correct 18.83mm track.

NARROW GAUGE

'Narrow gauge' railways have a track gauge that is less than standard gauge, and many different gauges have been used on such lines, in Britain and around the world.

Data for public narrow gauge railways in the British Isles around 1920 shows the following mileage for different gauges.

These gauges cannot really be categorized, but there are arguably two groups (highlighted blue and yellow in the table below) that have seen widespread use in slightly different applications:

- Gauges adopted for large-scale national or regional networks, operating trains of similar

This photograph clearly illustrates the difference in size between standard gauge and narrow gauge wagons. R. SHEPHERD

size and weight to standard gauge, but making use of the narrower track gauge to permit tighter curves, thereby reducing civil engineering costs in difficult terrain. These gauges include

Gauge (mm)	381	508	597–610	686	710	724	762	800	914	1,000	1,067	1,200
Mileage	7.25	0.25	75.8	25.5	3.25	8.25	21.8	5	572	0	31	6.5
Per cent mileage	0.96	0.03	10	3.37	0.43	1.09	2.88	0.66	75.6	0	4.1	0.86
Per cent groups			17.77						79.7			

A loco and train similar in size to British mainline stock on the metre gauge Brünig railway in Switzerland.

the 3ft (914mm), used in Ireland, the Isle of Man and some colonial networks, as well as metre gauge (1,000mm) and its imperial near-equivalent 3ft 6in (1,067mm) used on many large-scale networks with considerable mileages
- Gauges adopted for industrial systems and shorter feeders into the main lines. Originating with the 1ft 11½in (597mm) gauge of the Ffestiniog Railway, serving slate quarries in North Wales and replacing a horse-drawn tramway, this gauge (or often 60cm, a fraction more, or 2ft (610mm)) was also used by the Welsh Highland, Vale of Rheidol and Lynton & Barnstaple railways, and on secondary lines overseas. It was widely used in particular industries – for example, sugar – as well as supporting trench warfare in World War I. Other similar types of line used various gauges between 2ft and 2ft 6in

In 00 scale, the yellow group of lines would correctly run on track of various gauges between 8mm and 10mm, and the blue group on track between 12mm and 14mm gauge.

MODEL SCALE/GAUGE COMBINATIONS

The track gauges for commercial standard gauge models, which form the vast majority of the model world, are 45mm (Gauge 1), 32mm (Gauge 0), 16.5mm (00 and H0), 12mm (TT) and 9mm (N). Obviously it is convenient for a narrow gauge modeller to use a track gauge with good commercial support, as components such as wheelsets, motors, gears, complete locomotive chassis, rail and so on from a smaller scale can be used to create a narrow gauge model with fewer special skills than are needed to scratchbuild everything.

In 00 scale, the two categories of narrow gauge lines identified earlier are catered for by two of these model gauges:

- The 12mm gauge locomotive chassis, rolling stock and track that came with the arrival of commercial TT models in the 1950s greatly simplified the creation of 4mm/1ft scale narrow gauge models to run alongside 00 scale main lines, commonly referred to as '00n3' or '0012'. This track gauge suited Irish and Isle of Man prototypes perfectly, as well as allowing modellers of the time to exercise their creativity with freelance models
- When commercial working N gauge models began to appear (with Lone Star Treble-O-Lectric in 1960, but perhaps more significantly with Arnold of Germany in 1962), 4mm/1ft scale modellers had a similar short-cut to narrow gauge lines of 2ft to 2ft 6in gauge, which could all reasonably be represented with N gauge's 9mm gauge track. This became known as '009'

A tourist train on the 2ft 6in gauge Puffing Billy railway near Melbourne, Australia.

A slate train travelling downhill behind a double Fairlie locomotive on the pioneering Ffestiniog Railway in North Wales.

All 4mm/1ft scale: standard gauge Hornby SR N Class 2-6-0 poses with two narrow gauge engines from etched brass kits – Paul Titmuss's 12mm gauge Londonderry & Lough Swilly 4-8-0 and the author's 9mm gauge L&B 2-6-2T.

Overseas, a similar path was being followed. The standard gauge H0 scale (1:87) models were supplemented by the following:

- 1:120 scale standard gauge on 12mm gauge track of TT scale, the track being adopted by H0 scale modellers for metre gauge lines (known as H0m scale – 'm' for *[voie] métrique*, or metre gauge track)
- 1:160 scale standard gauge on 9mm track of N gauge, the track being adopted by H0 modellers for 60cm–76cm lines (H0e scale – 'e' for *[voie] étroite*, or narrow gauge track)

More recently, the 6.5mm gauge track of Z gauge has been adopted by H0 modellers for lines below 60cm (H0f scale – 'f' for *Feldbahn*).

A Tralee & Dingle 3ft gauge 2-6-0T leaves Annascaul, on Paul Titmuss's 00n3 Irish layout.

00 and 009 models, showing how they can be used side by side on a standard/narrow gauge layout.

> **SCALES THAT USE 9MM GAUGE TRACK**
>
> (The scales highlighted in bold type are covered in this book.)
>
> N – 1:150*: used to model standard gauge lines at 2mm/1ft
>
> TTn3 – 1:100*: used to model 3ft–3ft 6in gauge lines at 3mm/1ft
>
> **H0e – 1:87: used to model 60cm–80cm gauge lines at 3.5mm/1ft**
>
> **009 – 1:76: used to model 2ft–2ft 6in gauge lines at 4mm/1ft**
>
> 09 or 0n15 – 1:43.5*: used to model 12in–18in gauge lines at 7mm/1ft
>
> * The commonly-used scale varies according to country.

Peter Leadley's Clee Valley Miniature Railway is in 09 scale. This means that 7mm/1ft scale figures, road vehicles and scenic items are used with a 9mm gauge railway. The models of 15in gauge locomotives can conveniently be based on N gauge models. MICK THORNTON

> **OTHER POPULAR NARROW GAUGES FOR 00/H0 SCALES**
>
> H0f – 1:87 on 6.5mm gauge track: used to model 50cm–60cm gauge at 3.5mm/1ft
> H0n30 – 1:87 on 9mm gauge track: used to model 2ft 6in gauge at 3.5mm/1ft
> H0m – 1:87 on 12mm gauge track: used to model 1m–3ft 6in gauge at 3.5mm/1ft
> H0n3 – 1:87 on 12mm gauge track: used to model US/colonial 3ft gauge at 3.5mm/1ft
> 00n3 or 0012 – 1:76.2 on 12mm gauge track: used to model 3ft gauge at 4mm/1ft

This book covers 009 scale, which is generally understood to be 4mm/1ft scale trains running on 9mm gauge track (for UK prototypes). 009 is referred to in speech either as 'Double-O-9' or as 'O-O-9' (i.e. with the letter 'O') and written as '009' (that is, a number with leading zeros). This convention is followed throughout this book.

Much of the information in the book is also applicable to H0e scale, with 3.5mm/1ft scale (1:87 scale) trains running on 9mm gauge track (for overseas prototypes). Some H0e models of 60cm gauge prototypes in fact adopt a scale somewhat larger than 1:87, to maintain proportions relative to the (overscale) 9mm gauge track.

Although not described directly in the text, many chapters are equally relevant for narrow gauge modellers who adopt other scales around 3–4mm/1ft and gauges between 6.5 and 12mm.

The 009 Society is the principal society for 3.5 and 4mm/1ft scale narrow gauge, and they certainly welcome as members all modellers using gauges up to and including 12mm, which they refer to as the '009 family'.

009 AND H0e

These two scales sound quite similar, and it is true that models can be mixed successfully (especially if the H0e models are of larger prototypes), but care should be taken when purchasing rolling stock to discover which scale a particular model is built to. For example, two different ranges of ready-to-run War Department Light Railways Baldwin locos

INTRODUCTION 15

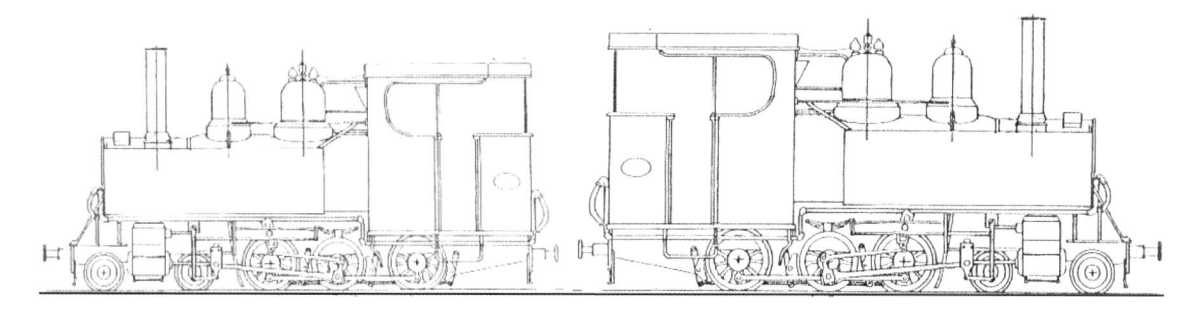

009 and H0e scales compared. Care is obviously needed if models in these two scales are mixed on a layout.

and rolling stock are currently available; one (aimed at continental modellers) is to 3.5mm/1ft scale, and the other (aimed at the British market) is to 4mm/1ft scale. Running these side by side would look rather odd.

> ## ALTERNATIVE NAMES FOR 009
>
> There are (or have been) various different naming conventions for narrow gauge scales, the European and US ones being defined in (different) formal standards, with other practices emerging, particularly in Britain. As a result, there are inconsistencies between the common names for narrow gauge in 4mm/1ft scale and narrow gauge in other scales.
>
> 009 is by far the most common name for 4mm/1ft scale models on 9mm gauge track, and is used throughout this book. However, occasional references may be found to 00-9, or 4n2.25 (4mm/1ft scale, with scale 2ft 3in (=2.25ft) track), or 4n9 (4mm/1ft scale, with 9mm gauge track).

THE ORIGINS OF 009 SCALE

It is not clear exactly when 009 modelling began. There were a few pioneers, probably professional precision engineers and toolmakers, who produced smaller and more detailed working models than their friends would ever contemplate. One such group was active in the Wimbledon Model Railway Club in the 1920s and 1930s, producing fine-scale 2mm/1ft scale models. Another member of that club was Jim Hoyland, a talented model maker, artist and illustrator, whose grandparents and aunt lived in Barnstaple. Jim spent his summer holidays staying with the family there, his aunt's house backing on to the Lynton & Barnstaple Railway's Pilton Yard.

The Model Railway News report of the 1932 Wimbledon Club Exhibition states: 'Scenic models were a prominent feature of the exhibition. Mr Hoyland's 3.5mm scale model of the Lynton and Barnstaple Railway was an excellent example of effective railway scenery.' This is perhaps the earliest example of a 00/H0 scale narrow gauge layout. We do not know the track gauge of this model, or whether it was genuinely 3.5mm/1ft scale (which the

Mr Hoyland's layout is best described as 'L&B-inspired' as it is not a scale model of a particular L&B location, but his artistic skills have created an evocation of the Devon scenery that was advanced for its time.

The 1950 4.5mm/1ft scale Alistair (right), pictured in 2013 on a surviving portion of P.D. Hancock's Craigshire layout alongside the 1952 4mm/1ft scale Exe by David Mander (left). The difference in scale between the two models is apparent. MICK THORNTON

Some time after building the chassis for P.D. Hancock's Alistair, Cherry's made further L&B locomotives – the first 009 ready-to-run models?
MIKE BAYLY COLLECTION

writer of the report may have assumed, as H0 was probably more popular than 00 for standard gauge models at that time). Maybe the locos' mechanisms were built for him by one of the 2mm/1ft scale modellers at the club, and maybe they ran on the 9mm or 9.5mm gauge track that these pioneers used.

The Model Railway News of February 1950 carried a report that Messrs Cherry's of Richmond, a well-known model engineering company of the day, had built the chassis for an L&B locomotive for a customer, to run on 8mm gauge track. In fact the article was in error, as the model was actually 9mm gauge, and the customer was the noted modeller and writer of magazine articles Philip Hancock (PDH). Mr H.B. Whall, one of the 2mm/1ft scale pioneers from Wimbledon, subsequently built the body for Hancock's locomotive, which he called *Alistair*.

One concession to practicality was that PDH's locomotive was built to around 4.5mm/1ft scale – so maybe the 9mm gauge was simply the result of this choice of scale (9mm = 2ft in 4.5mm/1ft scale). But we also know that PDH had previously built a 9mm gauge outside-framed 0-4-0T chassis, to fit an H0 scale shunting engine body.

During the 1950s, 8mm and 9mm gauge track were both used by different 4mm/1ft scale narrow gauge modellers, but the advent of commercial N gauge from around 1960 led to the general adoption of its 9mm gauge.

STYLES OF 009 MODELLING

STANDARD *VERSUS* NARROW GAUGE

Around 1920, less than 4 per cent of the public railway mileage in the whole of the British Isles was narrow gauge. In mainland Britain, the proportion of narrow gauge was only about 1.3 per cent. In addition to the public network, there was an unknown mileage of standard and narrow gauge industrial lines. Curiously, recent data suggests that around 40 per cent of currently operational UK heritage railways and 30 per cent of preserved rolling stock are narrow gauge, the remainder being standard gauge. This apparent imbalance illustrates perfectly why narrow gauge lines were originally built – they are easier and cheaper to build, equip and maintain than standard gauge lines, and therefore more feasible for today's volunteer organizations.

The majority of railway modellers base their layouts on the standard gauge railways that cover much of the country, and the number of modelling magazine articles on narrow gauge topics is small compared to standard gauge. Around 70 per cent of magazine articles are about standard gauge, 20 per cent about techniques applicable to both standard and narrow gauge, leaving no more than 10 per cent about narrow gauge models.

The eclectic mix of locomotives and rolling stock used on British narrow gauge lines makes it difficult for a manufacturer to select one obviously popular prototype for commercial production. This, together with the inherently smaller market, has resulted in trade support for modellers being primarily directed towards standard gauge.

REALISTIC *VERSUS* FREELANCE

In earlier times, when railway modellers had to scratchbuild everything, each individual could decide whether to make a realistic model or a fanciful one, but limited availability of materials and products might prevent the achievement of complete accuracy. Even early ready-to-run (r-t-r) locomotives were often of a generic design, rather than a specific prototype. But r-t-r stock and kits are now almost invariably of actual prototypes, and successive generations of r-t-r models have attained ever greater accuracy. Therefore in standard gauge modelling, realism became possible without exceptional skills, and as a consequence fanciful designs of rolling stock are rarely seen today.

To the ordinary modeller, creating an accurate model of a real location can seem daunting, even if the correct rolling stock can be bought ready-to-run. So many modellers give themselves licence to deviate from strict realism by choosing to model an imaginary but plausible line, perhaps set in a specific real location, or generically in an area of the country – 'somewhere in East Anglia' for example.

British 2ft to 2ft 6in gauge lines were mostly relatively short and self-contained feeders to the main-line network. So there is no reason why a fictitious narrow gauge line 'somewhere in East Anglia' should not have had engines or coaches like those of an actual line elsewhere. Most of the trade support for 009 has been for locomotive and rolling stock kits that follow prototype designs, although some involve compromising the accuracy of the model in the interests of using an N gauge chassis. These kits require assembly and painting, and so there are always opportunities to 'personalize' each model, such as (for example) painting an engine blue and naming it after the family pet.

So freelance modelling has remained common among 009 modellers. But in parallel with that perfectly valid style of modelling, others have striven to create accurate models of actual narrow gauge lines, or imaginary lines inspired by actual railways.

This view is confirmed by a small survey of articles and individual photographs published in twelve issues of 009 News (the members' magazine of the 009 Society) during 2016, which suggests the following:

	Per cent
Prototypical layouts	13
Prototype-inspired layouts	24
Freelance layouts	63
Prototypical stock and structures	61
Freelance stock and structures	39

It appears that a higher percentage of 009 locomotives and rolling stock are freelance than is the case for standard gauge models, whilst the percentage of narrow gauge layouts that attempt to represent an actual line, or the style of an actual line, is similar to that for standard gauge.

THE FUTURE OF 009

Recently there has been an increase in trade support for 009, with prototypical r-t-r rolling stock and locomotives being introduced by suppliers. There is no doubt that these new products will raise the profile of 009, will improve the average standard of 009 modelling, and will increase the number of layouts built in this scale. By bringing greater realism within reach of more modellers, it will also reduce the proportion of freelance 009 models.

But for most people, 009 modelling is unlikely ever to be achievable using only off-the-shelf models. Therefore, this book aims to help modellers achieve whatever level of realism they desire in this scale.

Glyn Valley Tramway locomotive **Dennis** *shunts some loaded granite wagons at Glyn Ceiriog – a compact prototypical layout using kit-built stock.*

CHAPTER TWO

MAKING A START IN 009

Some people will already know precisely which narrow gauge railway they wish to model. This chapter is for those who are attracted by the idea of a narrow gauge line, but have not decided on the subject to which they wish to devote their time and energy.

TYPES OF NARROW GAUGE RAILWAY

We can easily identify a number of different types of narrow gauge line, by categorizing them according to their location and their purpose. This section describes the different types of narrow gauge line.

UK, CONTINENTAL AND COLONIAL RAILWAYS

In the UK, the standard gauge network served even quite small towns by means of branch lines.

In continental Europe, some governments regulated railway-building earlier than in Britain, decreeing that secondary lines should be 1m gauge (see overleaf for the example of France). 1:87 scale modellers represent these 1m and 60cm lines with H0m and H0e scale layouts respectively.

Even a small village such as Carrog in North Wales had a standard gauge passenger and wagon-load freight service.

ABOVE: **In France, separate secondary lines linked small towns and rural areas that were uneconomic for the main lines to serve, such as here at Cayeux-sur-Mer. These metre gauge lines often ran along the roadside.**

BELOW: **There were narrower gauge lines in France, usually 60cm gauge. Early ones were often financed, built and operated by companies such as Decauville, whilst later lines – to support agriculture – used ex-World War I equipment.**

MAKING A START IN 009   21

Australian modellers usually adopt H0 scale (1:87) standards for both broad and standard gauge railways, and H0e scale for the 2ft 6in gauge lines.

The 3ft 6in gauge of South African main lines was supplemented by substantial 2ft gauge feeder lines in remote areas. Their use on British heritage lines means there are 009 kits available for some South African Railways 2ft gauge stock.

MAKING A START IN 009

The Lynton & Barnstaple was a well-engineered, 19-mile, narrow gauge, common-carrier line, with full signalling, comfortable rolling stock and substantial structures. It operated a service of five or six mixed or passenger trains per day on its 1ft 11½in gauge.

Although a common-carrier apparently similar to the L&B, the 2ft 6in gauge Welshpool & Llanfair rarely ran more than one daily mixed train, only owned three passenger coaches, and had minimal signalling.

Across its empire, Britain built and operated many railway networks, and for some time there was a free-for-all between the engineers employed to advise civil servants on the standards they should adopt. Whilst these engineers saw the opportunity to build main lines to wider-than-standard gauges to ease the constraints that existed in Britain, realism inevitably set in, and many colonies adopted narrower gauges for economic reasons.

As an example, main lines in Victoria, Australia, were initially planned as 5ft 3in gauge double track, with high standards of civil engineering. As reality took hold, single-track broad gauge lines with lighter axle loads were built, and plans were made to further reduce costs by using 2ft gauge feeder lines to serve some agricultural and mining areas. However, the intervention of Mr Everard Calthrop, a noted English engineer of the day, resulted in them being 2ft 6in gauge.

The 2ft 6in gauge was also used in other colonies, to open up the interior at reasonable cost (for example in West Africa). Such lines are usually modelled in 1:76 scale using 009 standards. With large British-built locomotives and long journeys, these colonial narrow gauge lines have an appeal to 009 modellers in search of exotic locations for their models.

MIXED TRAFFIC LINES

Some narrow gauge lines were common-carriers, just like their standard gauge counterparts.

MINERAL/FREIGHT LINES

Many narrow gauge lines had their origins in a freight traffic flow, such as slate (Ffestiniog, Talyllyn, Glyn Valley), stone (Glyn Valley), or milk (Leek & Manifold). Passenger traffic on these lines may have originated with the need to carry men to their workplace, leading to an advertised passenger service.

PRIVATE INDUSTRIAL SYSTEMS

Within large quarries (e.g. slate quarries in North Wales) and sandpits (e.g. at Leighton Buzzard), narrow gauge railways moved the heavy materials to processing plants, and the products to transhipment sidings, to the main line or to ships.

A passenger train including vintage workmen's carriages on the Ffestiniog Railway.

'V-tipper' wagons (skips) seen after unloading sand at Leighton Buzzard, where an extensive industrial narrow gauge system once operated.

Overseas, industries such as sugar refining still use extensive narrow gauge railways to carry the seasonal cane or sugar beet crops to processing plants.

A demonstration World War I portable trench railway at Apedale, Staffordshire.

MILITARY SYSTEMS

Army depots, munitions stores, dockyards, firing ranges and other military installations have all used 2ft and 2ft 6in gauge railways as the basis of their internal transport systems. But these small-scale applications pale into insignificance beside the very extensive 60cm gauge railway networks on both sides of the trenches in France and Belgium in World War I. These networks have long been popular subjects for both 009 and H0e modellers.

After the Armistice in 1918, a huge quantity of 60cm gauge railway equipment, including steam and petrol locomotives and rolling stock, was available

A scene on the War Department Light Railways in Northern France, modelled in 009 or H0e scale, in the museum at Cappy, Haute Somme.

The last days of the Ashover: an industrial diesel loco at Fallgate stone-crushing plant in 1968.

second-hand. Many other narrow gauge railways were built, or existing lines re-equipped, using such material. Examples include the Ashover Light Railway and several industrial systems.

CONSTRUCTION PROJECTS

Often overlooked by modellers, significant narrow gauge lines existed for relatively short periods in conjunction with large construction projects, in the days before efficient road transport was available. So a main-line railway might have been preceded by a narrow gauge construction railway. Similarly, many dams, tunnels, new roads and sea defences will have employed narrow gauge (often 60cm) lines during their construction. As an example, the Lynton & Barnstaple Railway was built using 3ft gauge lines at

Devon County Council Kerr Stuart 'Wren' locomotive at work on the Parracombe bypass construction project. R.M. STONE

L&B construction railway, Martinhoe Cross cutting.
MAJOR, DARKER & LORAINE

certain excavation sites, and a 2ft gauge construction railway, with three steam locomotives.

Later in its life, the L&B was crossed for a time by a 2ft gauge construction railway with several steam locomotives. This was used to carry stone from a nearby quarry to build the embankments of the 1920s road improvement project that contributed to the L&B's closure a few years later.

TOURIST AND HERITAGE LINES

Modellers favouring a modern layout may choose to model a real or imaginary tourist or heritage railway.

AVAILABLE LOCOMOTIVES AND ROLLING STOCK

The availability of r-t-r locomotives and rolling stock may influence the choice of line to model. For example, there is no doubt that the recent availability of 009 products means that a realistic model of the Lynton & Barnstaple, the Glyn Valley or the War Department Light Railways is now possible without the need for special skills.

26 MAKING A START IN 009

Overseas, there are short lines that cannot be considered as heritage lines, as their purpose is to take tourists to beaches using a variety of surplus rolling stock from industrial lines, refurbished for passenger use. An example is Le P'tit Train de St-Trojan, Île d´Oléron, France.

A UK heritage railway provides a subject for a realistic model with frequent train services, and the perfect excuse to run 'visiting locomotives'. Here, a Darjeeling Himalaya train is seen at Dinas on the Welsh Highland Railway.

Enticing though the L&B is, it is likely that some prospective 009 modellers will already have a preference for a particular line, and will therefore be faced with the question of how to achieve this aim with his or her existing skills.

THE DIFFERENCE BETWEEN 009 AND 00 MODELLING

The fundamental skills needed for 009 modelling depend on the availability of suitable commercial products in the various disciplines. Many aspects of modelling in 009 are exactly the same as those needed for prototypical modelling in 00 or similar scales. The following table identifies the similarities and the differences. The 009 column is coded red/orange/green according to the additional skills a 00 modeller might find were needed when attempting 009 modelling (green = minimal difference, orange = some differences, red = significant extra challenges).

The example projects described later in this book address each of these aspects of 009 modelling, but focus particularly on those identified in the table as needing different or additional skills.

Some models are even set in the near future. Tony Peart modelled the L&B's present Killington Lane terminus, as it may be once the line extends beyond it.

Parts Available and Skills Needed for 009 Modelling

Skill	00 Modelling	009 Modelling
Baseboards	Usually scratchbuilt	Usually scratchbuilt
Track and points	Most modellers buy 00 products off-the-shelf. Materials are available for those who want to scratchbuild	Most modellers buy 009 products off-the-shelf. 00 and N materials are available for those who want to scratchbuild
Point operation	Point motors are available off-the-shelf	The same point motors are equally applicable to 009
Signalling	A small range of off-the-shelf items is available. A wider range of component parts is available	Signals are less likely to be needed in 009, but 00 components are equally applicable to 009
Fiddle yards	Usually scratchbuilt	Usually scratchbuilt
Structures	Some kits are available, but are unlikely to include everything needed for an accurate model of a specific line	Fewer directly suitable kits are available
Scenery	A wide range of materials is available to help the modeller	The same materials are equally applicable to 009
Sky and backscene	Some materials are available, but many modellers make their own to add character to their layout	The same materials are equally applicable to 009
Detailing (street furniture, figures and so on)	Many items are available to help the modeller	The same items are equally applicable to 009
Locomotives	Many ready-to-run models are available, but are unlikely to include every loco needed for an accurate model of a specific line. A wide range of kits is also available	Few ready-to-run 009 locos are available. Some kits are available, but many use unprototypical N gauge chassis. Finding a ready-to-run outside-framed chassis for the desired locomotive is unlikely
Rolling stock	Many ready-to-run models are available, but are unlikely to include every item needed for an accurate model of a specific line. A wide range of kits is available	A very limited range of ready-to-run stock is available. A range of kits is available
Controls	Ready-to-run locomotives are suitable for DC or DCC operation. Control equipment is widely available	Ready-to-run locomotives are suitable for DC or DCC operation. Space for DCC decoders and sound systems may be limited in smaller locomotives. Control equipment is equally applicable to 009

THE SKILLS REQUIRED

A modeller contemplating 009 might wish to consider the skills necessary to build a 009 layout, and how relevant or otherwise the equivalent 00 modelling skills were to that aim. One way to do this would be to assess one's skills and experience in the areas listed in the table, and to identify the new skills that might be needed to complete a 009 layout successfully.

Lack of a particular skill should not prevent the modeller from tackling a new project. It is good to set about acquiring new skills, and simply requires a methodical approach to progress step by step, and sometimes to undertake small projects as training exercises before tackling the task itself.

A NEW SKILL

A great deal of the success of a diorama model rests on the effectiveness of its backscene. Using a photographic backscene may not be an option, for instance if the trees at the location have grown and obscured the earlier view. Also, because of the area of backscene involved, it will not be easy to achieve in watercolours. So the best option is to learn to work with acrylic paints. Fortunately, various on-line video tutorials are available.

Having selected a series, work through some of the material provided, particularly on the theory and practice of colour mixing, matching colours and painting techniques (brush types, palette management and so on). Soon you will be tackling exercises such as painting snow scenes, copying other artists' work, and so on. It isn't easy to begin with, but with practice the mixing of paints becomes second nature, and it is time to consider tackling the large backscene.

This may not all go according to plan first time, and some rework may be needed. But it is satisfying when you reach the point where the backscene adds to the effectiveness of the model.

WHERE TO WORK

To build small-scale models such as 009, a comfortable place to work is needed. Some tasks must, of course, be carried out on the layout itself, wherever it, or one of its modules, is permanently or temporarily located. But in this small scale, many other tasks can be done at other places around the home. The table on page 29 describes some of the possible places to work.

Everything needs to be to hand whilst making models. One solution is a portable workbench.

THE PORTABLE WORKBENCH

Working on a tray is possible for some tasks, but the quantity of small tools needed for other modelling work encroaches on the limited area. Also, a length of 009 track is desirable for testing rolling stock during construction.

A simple solution is to make a small portable table-top bench out of plywood. A base of about 24 × 12in (60 × 30cm) is adequate for 009, with a height of 12in. The structure is strengthened with stripwood, and fitted with rubber feet to provide grip whilst preventing damage to table tops. The neatest arrangement is a plywood box with a carrying handle. The front panel hinges down to form the working area, whilst stripwood sides reduce the risk of tiny components escaping on to the floor. The table-top bench should contain the following:

A vice: To hold workpieces firmly. A machine vice may be heavy enough not to need fixing down, or a smaller vice may be bolted to the front edge of the bench.

A plastic pen-holder: Can contain all the frequently-used hand tools and paintbrushes, whilst bigger tools and materials may be fetched from elsewhere when needed.

A fluorescent or LED adjustable table lamp (for example an anglepoise type): Can be located adjacent to the bench.

MAKING A START IN 009

Possible Places to Work

Baseboards for the layout	Space to manoeuvre large pieces of timber and the freedom to make dust are essential. A folding bench in a well-lit garage is ideal
	In the summer, a folding bench set up in the garden is a pleasant alternative
Locomotives, rolling stock and buildings	A well-lit table serves well, but should be protected against accidental damage from the hot soldering iron, splashes of glue or paint, or drills penetrating the surface
	A table in a conservatory gives good light during the day, but needs good table lighting after dark, as the glass sides and roof do not scatter light back into the room as walls and a ceiling would indoors. However, it may be more sociable than hiding in the garage or upstairs during the evenings
	A simple portable workbench containing commonly-needed hand tools, minidrill and soldering iron makes the task of setting up for modelling, and clearing away afterwards, quicker and easier
Specific tasks involving power tools	Occasional noisier work with power tools may mean moving to a different location away from other family members
	A lathe or pillar drill needs to be fixed to a sturdy timber base, ideally with a rim round it to discourage small workpieces from making a bid for freedom…
Specific tasks involving a limited range of tools	A tray on the lap in the living room is perfectly feasible when building items out of styrene sheet, assembling plastic kits, or painting models
	Simple tasks such as these can also be undertaken away from home, for example in a hotel room during the evening when on a business trip

A four-way individually-switched mains extension lead: Fixed inside (or to the rear of) the bench, this conveniently provides sockets for soldering iron, light, controller for the test track, and for the minidrill. Mains cables (especially for soldering irons) are bulky and rigid, so can take up much of the space within the box if the sockets are located inside.

When visitors are expected, such a bench can be quickly unplugged, closed and stored tidily, or moved out of the way.

TOOLS REQUIRED

The following hand tools are needed for 009 modelling:

- Craft knife, ideally with a snap-off extending blade, to provide a new cutting edge periodically.

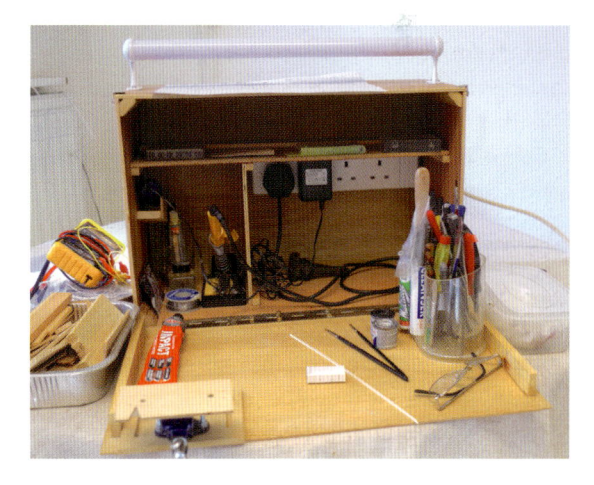

A portable bench opened for use. Soldering iron and minidrill are in the left-hand section, the power sockets in the right-hand one. Hand tools are in the desk tidy: the upper shelf holds the 009 test track and sets of drills, as well as (when stored) trays of wood and plastic off-cuts and electrical wire, test leads and multimeter.

Also, one with a fine-pointed blade, for cutting into corners
- Needle files (flat, half-round, round with a fine point, and wedge-shaped with a thin edge)
- A coarser file for wood and plastic
- Piercing saw, plus plenty of blades of different teeth per inch (TPI)
- 6in steel rule (one that is legible in a range of lighting)
- Micrometer
- Scriber
- Small steel engineer's square
- Centre punch
- Small pin hammer
- Scrapers to remove excess solder (broken needle files, honed on an oilstone)
- Pin chuck and sets of small twist drills (more than one of each size)
- Hand drill and set of larger twist drills and a countersink
- Small sharp scissors (have a pair dedicated to modelling!)
- Glass-fibre burnishing pen and fine emery paper
- Small paintbrushes

It saves time (and money) to keep boxes of wood, plastic and metal off-cuts to hand. The boxes are replenished by successive projects, and the off-cuts find uses later.

Some 009 tasks, especially building locomotives, need some extra tools:

- Cheap analogue electrical multimeter, capable of reading DC and AC voltage, current and resistance
- Taper tap and die for small threads (6, 8, 10, 12BA, or metric equivalents). It saves time to keep the tap and die, as well as tapping and clearance drills, in a plastic bag with the stock of nuts and bolts
- Tap holder and die holder
- Small robust lathe, with three-jaw self-centring chuck, drill chuck and associated tools. Alternatively, most tasks can be accomplished with files and a minidrill held securely

WORKSHOP RULES

Some common-sense 'golden rules' are worth stating:

Always work safely. There are hazards associated with using all tools, and these should be understood. Small drills may break, or pieces of swarf may fly into an eye, so safety (or reading) glasses are advisable for some tasks. Some substances (such as flux, solvents, adhesives) may be dangerous if mishandled. Dust from cutting certain materials is said to be dangerous to inhale.

Choose the method of construction that will give the most robust result. Consider how strong soldered joints will be, and look for every opportunity to run a fillet of solder along the unseen side of joints.

Double-check key dimensions before picking up a saw or drill – it is surprisingly easy to misread longer dimensions on a steel rule. Hold marked-out pieces against the drawing or against the model, to spot obvious errors.

Do not imagine that you can work by eye. Mark everything out using an engineer's square.

Use sharp tools (drills, scribers, centre punches), resharpening or replacing them when worn.

Hold work firmly, or accuracy will suffer and saw blades, drills and needle files will break more often. In engineering, a significant proportion of the construction time is spent making jigs to hold items securely for machining or assembly. Small-scale modelling is easier, and finger pressure will sometimes hold items, but even so, time spent aligning parts accurately will be repaid.

Finish pieces by careful hand-filing, until they fit in place. You can work to better accuracy by feel than purely by measurements. A useful technique is 'draw filing', where the file is held across the piece, and moved steadily to and fro along the length of the edge. This smoothes out file marks and leads to a straighter edge.

When soldering, ensure the components are held in alignment without using the fingers; when solder melts is not the time to be holding metal parts!

Have a second attempt at a component if you are unhappy with the first. Cutting out another piece of metal takes just a few minutes, whereas a model with a blemish will always be flawed. Modellers' scrapboxes are full of odd-shaped bits of metal that never made it into the final model.

Wash hands thoroughly after modelling work.

Of course, everyone bends these rules occasionally when trying to save a few minutes, but sometimes they regret it.

SOLDERING

Some modellers may feel that soldering is beyond their skills, but the principles are very simple:

- Start with simple 15W and 40W soldering irons, with copper bits. Place the iron in a proprietary stand when not in use, so that it can be picked up and put down without taking your eyes off the work
- Select the appropriate size of iron for the task in hand. The aim is to make each joint as quickly as possible, before any other soldered joints are loosened, or nearby plastic components such as wheel centres are softened. The smaller irons have finer bits that are better for small parts and edges of platework, but they cannot heat up a large mass of heavy-gauge metal quickly enough
- Fine electrical multicore solder works well for this scale
- Thoroughly clean both pieces of metal to be joined, using files, emery paper or a glass-fibre burnishing tool. Clean the metal either side of a joint, if a fillet of solder is to be used to strengthen it
- Baker's Fluid is the best flux for nickel silver and brass. It cleans surfaces most effectively as it boils off under the bit. Carr's and other companies offer alternatives. Arrange the flux container so that it cannot get knocked over (the liquid is corrosive), for example by standing it in a plastic tub. Dip a piece of metal – such as thick wire – in the flux and apply a drop to the work
- Tin the surfaces to be joined by applying some liquid flux right along the edge, melt a small amount of solder on the iron's bit, and run it along the edge to create an even coating of solder. Repeat this for the mating edge. The aim is to avoid blobs that will prevent parts being correctly aligned
- Position the components carefully, using a jig to hold them in place if at all possible. The 'jig' may be nothing more than a rectangular block of balsa and some dressmakers' pins
- Remember that, as the solder melts, you want the joint to close up tight, so the jig must allow pressure to be applied to achieve this. Run flux right along the joint, apply a little more solder to the iron, and run the bit along the non-visible side of the joint, if possible. The flux will hiss as it boils off, and you will see the solder melt
- If the joint is long, 'tack' each end to hold the alignment first, and then make the entire joint. In this case, just apply a tiny blob of solder near each end of the joint, check everything, and then solder it properly
- Always clean the excess flux off the work immediately after a soldering session, immersing it in water in a bowl. Do not hold small items under a running tap, as they may disappear down the plug-hole!
- From time to time the iron's bit needs re-profiling, as it accumulates scale. Use a coarse file to carefully recreate a tip with smooth faces, and tin the copper before it tarnishes

GOOD ENGINEERING PRACTICES

Railway modelling is undertaken for pleasure, but trying to be organized repays the effort. Some modellers enjoy spending time at a drawing board or computer, producing scale drawings of the main components for their models, but others may not.

Taking the example of a 009 locomotive project, a simple approach based on good engineering practice is outlined. Similar principles apply to rolling stock, lineside structures and details. Thus a method of organizing each project, which allows reference back later, could be to gather relevant information into a project file, and to gather parts for the loco, as they are acquired, into a project box.

THE PROJECT FILE

Gather relevant information into a project file, such as a transparent document wallet, and add to the contents as the project progresses. Keep documents and drawings up to date, to reflect the 'as-built' state, dating them after each update.

The typical contents of a project file for a 009 locomotive might be:

- Drawings of the prototype, both large scale and reduced to 4mm/1ft scale
- Key photographs of the prototype, printed A4 size, preferably of the actual loco at the date it is being modelled
- Chassis sketch, freehand in pencil on 5mm-squared paper
- Body sketch, showing how the structure will be assembled, freehand in pencil on squared or isometric paper
- Dimensioned sketches of critical components to be made (especially ones to be turned on the lathe)

THE PROJECT BOX

Gather parts for the loco, as they are acquired, into a project box. A plastic box with a tight-fitting lid (as obtained with take-away meals) is ideal for a 009 locomotive or rolling stock project. Store the various types of part in resealable plastic bags within the box, to minimize the risk of small items being lost. Initially include alternative parts or materials, removing unused ones later.

The typical contents of a project box for a 009 locomotive might be:

- Source kit (if applicable)
- Chassis (if applicable) or motor, gears and wheels
- Bought components from stock (lamps and handrail knobs, for example)

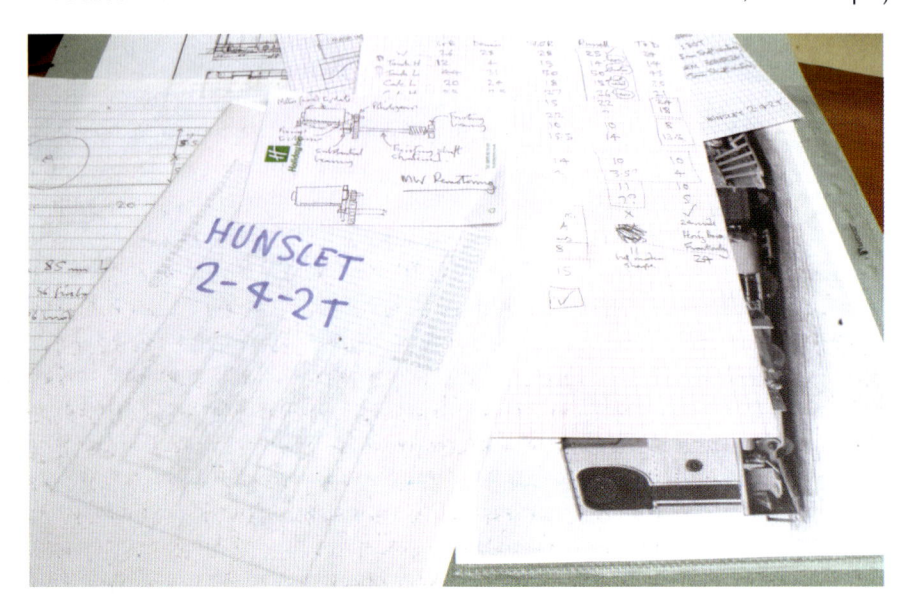

A typical project file and some of its contents, in this case for a yet-to-be-built model. This is a 2-4-2T of a design tendered unsuccessfully by Hunslet for the L&B contract.

MAKING A START IN 009   33

The project box for the Hunslet loco, using parts from two different whitemetal body kits, along with some of the parts for a scratchbuilt chassis. Alternative worm gear options are included at this stage.

- Any specialized materials, such as brass tube of the correct size for the boiler
- Couplings
- Mock-up

DRAWINGS

Not every published drawing of an obscure narrow gauge prototype is accurate, and recourse is needed to photographs. Sometimes key dimensions may have to be scaled from photographs.

The section 'Making Drawings from Photographs' in Chapter 3 gives more information on this.

Several different types of drawing are helpful:

Chassis Sketch

For a 009 loco, side, end and plan views of the chassis, drawn 2.5 × full size on 5mm-squared paper (that is, each square equals 2mm), seem to work. The outlines of wheels, gear sets, motor and so on are added, and adjusted until a viable drive train has been designed. Then add the frame spacers that will strengthen the chassis and support the various components (motor, gears, power pickups and so on).

As the design evolves and the construction progresses, the sketch is kept up to date to reflect the actual arrangement adopted in the model.

Body Sketch

A similar approach can be used when designing the loco bodywork, but it may be easier to use isometric paper, and draw an exploded view of the structure. As work progresses, this sketch is also kept up to date.

Component Sketch

When key components are being made (marked out on sheet metal or turned on the lathe), it is useful to have a dimensioned sketch of the component to hand, to avoid continual references to larger-scale drawings, and multiple conversions of measurements.

Examples of each type of sketch are included in the descriptions of locomotive projects in Chapter 6.

Mock-up Drawings

It may be helpful to print 4mm/1ft scale drawings of the model on to thin card, and use these to make a scale 'mock-up' or 'space model' of the body structure. If adapting a kit, it is possible to 'build' the bodyshell from a mixture of the kit parts and balsa.

A simple balsa block 'chassis' may also be made at this stage, using the drawings to provide the shape, and further balsa blocks can be added to represent the motor and drive-train components, according

The mock-up of the Hunslet. The modified whitemetal body parts are assembled round a balsa boiler/tank block, and at this stage the chassis mock-up is a simple balsa block.

to the chassis sketch. The chassis mock-up can then be tried in position under the basic body structure, as it is being assembled, to check key dimensions before any metalwork is started.

To provide additional encouragement to continue with the project, pose the mock-up on the layout, and the ultimate goal becomes clearer.

WHITEMETAL KITS: GLUE OR SOLDER?

Manufacturers usually suggest assembling whitemetal kits with glue (epoxy or cyanoacrylate), or low melting-point (LMP) solder. Experienced modellers would generally use LMP solder, although both types of adhesive are useful in particular situations. The more parts that are assembled in a single session with epoxy, the greater the risk of one of the parts becoming misaligned before the epoxy hardens. Also, it is easy to leave a fingerprint in hardened epoxy on the surface of the model.

Construction with LMP solder can be rather satisfying. The correct solder (supplied as a straight or coiled stick of metal) is needed, together with the appropriate type of liquid flux, to clean the surfaces and encourage the solder to flow into the joint.

Some modellers will have temperature-controlled soldering irons that can be used at the appropriate setting for LMP solder, but there is a simpler technique that works perfectly well. This involves making a unit to connect a 230V light bulb in series with a 230V mains socket to reduce the flow of current. A 15W soldering iron, which would suit a 009 kit, needs a 230V 15W filament lamp plugged into the lamp socket, and the extra resistance of this in the circuit means that the soldering

The various items needed for low melting-point soldering. The glowing bulb shows that the iron will reach a suitable temperature for whitemetal.

Wiring diagram for the LMP soldering device.

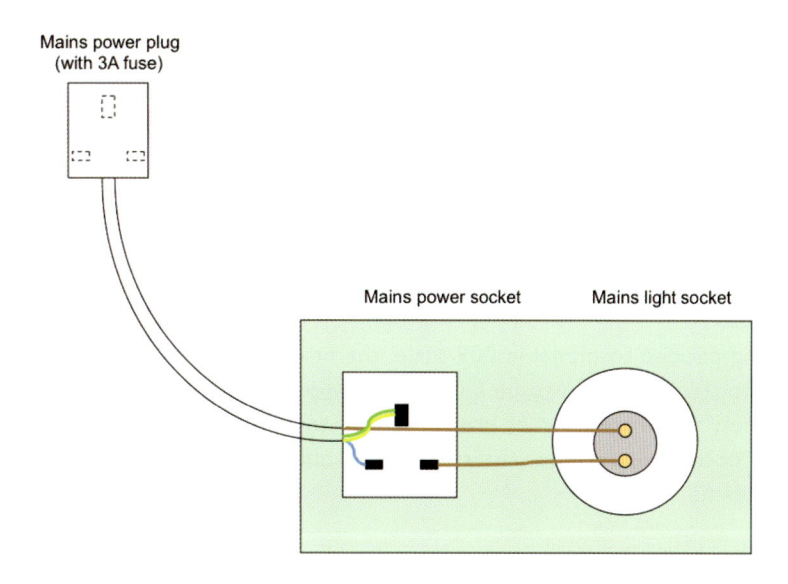

iron reaches a temperature below the melting point of the whitemetal kit components, but above the melting point of the LMP solder.

Always check the iron's temperature on a spare piece of whitemetal before starting.

Once the two components mate neatly, the metal round the joint should be cleaned with a glass-fibre burnishing brush. The components are carefully aligned and held in position (with right-angle blocks or BluTack if necessary) and flux is deposited along the inside of the joint. Then, checking that the re-assuring glow of the lamp confirms the iron is not too hot, the iron's bit is loaded with some LMP solder and applied to the inside of the joint. For a short joint, the iron is moved to and fro along the seam until the solder runs, but if the joint is longer, the joint is 'tacked' near its two ends before returning with more solder to run along the entire length of the joint in two halves, from the centre outwards.

It is apparent when the solder flows into the joint, and the iron should be removed as soon as possible once it does, in case the rising temperature approaches the whitemetal's melting point. At the low temperatures involved, the work cools down quite slowly compared to normal soldering, so if holding items in position by hand, keep hold until the surface of the solder suddenly changes from shiny to dull before relaxing.

Mistakes can be rectified, although it can be difficult to clean excess LMP solder off a part after it has been unsoldered, but a 'solder sucker', as used in repairing electronic circuits, can help. In the worst case, items can be separated by immersing them in hot water – somewhere between hand-hot and boiling – but of course this method cannot be used on a nearly complete model without undoing *all* the work so far accomplished.

It can be difficult to keep adding many small parts using LMP solder, as soldering can unsolder earlier work. Cyanoacrylate adhesive can be useful to fix the later parts to be added. Epoxy is also useful, as it can help fill an imperfect joint whilst fixing parts together, and can be filed to shape once hardened. Epoxy might be good for attaching a dome to a boiler, for example, to fill any gaps around the dome's base.

After a session of assembly with LMP solder, the model should be rinsed with cold tap water (in a bowl, in case any parts become detached!) to remove any remaining flux.

CHAPTER THREE

PLANNING A LAYOUT

Railway modelling is a hobby, undertaken for pleasure, and the builder may adopt any approach he or she wishes.

Having decided to model in 009 scale, the next step is to plan the layout to be built. This chapter shows how this process can be broken down into a number of choices, and how a realistic and workable layout can be designed.

PROTOTYPICAL OR FREELANCE?

The first choice to make is whether the narrow gauge line should be an accurate model of an actual line, or not, and there are effectively three paths a modeller can take: prototypical, prototype-inspired, and purely imaginary.

Each person viewing a model layout may privately decide to what extent the model captures the intended atmosphere. Normal good manners and tact should prevent offence being given by thoughtless criticism.

THE PROTOTYPICAL MODEL

The modeller may decide to build a layout that represents an actual line, an actual station or location, and uses the correct rolling stock. One attraction of this is the challenge of undertaking research using historical sources – for example maps, documents and photographs – and perhaps archaeological sources, such as surviving buildings and other remains.

Such a model need not be totally to scale. Some compression of platform and siding lengths, and reduction of curve radii, is inevitable, and very few people could consider a model with true-scale distances between adjacent stations (1 mile is about 70ft (20m) in 4mm/1ft scale).

The track layout should reflect the prototype, although sidings may be foreshortened, and sheds may be modelled in low relief, as seen here. A large yard might have the number of sidings reduced without spoiling the appearance.

Some areas of the prototype can be left to the viewer's imagination, as here, where only half a passing station is modelled (a so-called 'cameo layout'). PETER AINLEY

Some modellers might worry about criticism of the finished prototypical model. If the layout is intended primarily as a private layout, the builder will be his or her own sternest critic, but at an exhibition, a casual remark delivered insensitively may be hurtful.

Before starting work on such a model, the builder could consider their possible reaction to a critical comment from a stranger:

(a) Would they wonder privately if the critic had ever actually created a model of any sort themselves?
(b) Would they want to go back to the historical sources and check whether the criticism were valid, and take satisfaction from rectifying any errors?
(c) Would they want to tear the layout apart and never try modelling again?

If the reaction were (a) and/or (b), the prospective modeller should continue with a prototypical approach. If their reaction were (c), a different approach might be preferable.

Perhaps one of the main benefits when exhibiting a prototypical layout is having the chance of talking to someone who remembered the railway or the nearby buildings, and who can provide information not available from other sources.

AN EXAMPLE OF CONSTRUCTIVE CRITICISM

I once showed my model of the L&B's Barnstaple Town station at an exhibition. A visitor whom I didn't know at the time spent a long while looking at the model, and watching it operating, and we got chatting. He was very kind about my modelling efforts, but tactfully mentioned that, after 1930, the L&B had its coal delivered by the Southern Railway, whereas my model (set in 1935) had a Great Western wagon unloading coal on to the narrow gauge coaling stage – which I had thought was a reasonable assumption, as the coal was probably Welsh steam coal. I subsequently spent an evening replacing the GWR wagon with an SR type, and also gained a very knowledgeable and helpful friend!

THE PROTOTYPE-INSPIRED MODEL

Modellers who feel daunted by the prospect of creating an accurate model may prefer to create a model that is clearly inspired by a particular prototype, but fictionalized to some extent. This would give licence to make changes, or to excuse inaccuracies. Variations on the prototype-inspired layout may be discerned, including the following:

Tony Peart's **Blackmoor Junction** *represents an actual location, but presumes that a proposed branch to Combe Martin had actually been built, requiring additional sidings and an engine shed.* CHRIS OSMENT

John de Frayssinet's **County Gate** *presumes that a line had been built to link the Lynton & Barnstaple to Minehead.*

PLANNING A LAYOUT

- A fictitious station on an actual line
- A fictitious (or planned but never built) branch or extension to an actual line
- An imaginary narrow gauge line typical of lines in a particular geographical area (for example, a gravel pit in Lincolnshire or a French roadside tramway)

Such prototype-inspired models might include accurate or adapted models of actual buildings, and run models of actual rolling stock. Narrow gauge lines (in Britain, at least) tended to be distinct and separate, each with its own style, unlike the main-line companies where a 'style' of structures, buildings and rolling stock would be apparent across a wide area or along a particular line.

THE PURELY IMAGINARY MODEL

Where no actual narrow gauge line forms the inspiration for a model, the builder has a free rein to determine every aspect of the scene, the structures, the buildings and the rolling stock.

Some such models are by choice set in an actual location (for example a narrow gauge line serving the fishing village of Port Isaac in Cornwall, or a heritage narrow gauge line built on the trackbed of an actual standard gauge branch), with the atmosphere established by models of actual buildings.

A Talyllyn train on Roger Christian's and Stan Williams' Tan-yr-Allt – an imaginary line set in mid-Wales countryside, with structures and scenery typical of the area. MICK THORNTON

Charles Insley's **Fort Whiting** *is a very effective imaginary colonial station operated by locomotives adapted from ready-to-run models and kits 'in the style' of particular builders, but without aiming for prototypical accuracy.*

Charles Insley's St-Etienne-en-Caux captures the atmosphere of a French secondary line, thanks to careful choice of buildings and types of rolling stock.
MICK THORNTON

Hugh Norwood's fanciful **Angst Lesspork**, *inspired by Terry Pratchett's* **Discworld** *novels, includes a number of recognizable features and figures. Here, Mick Thornton, on a visit across the 'many dimensional worlds of the multiverse', photographed his own Roving Reporter's Railcar.*

RESEARCHING A PROTOTYPE

The example layout described in this and the following chapter follows the prototypical approach, because that presents the greatest number of challenges. Other approaches allow simplifications. Except in the case of a purely imaginary layout, the prototype or locality must be researched. As significant time will be spent building the model, it is worth getting this right before starting work.

A prototypical layout will inevitably need the greatest amount of research, whilst layouts set in scenery typical of an area may need less detailed research.

INTERNET SEARCH

Nowadays an on-line search about an actual narrow gauge line will give an immediate indication of the amount of information available about it. Such a search may reveal some, or all, of the following types of information:

- A Wikipedia entry about the line. This may be minimal, or it may be extensive. It will usually be quite accurate, but possibly not in every detail
- Reference to a support society, or heritage railway group
- Mention of the line in local history websites for the area

- References to books about the line, and magazines including articles about the line (a few magazine articles are reproduced on-line, but on-line auction sites usually list the contents of magazines offered for sale)
- Photographs of the line, and photographs of models of the line
- Movie clips of the line (sometimes even including period ciné film of trains operating on the line), and of existing models of the line

When trying to understand the context, contemporary maps can show the buildings, roads and even field boundaries at the chosen date for the model. The National Library of Scotland provides a useful free website which allows two maps of the UK from a selection covering various dates to be compared side by side, on screen, the mouse pointer moving over the same location on both (http://maps.nls.uk/geo/explore/side-by-side/).

Another example of material available on-line is the collection of aerial photographs from different periods (see https://britainfromabove.org.uk).

BOOKS AND MAGAZINES

The most obvious source of information is the various books about a line (second-hand, if not currently in print). These generally fall into two main categories: first, histories of the line, which usually include the origins, construction and key events during the life of the railway, a description of the infrastructure of the line, the locomotives and rolling stock used on it, and any notable operating practices. And second, albums of photographs of the line, which provide an invaluable resource for modellers. Modern albums often reproduce images more clearly and much larger than older publications, which probably had to rely on second- and third-generation prints.

As well as books specifically about the line in question, a prospective modeller will find magazine articles on the subject, and individual photographs within more wide-ranging albums (for example, albums about a photographer who visited many lines).

Where other models based on the line exist, articles about these will be instructive when contemplating a new model of the same line. Such articles may highlight particular difficulties, and may suggest modelling a different section of the line from the section originally considered.

SOCIETIES

Narrow gauge lines very often have societies dedicated to preserving their memory, which are making plans to reopen them, or are actually running them as heritage lines.

If such a society exists for the subject of a model, joining it can give access to historical resources, surviving artefacts and photograph collections, and also to a number of knowledgeable individuals who may be willing to help another member, but who are perhaps less willing to help a non-member.

If no specific society exists, more generic organizations such as the Narrow Gauge Railway Society (http://www.ngrs.org) have libraries of books, drawings and photographs, which may prove invaluable to the modeller.

ON-LINE DISCUSSION GROUPS

A heritage railway may have on-line groups (whether formally associated with it, or independent) enabling discussion between those sharing an interest in the line. Such groups can be a valuable knowledge base for a modeller.

Before posting queries on such a group, it is advisable to assess the interests of existing group members and the range of topics discussed. Some will focus on the rebuilding and operation of the modern-day line, while others will cover its heritage. Relatively few 'prototype' groups will welcome being swamped by modellers discussing the finer points of model making, but may willingly answer questions about historical facts.

Some lines have separate modelling discussion groups, which cover practical modelling issues, as well as aspects of historical research overlapping with heritage groups.

LOCAL HISTORY CENTRES

An interesting aspect of modelling an actual line

On visible sections of a layout, the appearance will suffer if trains negotiate excessively tight curves. The smallest radius for satisfactory appearance may be greater than the absolute minimum radius.

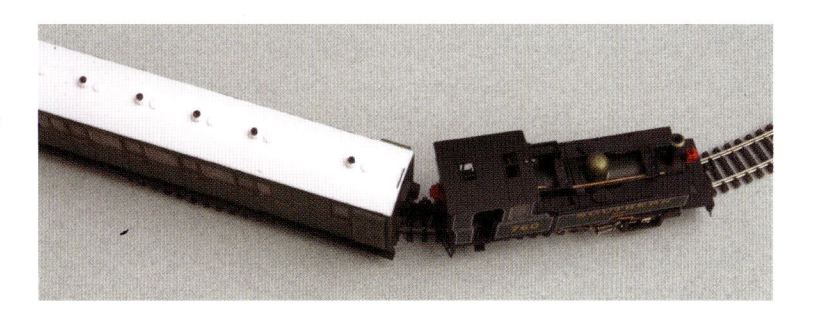

is the opportunity it gives to research its history locally, using libraries, local studies centres and county records offices. With many such archives being digitized, much research can be carried out from a home computer. For example, photograph collections held in the National Archives in Kew (and corresponding archives in Scotland and Northern Ireland) are increasingly being catalogued, and copies offered for sale. Such images, even viewed in low resolution on the screen, may provide useful details about a location.

Many other sources are available which can help modellers with details of their layouts – for example, copies of local trade directories (such as *Kelly's Directory* for a town) can give the names of local coal merchants, shopkeepers, hotel-keepers and so on, at a given date.

Local history and archaeology groups may have researched a narrow gauge line in their area, or may be willing to undertake new research as a project for their members. Similarly, evening classes studying local history may reveal levels of unpublished detail about an area, or at least may assist the modeller with carrying out private research.

KEY PARAMETERS

An early task in designing a full-size railway is to define its key parameters. Few modellers would consciously do this when planning a model, but the following factors should be considered: minimum curve radius, maximum train length, kinematic envelope and structure gauge.

MINIMUM CURVE RADIUS

Each type of model locomotive or rolling stock will only reliably negotiate curves above a certain minimum radius, due to physical constraints of the prototype and model designs, including coupling on curves. The minimum radius for reliable operation may be larger through points than on plain track.

Using examples of the intended rolling stock and locomotives, tests should be carried out to determine these radius values, so that the layout can be designed from the outset with adequate curve radius.

MAXIMUM TRAIN LENGTH

Various layout features (platforms, run-round and passing loops, fiddle yard sidings and so on) must accommodate the longest trains to be operated on the line, so the required train configurations must be considered. The prototype line may have operated occasional longer trains (such as double-headed summer Saturday specials and market-day trains) and the way in which these were worked should be studied, or, if no information is available, at least thought about. Then a decision can be made as to whether these workings should be possible in the model.

Compromising on Train Length

The long 1-in-50 gradients on the Lynton & Barnstaple meant that the load hauled by one engine was limited to five bogie vehicles. Double-headed trains of up to nine coaches were occasionally operated. In 009, such a train would be 1.66m (5ft 5in) long, and a layout accommodating trains of this length would be sizeable.

A modeller needs to decide whether to reproduce *all* these operations in model form. Whilst a single train of nine coaches could be worked through a shorter passing loop, two such trains could not pass easily in the loop. Therefore the means for marshalling and disposing of such a train at the termini must be considered:

- Will 'off-stage' fiddle yard areas accommodate such a train?
- Will the model locomotives haul such a train?
- How will the engines be released from the train on arrival?
- Will the train be split approaching the terminus, with one engine hauling a portion into each of two platforms? Or will one engine be expected to haul the whole train into the platform?

However, photographs may show two or three coaches in the winter, with some longer trains in the summer and on market days. So maybe one locomotive and either three coaches, or two coaches plus a few wagons, would capture the atmosphere of the line.

Limiting trains to this length means passing loops able to accommodate a total train length of 640mm (25in), and run-round loops capable of accommodating at least three coaches (474mm/18.7in).

KINEMATIC ENVELOPE AND STRUCTURE GAUGE

These terms sound complicated, but are actually straightforward. The locomotives and rolling stock used on a line will vary somewhat in height, width and so on, so consideration must be given to the largest items of rolling stock to be used on the model. Even a modeller building a prototypical model may wish to run a wider range of stock, or may wish that their friends' stock with different characteristics can run on the layout.

As well as the overall height and width shown on a drawing, other characteristics of the rolling stock (overhang on curves due to the length of carriages, for example) will affect the cross-section to be accommodated on curves. Overhang near rail level can be particularly important for narrow gauge models, to ensure that all vehicles pass clear of objects such as point rodding near the rails, and that low-level features of locomotives (such as cowcatchers) clear any platforms that stand above rail level. This is especially important when negotiating engine-release crossovers within platforms.

Also, some allowance must be made for vehicles rolling and yawing when in motion and on curves,

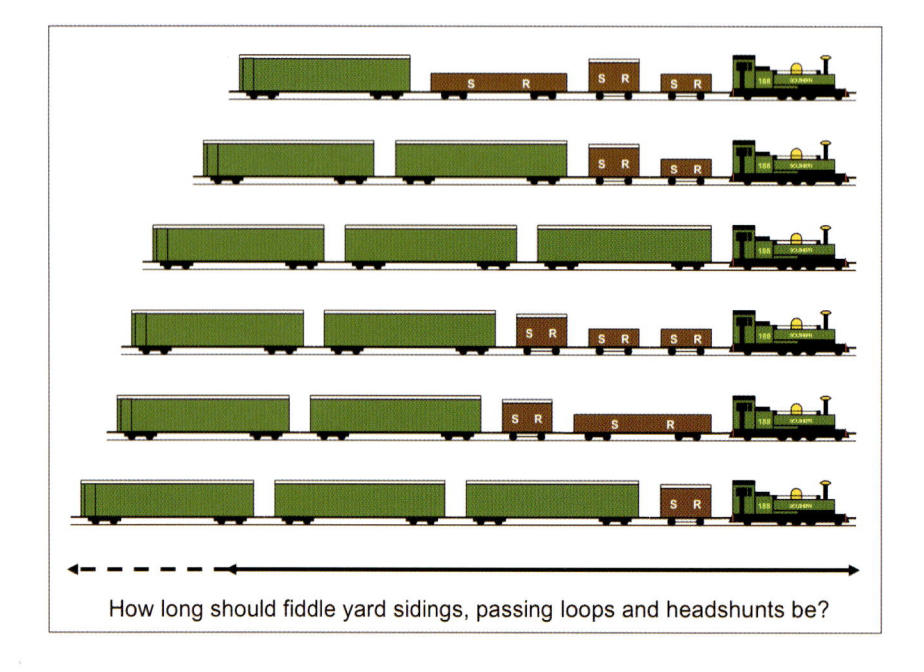

How long should fiddle yard sidings, passing loops and headshunts be?

An illustration of how the length of passing loops and fiddle yards may restrict the train formations that can be operated.

PLANNING A LAYOUT

The kinematic envelope and structure gauge may be combined on one drawing. This shows such a drawing for a UK 009 layout, although others may choose to accommodate bigger rolling stock.

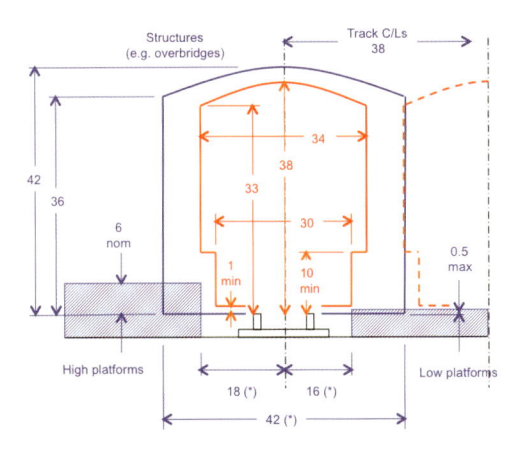

Notes:

Blue dimensions are minimum values unless otherwise stated

Red dimensions are maximum values unless otherwise stated

Dimensions marked (*) are increased as necessary on curves

This structure gauge is designed to suit the L&B and other UK 2ft gauge rolling stock.

It will not allow an SAR NGG16 Garratt to operate.

It may not accommodate models of prototypes of greater than 2ft gauge, which may be significantly larger.

NOT TO SCALE

and for wheels following the track differently when propelling.

All these factors combine to define the 'kinematic envelope' of the rolling stock.

It is useful to measure model rolling stock or drawings, to carry out tests on curved track, and then to draw the kinematic envelope to be accommodated on a new layout, to avoid nasty surprises when the first trains are run.

The structure gauge is the 'other side of the coin' from the kinematic envelope, and shows the closest incursion of structures on the line towards the rails (for example the size of overbridges, doors to sheds, platforms).

LAYOUT CONSTRAINTS

There are several constraints on the design of a new layout.

AVAILABLE SPACE AND VIEWING POSITION

A layout around the perimeter of a spare bedroom or garage will provide the longest end-to-end journey, excluding loops and spirals (see diagram overleaf), and its location may define the viewing position.

OPERATOR POSITION

A private layout is *de facto* operated and viewed from

If the layout is to be assembled and operated at home, it must fit in the available space in a room where its presence will be tolerated for periods of time, such as a spare bedroom.

PLANNING A LAYOUT

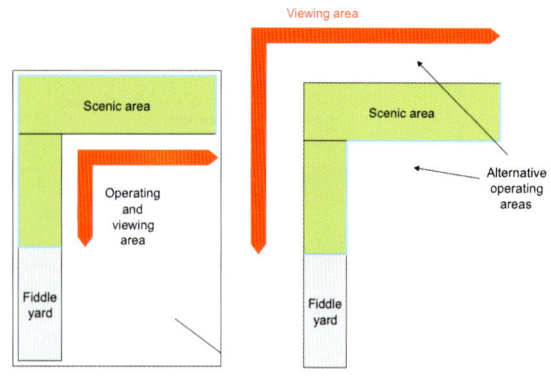

In a room, a layout is viewed from within, but at a model railway show it is better if the public can view it from two or more sides.

the same side. This normally means the backscene is to the rear, as seen by the operator. However, an exhibition layout may be operated from behind the backscene, whilst the public view it from the front. A layout to be used both at home and at exhibitions may therefore need to be designed with that in mind. Other factors affect whether to operate an exhibition layout from the front or rear, and these are discussed in Chapter 10.

MODULARITY

009 does allow very compact layouts, but larger layouts must be built as a number of separate modules, for several reasons:

- To limit the size and weight of each module, taking account of the builder's age and possible future home downsizing
- To allow work to be carried out on a single module in a convenient location (which may not be the same as the intended operating location)
- To allow transport of the modules (for example, in a car)
- To permit the modules to be stored easily when not in use

In many model railway scales, formal standards exist for layout modules, and some of these are widely adopted. These can have two aims:

- To allow an individual to set up different layout configurations from a number of modules, to suit particular needs
- To permit a layout to be assembled from modules built by different individuals who follow the same standard. This can be for private collaborations, a club effort, or for an exhibition

A modular H0e club layout from Amiens, France, based on the P'tit Train de la Haute Somme. Each of the three modules gives the viewer a 'window' on to a different scene on the line. MICK THORNTON

There are currently no widely adopted modular standards for 009 layouts, although one modeller has produced a set of standards – called *Freem009* – which he is using himself for a modular layout, and which others may choose to follow (see link below). This standard provides a useful indication of the areas that need to be defined, if interchangeability is sought at the module level.

(http://www.rmweb.co.uk/community/index.php?/topic/124103-freem009-a-modular-system-for-british-009)

LAYOUT CONFIGURATIONS

The next stage of planning is to define the layout configuration. There are two basic layout types, which may also be combined within one layout: end-to-end layouts (*see first diagram*) and continuous layouts (*see second diagram*).

CAMEO LAYOUTS

Those without the space for a full working layout

PLANNING A LAYOUT

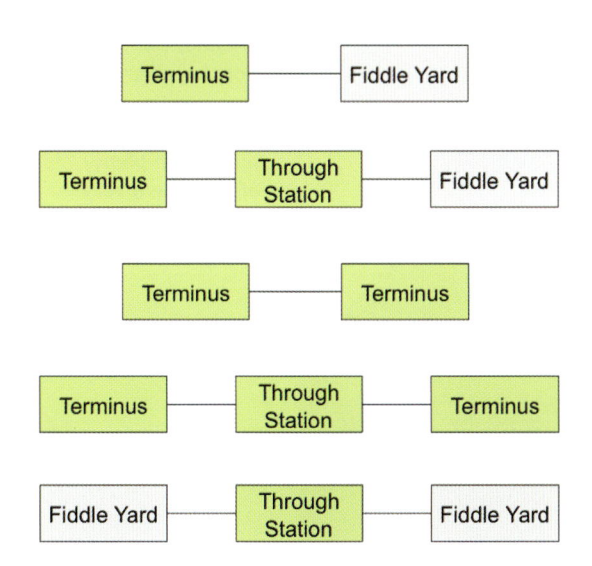

```
Terminus ——— Fiddle Yard

Terminus ——— Through Station ——— Fiddle Yard

Terminus ——— Terminus

Terminus ——— Through Station ——— Terminus

Fiddle Yard ——— Through Station ——— Fiddle Yard
```

Actual narrow gauge lines run from A to B, to meet their intended purpose as transport systems. Some may include branches, triangular junctions, turn-back loops, and other, more exotic features. The basic end-to-end layout configurations are shown here.

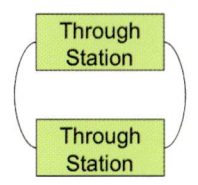

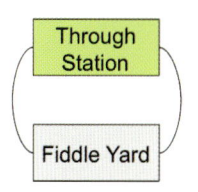

```
  Through Station
 /                \
  Through Station

  Through Station
 /                \
  Fiddle Yard
```

Few actual lines include a continuous circuit. However, such a layout suits both exhibition and home use, providing a regular train service with minimum operator input – good for 'watching the trains go by'. The basic configurations are shown here.

may nevertheless create a 'cameo layout', in which a single view of part of a station conveys the impression of a larger area of the railway. Key to such layouts is the idea of 'staging' the scene within a viewing frame – like a theatre stage. Such layouts are usually end-to-end ones. The following are possibilities:

- A locomotive depot, where engines are prepared to depart off-stage to operate the service trains, and to bring wagons of coal to refuel the engines
- One end of a station, with the other end off-stage
- A goods yard, where engines shunt wagons and prepare trains, but the viewer does not actually see the trains running from A to B

*John Bruce's very effective scenic cameo layout **Wherewithial Quay** demonstrates that 009 layouts need not be large in size.*
MICK THORNTON

Michael Campbell's **Southon Yard** *micro layout consists of a loco shed and works scene with plenty of detail in a very compact space.*
MICK THORNTON

MICRO LAYOUTS

Micro layouts often form the subject of competitions at shows to make a working model in a precisely defined small area. These layouts may be designed to fit in a small available space (for example a bookshelf or coffee table), or made to fit in a given area (for example a 1ft square or an A4 box file).

Such layouts can be very effective for industrial scenes, and some have even been built to show the railway inside a building (for instance a loco shed or repair shop). They are less well suited for lines with larger narrow gauge locomotives and rolling stock.

Because of their small size, most micro layouts are end-to-end. The exception is the operationally limited 'pizza layout', in which a train runs continuously around a circular track, through varied scenery on a round baseboard.

FIDDLE YARDS

Many modellers accumulate a larger collection of rolling stock than is appropriate for the size of layout they have space for. They may also wish to avoid placing stock on, or lifting it off, the track by hand within the scenic area of a layout.

A fiddle yard is a non-scenic section of a layout, accessible to the operator, which can be used to store spare stock and to marshal trains to be dispatched into the scenic layout area, thereby providing a suitable variety of trains to serve a small layout.

A fiddle yard may be single-ended (as part of an end-to-end layout) or double-ended (usually as part of a continuous layout), with several different configurations in each category.

Single-Ended

Fan of sidings: A set of sidings reached by pointwork.

Sector plate: A set of pivoted siding tracks, which can be turned to give access to different sidings from the same approach track. This minimizes the required length, as pointwork is not needed in the non-scenic area. The turntable is a variant where the set of sidings is pivoted at its centre, and can be turned to allow complete trains to be sent back where they came from without re-marshalling. This only suits a line whose locomotives and stock can couple either way round, and strictly speaking should only be used for models of lines whose locomotives and stock were turned in the course of traffic (for example lines with turntables, triangles or balloon loops).

Traverser: This allows several storage siding tracks to be slid sideways, to align one of the sidings with the entry/exit track. A sector plate offers similar capabilities, without the constructional difficulties of the slides.

Cassettes: Trains run on to separable 'cassette' sections of track in the fiddle yard, so that an entire train can be unplugged from the approach track after arrival, and moved around on a flat surface to allow another cassette carrying a train to be connected ready for departing. The removed train can then be re-marshalled before being plugged back into the departure track. The need to handle or re-rail stock can be minimized by providing separate 'loco' cassettes, and even by sub-dividing the 'rolling stock' cassettes.

Double-Ended

Fan of loops: A fan of sidings, but with pointwork at both ends, which increases the overall length of the fiddle yard. A mixture of loops and single-ended sidings may be provided, if that suits operational patterns. Very large fiddle yards may store more than one train per loop, isolating them by DC track sections or by the use of DCC control.

Traverser: This configuration replaces the sector plate for continuous layouts, permitting access to each track from either end without any length wasted by pointwork.

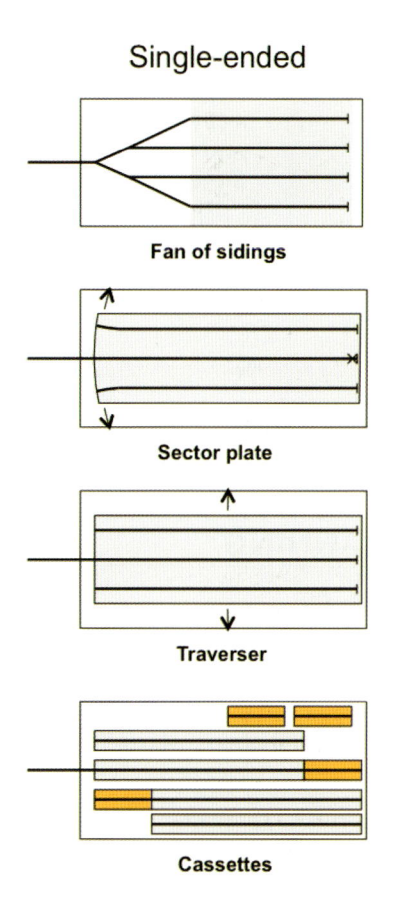

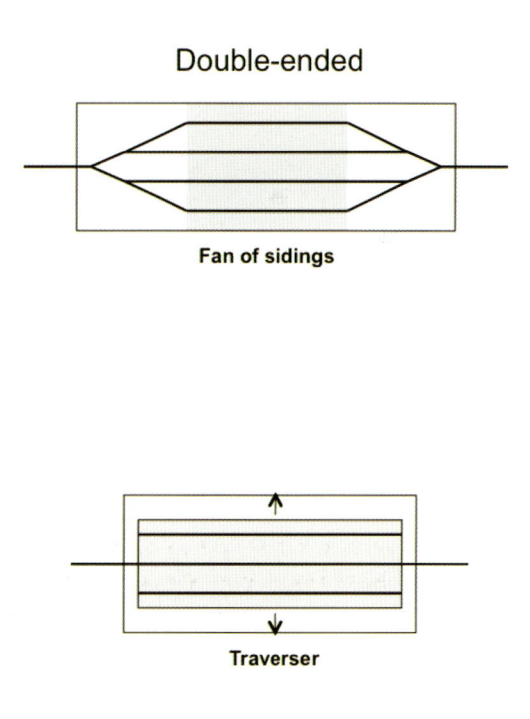

Fiddle yard configurations.

PLANNING A LAYOUT

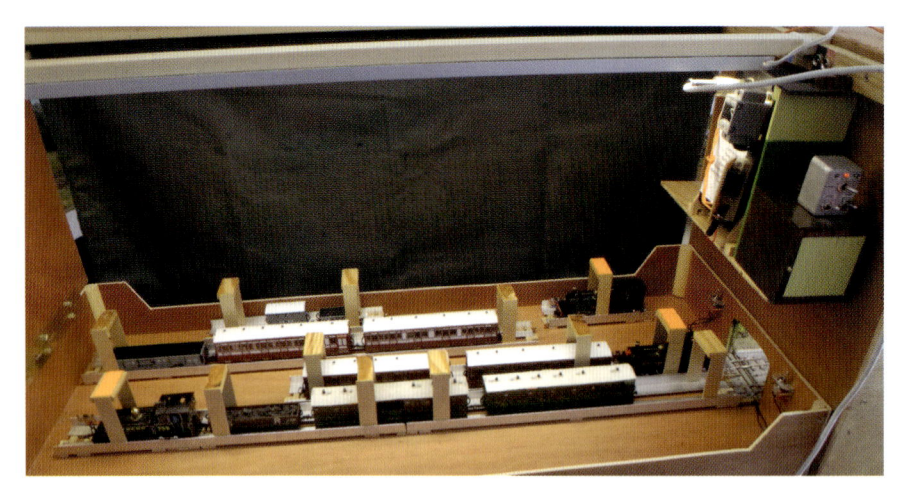

Cassette-type single-ended fiddle yard in use.

A 009 turntable fiddle yard by Richard Glover. MICK THORNTON

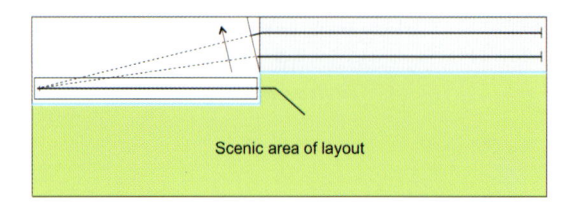

Cameo layouts may use a fiddle yard reached by a sector-plate headshunt – a kick-back fiddle yard. This allows engines or trains to move off-stage within the confines of a small layout.

LAYOUT PLANNING

SPACE MODEL OF PLANNED LAYOUT

Having decided the size and configuration of a new layout, it can be helpful to build a 'space model' of it. A reduced-scale space model can be used to confirm that details such as folding or stacking base-boards will actually work as intended. For example, a folding baseboard may not work if tall structures are located on either side of the fold.

PLANNING A LAYOUT

A full-size space model can confirm that sightlines give good visibility of trains and sidings, and that scenic breaks can be made to work. Such a model is quickly built from cardboard boxes and parcel tape.

For a cameo layout in a box, this 1:10 model was used to check that removable side panels would allow the layout to be viewed from one side or the other, and that the fiddle yards could be 'hung' on the ends of the box and concealed by curtains.

A scale of 1:10 is appropriate for a space model of a small layout, and such a model can be built quickly from card, balsa or thin ply. An evening spent making such a space model could save abortive expenditure and work later.

FULL-SIZE LAYOUT PLAN

It is essential to draw a new full-size layout in the centre of a large sheet of paper: this allows the baseboard edge positions and alignment to be adjusted later. The points to be used (or full-size templates, available to download and print for some Peco 009 items) are laid out on the paper, and the track linking them can then be sketched in, checking the radius of any tight curves. If large structures are to be included – for example scale models of actual buildings, which will look wrong if scaled down – cut their scale-size shapes out of paper, and place these on the drawing.

An iterative process of juggling the various elements around allows a workable design to be reached. On seeing the various items laid out, the baseboard edges may need to be moved relative to the track. Points must not cross baseboard joints, and neither should buildings (unless they are to be removable). For reliability, the fewer tracks that cross baseboard joints, the better.

The following checks should be made on the full-size plan: that maximum-length trains fit in run-round loops and fiddle yard sidings; that sightlines work (visibility of the scene, scope for disguising scenic breaks, and so on); that radii conform to a minimum curve. These checks are made easier by placing actual model locos, rolling stock and scale-size paper space-models of buildings on the plan.

The final step is to mark the chosen positions of the three ends of each set of points, the track centre-line at intervals between the points, and the corners of structures.

PROJECT: RALEIGH WEIR, A LYNTON & BARNSTAPLE DIORAMA

In Chapter 4 the stages of work involved in building a small diorama layout will be described, but first it is necessary to plan this layout. The key requirements are as follows:

- To show a prototypical scene on the Lynton & Barnstaple whilst under construction in 1897–8, including the contractor's temporary worksite and engine shed at Raleigh Weir on the outskirts of Barnstaple

- To allow contractor's locomotives and a variety of works trains of skips and other wagons to run on a small continuous circuit, suitable for exhibitions
- To allow an L&B Manning Wardle locomotive and one L&B carriage to pass through periodically, conveying dignitaries inspecting the work on the line
- Scenically, to show a newly-built railway cutting through an established landscape

The L&B worksite at Raleigh Weir, Barnstaple.
MAJOR, DARKER & LORAINE

TECHNICAL DETAILS

Length of contractor's loco	60–65mm (2.4–2.6in)
Maximum length of works train	200mm (7.9in = eight skips)
Maximum number of works locos/trains	Three
Length of L&B loco	108mm (4.25in)
Length of L&B coach	158mm (6.2in)
Minimum curve radius (works train)	9in (23cm)
Minimum curve radius (L&B train)	12in (30cm)
Structure gauge	Standard L&B

ANALYSIS

The layout for this diorama should observe the following parameters:

- The works trains will negotiate Peco 9in radius 009 Setrack track and points, which can be used on all non-scenic track. The L&B loco and train will not reliably negotiate 9in radius curves, but this train does not have to run continuously, so can shuttle to and fro across the scene between sidings of larger radius
- The realism of the scenic section requires fine-scale (scratchbuilt) track
- A fiddle yard of two electrically split loop tracks is needed, to allow up to three Up and Down contractor's trains to run in varied sequences, or to allow a continuously running contractor's train to pass the other two
- For portability and light weight, the layout will use lightweight foam insulation baseboards, and must be split into sections no more than 4ft (1.2m) in length for ease of transport in a small car
- The 9in radius curves at the ends of the circuit suggest that a 2ft (60cm) deep layout is feasible. The length of the scenic section is undefined at this stage, but needs to be at least 3ft (90cm) to be visually interesting

After making some preliminary sketches, two options were considered:

Option A: A layout with a siding at each end of the oval for the L&B train, and the fiddle yard on the straight section behind the Raleigh Weir scene.

Option B: A layout with the fiddle yard at one end of the oval, in addition to the siding for the L&B train. This option offers the possibility of adding a second construction scene later, opposite the Raleigh Weir scene.

PLANNING A LAYOUT

After making a space model of Option B, the final decision was to adopt Option A, for the following reasons:

- The end baseboards are more compact
- It uses less material, is lighter in weight, and is smaller to store later
- The fiddle yard sidings are longer
- Trains are re-marshalled on straight track in the fiddle yard, making coupling easier

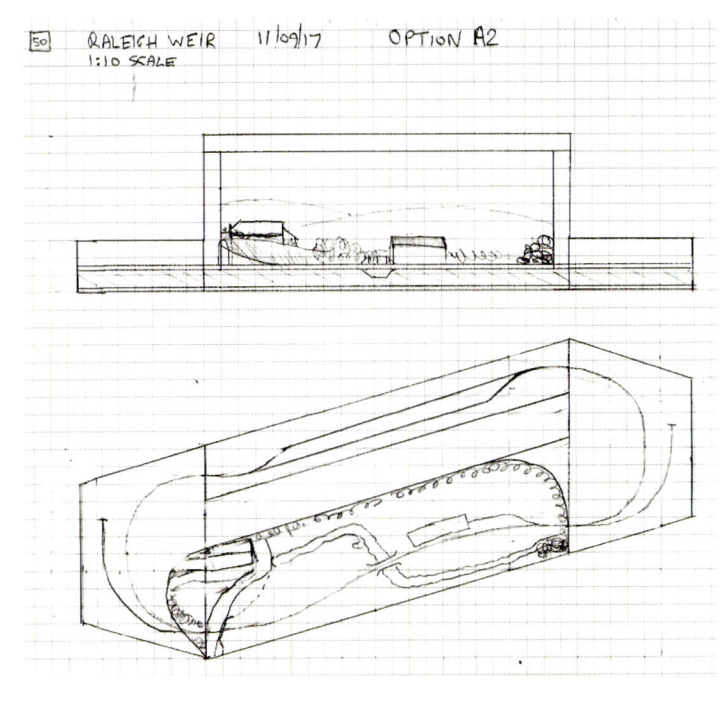

An overbridge forms a scenic break at one end of the scene, but trees must be used to disguise what should actually be a bridge across the river at the other end.

The use of Peco Setrack means that the ends of the oval must each form an exact 180-degree curve. The gentle S curve of the L&B route at the location is facilitated by angling the ends of the straight baseboards at about 15 degrees, forming a parallelogram, rather than a rectangle. This gives visual interest to the scene.

The geometry of the Peco Setrack used in the fiddle yard governs the precise length of the scenic section and the fiddle yard and its S curves. Analysis shows that there is a choice of making the fiddle yard (and therefore the scenic section as well) around 900mm (35in) or 1,100mm (43in) long.

Consideration of the length of the fiddle yard loops relative to the 200mm (7.9in) maximum length of each contractor's train leads to 1,100mm (43in) long boards being chosen.

The space model is shown in the two photographs.

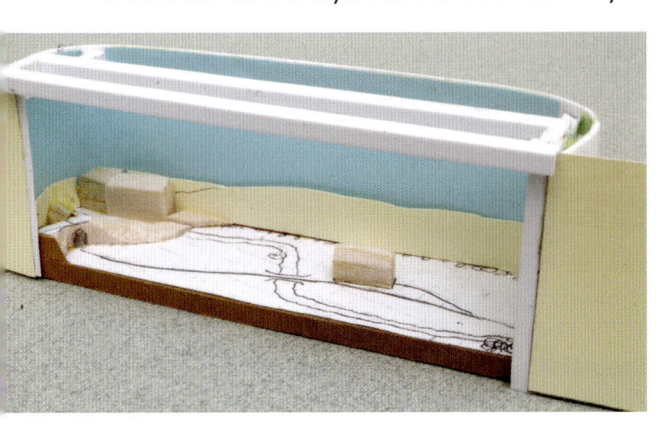

Raleigh Weir layout Option A plan.

A space model, constructed in an hour or two from balsa, styrene and card, gives a quick appreciation of the likely appearance of the finished layout.

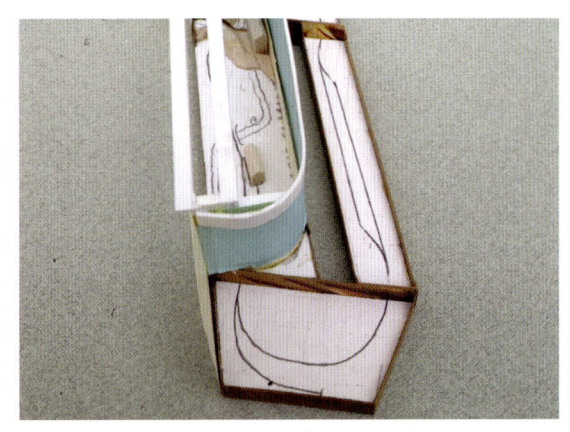

An end view of the same space model.

MAKING DRAWINGS FROM PHOTOGRAPHS

Some narrow gauge railways, particularly those serving private industries and estates, were remote and rarely visited, and a few photographs may be the only source of information about a particular locomotive, wagon or building. It is sometimes possible to make drawings by scaling from such photographs.

The first task is to obtain a few key dimensions of the subject. Possible ways to do this could include the following:

- A manufacturer's specification or a client's order for a locomotive or wagon may specify its overall length, width, wheel diameter or wheelbase
- The ground plan of a long-demolished building may be identifiable on old large-scale maps
- It may be possible to determine the size of a building by counting bricks, or by scaling from the presumed size of doorframes or of people standing nearby

THE EFFECTS OF PERSPECTIVE

Posed photographs of locomotives frequently show a front three-quarter view, and the probability is that a picture of a building will also show one side and one end, rather than a direct side elevation. This complicates matters, because of the effects of perspective. There are two key principles to remember: vanishing points, and diagonals of rectangles.

Vanishing points: All the horizontals in a perspective picture can be traced back to two vanishing points, one to the left of the picture, the other to the right. A three-quarter view will have one vanishing point for horizontals on the side of the object and the other for horizontals on the end of the object. A tall object will have similar vertical vanishing points for verticals.

Diagonals of rectangles: Imagine a rectangle (perhaps the United Kingdom flag – the Union Jack). Seen flying at the top of a flagpole, above and at an angle to the viewer, it appears distorted by the effects of perspective. But we know the diagonals of the flag still cross at its centre, and this principle can be used to scale measurements from photographs. As locomotives, rolling stock and structures are man-made, they have many vertical and horizontal straight-line edges.

EXAMPLE: CREATE A DRAWING OF AN L&B CONTRACTOR'S WAGON

We will create a scale drawing from a single photograph, to illustrate the process. A drawing produced from a single image will necessarily be an approximation. Because there is no alternative, the modeller must work 'by eye' where geometric precision is impossible.

The aim of the example is to create a drawing of the crude open wagon seen behind the engine at Blackmoor station, apparently running on two skip chassis 'bogies'. MAJOR, DARKER & LORAINE

No dimensions are known for this wagon, but a dimensioned drawing exists for the locomotive *Slave*, seen to the right of the wagon in the photograph. The portly man with a bow tie, obscuring part of the wagon, may also help with the scale, as his height can be estimated.

Step 1: Establish vanishing points
Three vanishing points are significant here:

- The wagon is viewed from a slightly elevated position, so verticals (the corners of the wagon

PLANNING A LAYOUT

body) converge towards a vanishing point some way above the scene
- The wagon is viewed from quite close to side-on, so that the horizontals converge towards a vanishing point far off to the right of the image
- The vanishing point to the left would be nearer, but there are few clear horizontals visible on the left-hand end of the wagon. This will make it difficult to establish the width of the wagon accurately

This example was worked on a computer screen with as large an image as possible, so the vanishing points are far off-screen and must be estimated. Drawing the lines on a printed photograph stuck in the middle of a large sheet of paper could enable the vanishing points to be established with more precision.

Less well-defined horizontals and verticals can then be drawn, as further lines radiating from one of these vanishing points. It is worth drawing in as many strong converging lines as possible – for example the top and bottom of the wagon body side, the rails, and even the top of the load of uniform-length sleepers in the wagon.

Step 2: Establish vertical dimensions

Any vertical dimension can now be estimated, provided one dimension on this scale is known reasonably accurately. The height of the locomotive *Slave* from the rails to the cab cant rail is (according to the drawing) 8ft (2.4m). So the projection of this dimension on to the front corner of the wagon (bold line) allows other vertical dimensions to be scaled.

Two checks can easily be made: on the basis of the above, the sleepers standing on end in the wagon scale to 5ft 6in (1.7m), which corresponds to the dimension on drawings of L&B track, and the man in the bow tie scales to just under 6ft (1.8m), which is plausible for a substantial figure. Using this scale, the height of the wagon sides above the rails works out at exactly 4ft (1.2m).

Step 1: By drawing lines along the longest clear straight horizontals and verticals on each visible face of the wagon, and extending these lines to where they meet (beyond the picture), the vanishing points are established.

Step 2: The nearest corner of the wagon is a good place to establish a vertical scale. By drawing lines from the two vanishing points along the main horizontals in the picture, a scale is created on the vertical at the front corner.

Step 3: Establish horizontal proportions
By dividing the object into a number of smaller rectangles, the location of each point on the side or end can be estimated. A rectangle seen in perspective can be halved by drawing its diagonals, and using their intersection as the mid-point. Each half can be halved again to determine quarters, and so on. Thirds can be derived also:

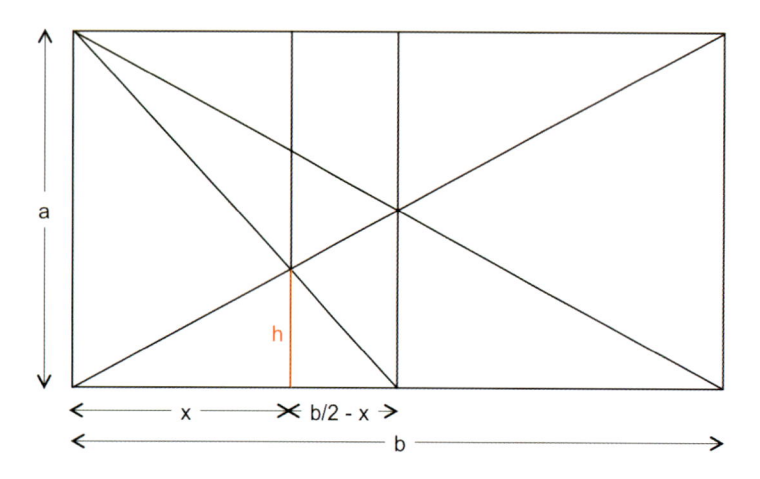

The one-third and two-thirds points of a rectangle lie where one diagonal of the whole rectangle intersects the opposite diagonal of half the rectangle. Like the mid-point, this still applies when the rectangle is seen in perspective.

Step 3: From the half, quarter and third points of the wagon side, other proportions (such as the width of the side doors, the position of the stanchions, and so on) can be estimated with adequate precision, and adjusted by eye when making the drawing.

Proof:
$h = Xa/b = (b/2 - X) 2a/b$, ie $Xa = ab - 2Xa$
Rearranging, $3Xa = ab$, or $3X = b$
ie $X = b/3$

Step 4: Establish horizontal dimensions
The absolute length and width of the wagon have not yet been established. Provided one horizontal dimension on each face is known, other horizontal dimensions can be determined. A known horizontal dimension on an adjacent object can also help establish the horizontal scale, by using the methods identified above to extrapolate larger rectangles from smaller ones.

The locomotive drawing shows that the distance from the cab back sheet to the front of the saddle tank is 9ft 9in. A 9ft 9in long rectangle is therefore drawn on the side plane of the locomotive. The diagonals of this rectangle determine its centre point, and a horizontal line radiating from the right hand vanishing point is drawn through it. Drawing a diagonal of the upper half of the original rectangle, and extrapolating this line to the base of the original rectangle (rail level), a further 9ft 9in distance is established.

Further smaller rectangles could be drawn, but the length of the wagon's body can be estimated to be 10ft 6in. Similar work allows the wheelbase of the 'skip chassis' bogies (2ft/60cm), and the bogie pivot centres (7ft/2m) to be determined.

The photograph cannot be used to establish an accurate width for the wagon, as the end is not clearly visible. However, as the wagon body appears about the same width as the locomotive cab, it is 4ft 6in (1.4m) according to the loco drawing.

PLANNING A LAYOUT | 57

Step 4: The length of the wagon is extrapolated from the known length of the locomotive. Its width is approximately the same as that of the locomotive's cab.

10ft 6in (scaled)
9ft 9in (known)
9ft 9in (extrapolated)
1/4 1/3 1/2 2/3 3/4

From these key dimensions, a scale sketch of the wagon can be produced, sufficient to permit a 009 model to be constructed.

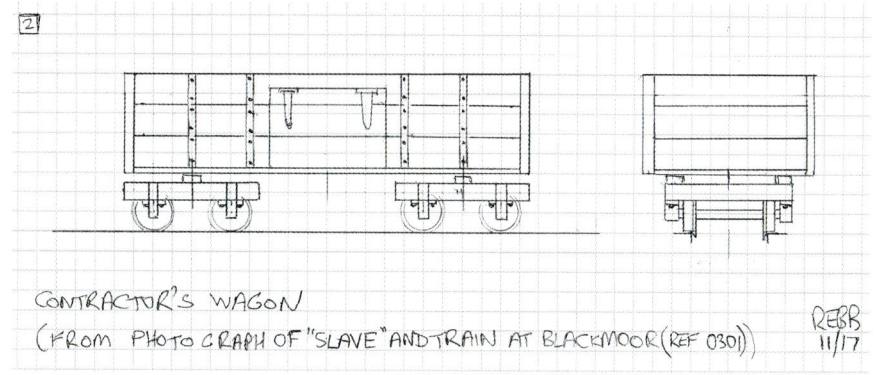

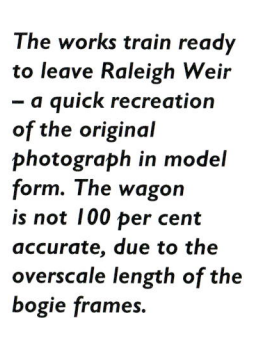

CONTRACTOR'S WAGON
(FROM PHOTOGRAPH OF "SLAVE" AND TRAIN AT BLACKMOOR (REF 0301))
REBB 11/17

The works train ready to leave Raleigh Weir – a quick recreation of the original photograph in model form. The wagon is not 100 per cent accurate, due to the overscale length of the bogie frames.

CHAPTER FOUR

LAYOUT CONSTRUCTION

The next task is to turn the plans for a 009 layout into reality. Few aspects of building a 009 layout differ radically from the tasks involved in building any model railway layout. The whole process is summarized in this chapter, and illustrated using the Raleigh Weir layout, focusing on the 009-specific areas such as the opportunities for small lightweight baseboards in this scale, and also the specifics of 009 trackwork.

A conventional construction sequence is followed – baseboards, track, wiring, structures, scenery, backscene, detailing – and it is advisable to plan carefully:

- Wiring and control (see Chapter 8) must be defined before track is laid, to ensure all necessary insulated rail joiners are installed
- Underbridges and terrain below rail level must be carefully planned and built before tracklaying
- The dimensions of structures must be known before track alignments are finalized, to ensure the structures will fit the available space

Some aspects of good working practices for 009 modellers are given in Chapter 2.

BASEBOARDS

Smaller layouts are more feasible in 009 (especially of industrial prototypes) than are possible in 00 scale, provided short trains are accepted. This may allow fewer layout modules and simplified construction.

Traditional construction: Soft boards such as Sundeala may distort over time, resulting in undulating track. It can be strengthened by adding a ply layer under the Sundeala, but this adds weight.

The underside of a traditional baseboard, with a Sundeala surface suitable to take pins and screws on a softwood frame. It is difficult to model terrain below trackbed level with this approach.

Honeycomb construction (see opposite): This approach needs very detailed design before cutting timber, as changes are hard to make later. Large areas of ply may have holes cut in them before assembly, to reduce weight.

NOVEL MATERIALS

For small layouts, novel materials can be used to give rigidity without excessive weight. For example, a small baseboard for a 009 layout may be fabricated from sheets of thin foam-cored board in place of ply. Alternatively, PIR (polyisocyanurate) or thermoset phenolic cavity-wall insulation block may be sawn to size, and its edges protected against accidental damage. Such blocks are extremely light and very rigid. They also tolerate many solvent-based adhesives such as Evostik – but always check before use. They do not hold pins and screws well, so a separate trackbed layer may be added to allow track and other items to be fixed securely in place.

BASEBOARD JOINTS

Whatever material is used for baseboards, the joints

With a honeycomb baseboard construction, a rectangular grid of deep top-quality plywood profiles forms the supporting frame and also the terrain profiles. The plywood trackbed is fitted only where needed.

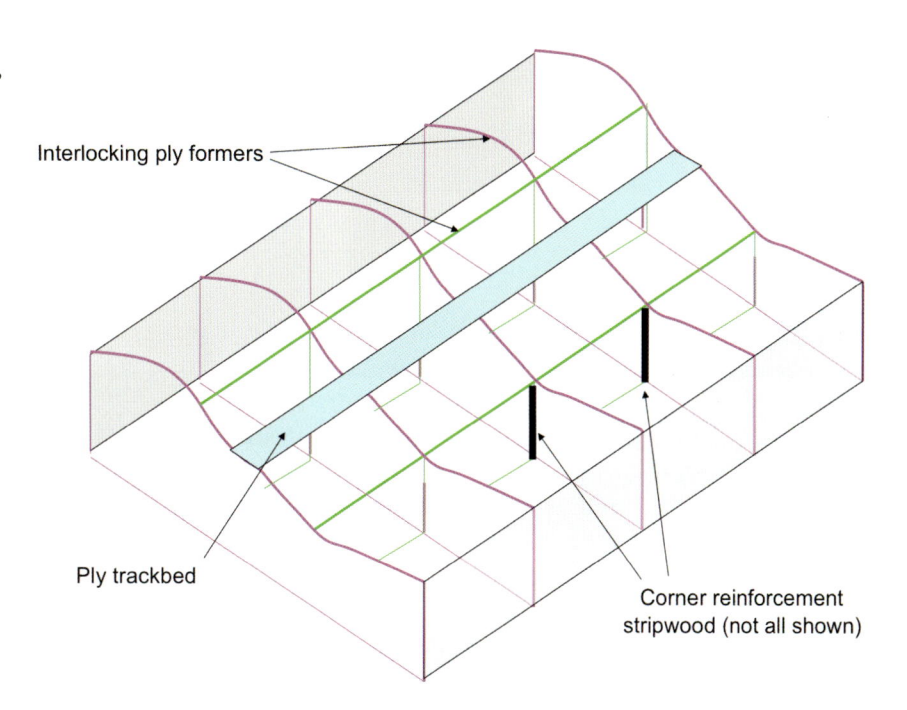

Interlocking ply formers

Ply trackbed

Corner reinforcement stripwood (not all shown)

between modules must be designed and built well, in order to keep the narrow gauge track aligned between boards. Two techniques are popular: hinges and dowels.

Hinges: Good-quality machined brass hinges with removable pins fitted are screwed to the two carefully aligned and clamped baseboards. Used in this way, they serve both to align the baseboards and to hold them together.

Dowels: The mating fascia panels for the two boards are aligned by dowels. Purpose-designed dowels or large (for example, M6) bolts can be used. Plain dowels only align the baseboards, but if bolts are used, washers and nuts can be used to secure them.

TRACK ACROSS BASEBOARD JOINTS

Most modellers align the rails at baseboard joints by fixing a copper-clad sleeper to the baseboard either side of the joint, and soldering the rails to these. The track alignment then relies totally on the accuracy and repeatability of the baseboard alignment. With a gauge as small as 9mm, this can cause derailments.

The rails at baseboard joints can be aligned by leaving a short length of track on one or both boards 'floating' (that is, not secured to the baseboard near the edge); sliding rail joiners then connect the adjacent rails after assembly of the two modules. This approach minimizes the risk of derailment at baseboard joints.

If the model is being built to a particular modular layout standard, even greater care is needed to ensure that any pair of modules (including those from other builders) will align correctly.

PROJECT: LIGHTWEIGHT BASEBOARDS FOR THE RALEIGH WEIR LAYOUT

Separate baseboards are needed for the Raleigh Weir scene, the fiddle yard, and the two end boards. All have rather unusual shapes, which are cut from two 1,220 × 450mm sheets of 50mm foil-faced PIR cavity-wall insulation block, bought from a local builder's merchant.

One piece is cut to form the two trapezoidal end boards. The other piece, cut along its length, allows the parallelogram scenic section and fiddle yard to

LAYOUT CONSTRUCTION

The sides that adjoin other baseboards are faced with 6mm plywood. Captive M6 bolts form alignment dowels, the boards being fixed together using washers and nuts. The ply includes apertures for the tracks to pass through.

The other sides of the insulation blocks are faced with 3mm MDF. The facings include stripwood corner strengtheners and supports for the insulation blocks. The wood/MDF is varnished to damp-proof the structure.

have a combined width of 450mm (17.7in), and a maximum overall length of 1,220mm (48in). The insulation blocks are cut to shape with a saw held against the edge of a tri-square on the surface of the block. Off-cuts from the blocks are used later to form raised terrain.

GAINING EXTRA SPACE

The parallelogram boards are intended to make the scene visually interesting, but can also enable further enhancements.

The overbridge at the left of the scene carries the lane to Raleigh Tucking Mill, an attractive stone structure set between the mill leat and the (lower) river. Space to include this mill is very limited, but by positioning the backscene within the 180-degree curved track on the end board, more space is created for the mill building and surrounding trees. This extra space also accentuates the impact of the newly constructed overbridge through the well-established landscape, rather than it just appearing to be a scenic break.

This change requires modification of the adjoining baseboard end panels. There is little advantage in annexing the equivalent space in the curve at the right-hand end of the scene, as the tree-lined riverbank forms a natural border between three-dimensional and two-dimensional worlds.

The profile of the fascia at the front of the scenic board includes scenic features like the overbridge approach and ground contours. So the bridge's location, the profile of its approach roads, and the ground contours, must all be worked out before cutting this fascia.

BASEBOARD WEIGHT

The aim was to build a lightweight layout. The weight of the components of the baseboard for the scenic section (1,100 × 325mm/43 × 12.8in) was as follows:

Insulation block, cut to size:	630g (22oz)
Wood/MDF framing and bolts:	1,080g (38oz)
Cork trackbed:	50g (1.8oz)
Total:	**1,760g (62oz)**

This is less than half the weight of a more conventional baseboard made from Sundeala on a softwood frame.

LAYOUT CONSTRUCTION

TRACK AND POINTS

SCALE TRACK

Most narrow gauge lines use flat-bottomed rail of 30 to 50lb/yard, although the Ffestiniog Railway had some 50lb/yard bull-head rail until recently.

Specialist suppliers offer various sizes of rail and of pre-cut copper-clad phenolic or glass-fibre sleeper strips, from which trackwork can be scratchbuilt. Even when using bought track for plain line sections, these materials can be useful when points with an unusual geometry (for example, curved points) are required to fit a layout into the available space.

However, most 009 modellers buy track from Peco, the leading supplier worldwide, or use an H0e track system from a European or Japanese manufacturer.

FLEXIBLE TRACK

The Peco range includes so-called 'Crazy' track, with the uneven sleeper lengths seen on an industrial line, and 'main line' track, with the size of sleepers (often shortened standard gauge ones) that would be seen on passenger lines. The sleepers of both types of plain track are moulded from soft plastic, so the track is flexible, and can be laid as required for the layout. Points in various radii are also available.

FIXED GEOMETRY TRACK

Peco also offer 'Setrack', with curves, straights and points of compatible geometry to enable a layout to be built quickly and easily. Note that the 9in curve radius may not suit larger 009 stock. Minitrains in Germany produce a similar range, but with even smaller radius curves suitable only for industrial layouts.

An advantage of fixed geometry track is that small radius curves are formed accurately. Laying them 'by eye' using flexible track may result in 'tight spots', which adversely affect operation.

TOP RIGHT: **Industrial and military lines often used very lightweight track (perhaps 15lb/yard).**

BOTTOM RIGHT: **The rebuilt Welsh Highland Railway uses new rail of 30kg/m, about 60lb/yard.**

LAYOUT CONSTRUCTION

Left to right: Peco Main line, Crazy and Setrack with Code 80 rail – that is, 80-thou (2mm) high – alongside scratchbuilt track with Code 55 rail (55-thou high). Typical 40lb/yard rail is about Code 40 in this scale, so the Peco track is seriously overscale. Most modellers tolerate this.

PROJECT: TRACK FOR THE RALEIGH WEIR LAYOUT

PECO SETRACK

The hidden areas use Peco Setrack with 9in radius curves and points for speed of assembly and to minimize space requirements.

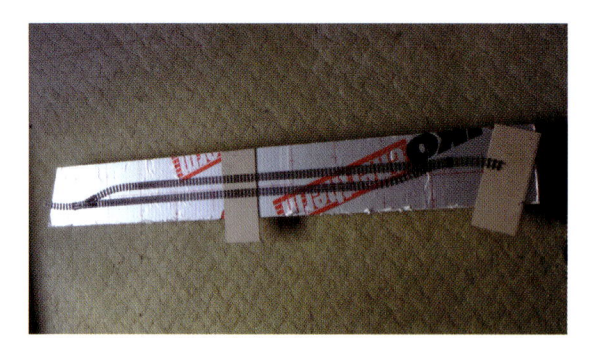

Here the track is first laid out on the baseboard.

The tracks across baseboard joints are aligned using 'floating' track with rail joiners. Here the fiddle yard to end board joint is seen with the floating track removed…

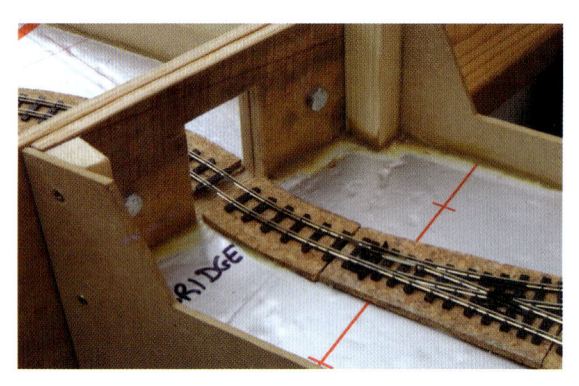

… and here connected.

A cork trackbed is glued to the foam baseboard, and the Setrack is connected, positioned on the trackbed, and pinned to the cork through the holes provided in the sleepers.

SCRATCHBUILDING TRACK

The scenic area uses scratchbuilt track with Code 55 rail (a compromise between accuracy and robustness).

The original track of the L&B used 30ft (9m)-long rails, each laid on ten sleepers 5ft 6in × 9in × 4½in (1.7m × 23cm × 11.4cm). The sleepers adjacent to rail joints were closer together than the remainder, with the rails clipped and bolted to these end sleepers. On straight track, the rails were spiked

LAYOUT CONSTRUCTION

Initially, a length of flexible track is temporarily connected to the Setrack on the adjoining end boards to establish the required curve. Marking along the sides of this track allows the trackbed to be fitted to the required alignment.

to the intermediate sleepers, whilst on curves they were bolted periodically (typically every fourth sleeper).

Track can either be built on a jig, or *in situ* on the layout. As almost all the plain track on this layout is gently curved, it is built *in situ*.

Because of the uneven sleeper spacing noted above, the (notional) rail joints at 30ft (9m) intervals, and the sleeper positions between, are marked out on the cork trackbed, and the sleepers are then glued in place.

One rail is then aligned to the required curve, and held in place with dressmakers' pins, and adjusted to set the rail the correct distance from the sleeper ends. It is then soldered in a few places, ensuring that it lies flat on each sleeper.

The second rail is pinned roughly to gauge, and is then soldered in place at intervals, with a track gauge positioned nearby. A second pass solders both rails to all remaining sleepers.

The panel of straight track over the mill leat bridge is separate, and is only installed once the bridge has been finished.

After completion of the track, it is possible to file a slight 'nick' in each rail at the joint locations. This allows the correct sound to be made by passing trains, which is worthwhile if quiet r-t-r locomotives are to be used.

The sleepers at the notional rail joints may be drilled for a short length of plastic rod to represent

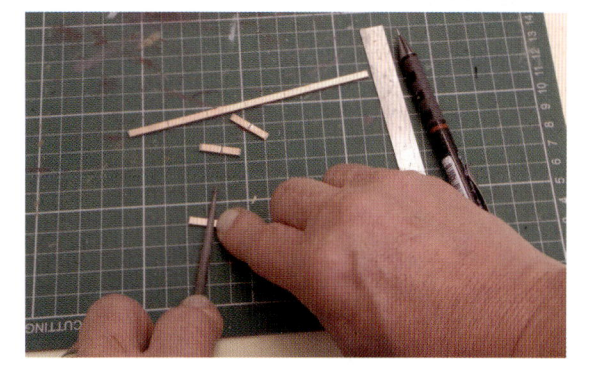

The sleepers are cut from C&L copper-clad strip of the correct cross-section. A cutting jig ensures a consistent length. The copper is filed away mid-sleeper using the convex side of a half-round file, to insulate one rail from the other.

the rail bolts. Intermediate sleepers may be drilled for a piece of thin nickel silver wire to represent each track spike.

The sleepers of the newly laid sections of track are painted with a 'new oak' colour paint (Humbrol 84), as the study of old photographs suggests that the sleepers were untreated hardwood.

Whereas the sides of rails on a model would usually need to represent dark rust, an attempt was made here to represent 'new' track, so the rails were painted mid-grey to represent 'mill scale' from the rolling process, and Precision Paints 'light rust' was overlaid thinly on the grey.

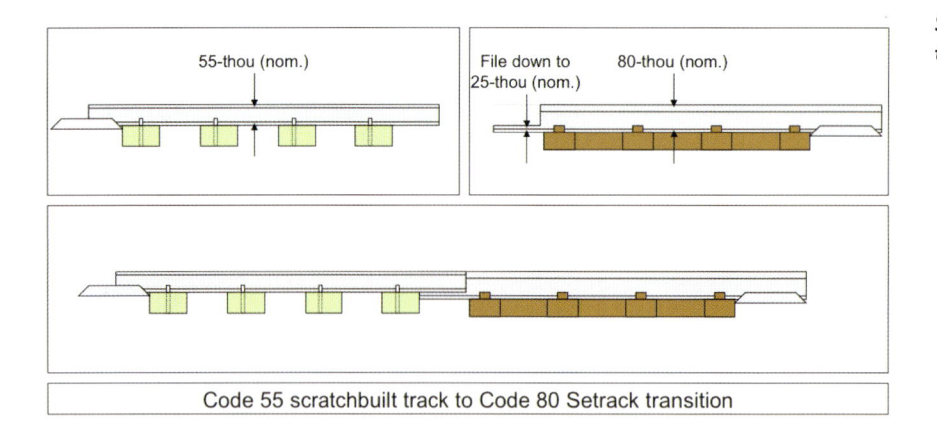

Special transition track sections.

Code 55 scratchbuilt track to Code 80 Setrack transition

Transition track under construction.

The remaining contractor's track, which will have been in place for some time, is painted more traditionally, to create a contrasting appearance.

TRANSITION TRACK – CODE 55 TO CODE 80

The Code 55 rail on the scenic section must be aligned and connected to the Code 80 Setrack on the end boards. This is achieved using special transition track sections, which can be removed for transport.

BUILDING POINTS

The layout needs one set of points with Code 55 rail to allow a contractor's locomotives to access the siding and locomotive shed. These points were 'temporary', being removed once construction of the line was complete. However, in the model (using 'artistic licence' – it is unlikely that this was permitted in reality) they must be robust enough to allow the heavier L&B trains to pass.

Step 1 (see diagram opposite): The alignment of the rails is drawn out full-size. In this case the geometry is based roughly on the downloadable template of the Peco 009 Y-Points SL-E497:

www.peco-uk.com/imageselector/Files/Track-templates/OO-9/SL-E497%20plan%20sheet.pdf

Sleeper positions are marked on the template – wider-spaced than the Peco design, with uneven ends, and including extended sleepers to carry a dummy point lever.

Step 2: Copper-clad sleeper strip is cut to length, insulated, and fixed to the plan with a Pritt

Step 3: The crossing (the 'frog' to modellers, for some reason…) is made from a single piece of rail held in a jig. The inner foot is filed away either side of the point, the thickness is reduced, and then the crossing nose is carefully formed with pliers. A needle file sharpens up the crossing nose.

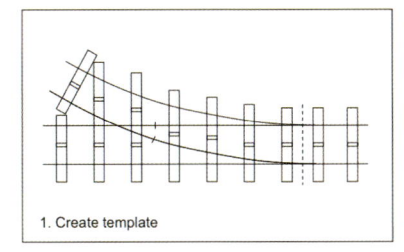

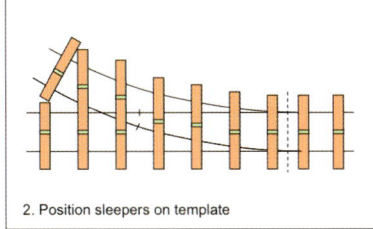

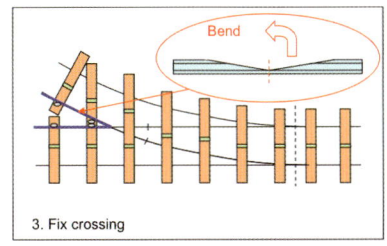

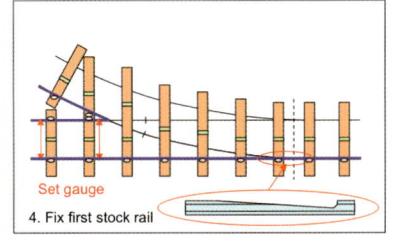

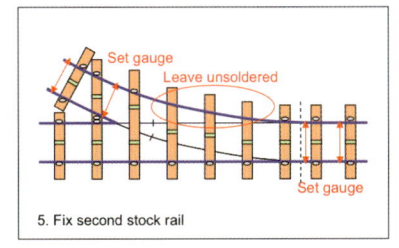

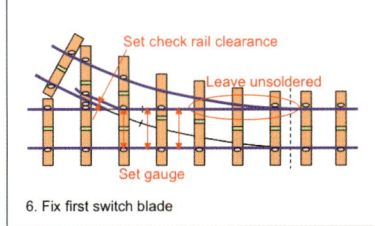

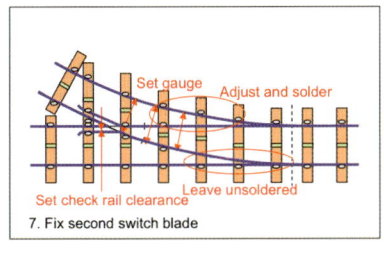

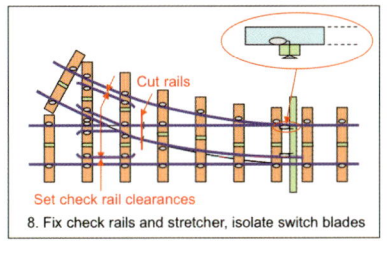

LAYOUT CONSTRUCTION   65

glue stick so that the paper can be removed later. Note that the Raleigh Weir points in the photographs have a slightly asymmetric 'Y' shape.

It is best to paint the sleepers and rails of the points before they are finally installed on the layout.

After laying the points, the stretcher between the switch blades is connected by a steel or nickel silver wire to a small slide switch mounted on the baseboard fascia. A change-over contact on this switch is wired to the track to connect the crossing to the appropriate stock rail, as the points are operated.

Other electrical arrangements are possible for scratchbuilt points. If the switch blades are not cut, the copper can be filed off the sleepers to isolate the open blade from the stock rail.

An electrical switch is still needed with this arrangement,

The sequence for building the points is shown in this diagram.

Step 4: The inside of each stock rail is filed away to accommodate the switch blade. On a model, a recess in the rail head accommodates the thickness of the closed blade. The end of this recess should be chamfered.

Step 4 (continued): The first stock rail is soldered in place, a track gauge maintaining the gauge past the crossing. When the second stock rail is added (Step 5) the gauge must also be correct at the toe of the points.

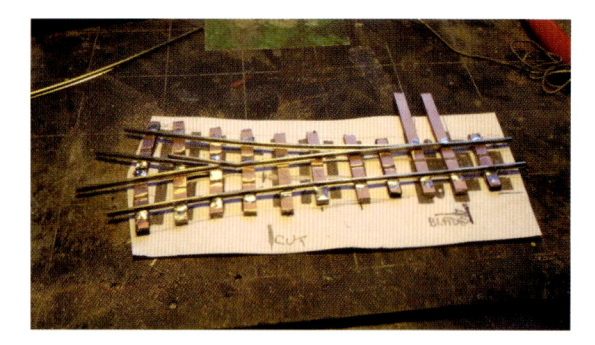

Steps 6 and 7: Switch blades are made by filing the foot off both sides over-length pieces of rail and thinning the blade towards its end. This may give it a vertical curve, which needs straightening. The other end of the rail is bent to form the crossing check rail. After checking on the template, each blade is trimmed and soldered in position.

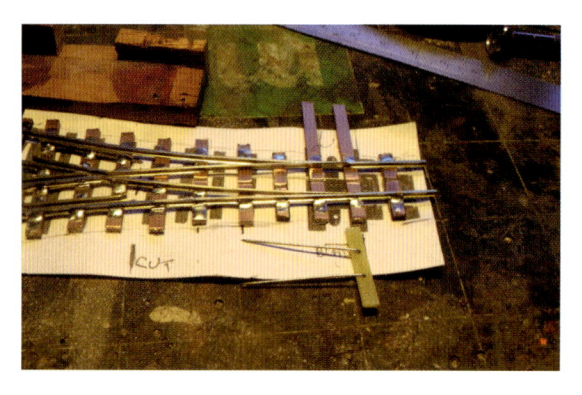

Step 8: Check rails are fitted, and the stretcher (tie-bar to modellers) is made by filing the copper off sleeper strip, and narrowing it to improve its appearance. Brass pins through holes in the tie bar are bent at right angles.

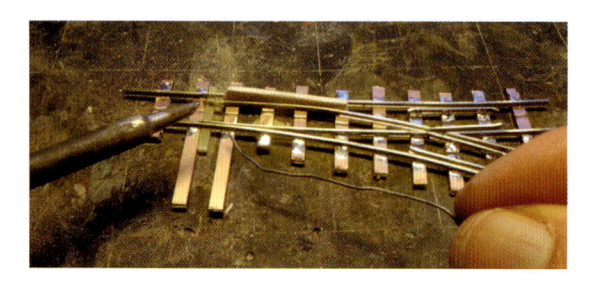

Step 8 (continued): Each switch blade is soldered to one of the stretcher pins whilst a scrap of wood holds the switch open. After assembly, the switch rails are cut between sleepers using a piercing saw, to isolate them from the crossing.

as contact between the switch blade and the stock rail cannot be relied on.

It should be noted that any contact between the back of a metal wheel and the open switch blade will short out the track power if this solution is adopted.

ELECTRICAL WIRING

Before the track is finally laid, the location of all insulated rail joiners must have been decided. This requires an understanding of how the layout will be operated and controlled, which is considered in Chapter 8.

BALLAST

Woodland Scenics Buff Fine Ballast is used, to represent new, locally quarried stone. The track is left unballasted in some areas, to suggest that work is still in progress.

STRUCTURES

Structures for 009 layouts are built using exactly the same techniques and materials as those for 00 scale, and various 00 kits and complete resin structures are available to save time for freelance modellers.

It is not the purpose of this book to describe these techniques in detail, but the basic methods used are noted in the following sections.

PROJECT: STRUCTURES FOR THE RALEIGH WEIR LAYOUT

ROAD OVERBRIDGE (DERBY LANE – BRIDGE 6)

This structure still survives, filled in and hidden by undergrowth. It is skewed, and old maps show that it was built alongside an existing lane, which was then diverted over it. The lane originally descended gently towards the mill, and although the new railway was emerging from a cutting here, the lane had to rise to cross the line before falling more steeply towards the mill.

A drawing of a similar bridge is printed on to thin card, and made up into a space model of a skew

LAYOUT CONSTRUCTION

The model has 1.5mm ply facings on a balsa internal core, and is faced with brick-embossed styrene sheet.

The skeleton of the bridge from above. Separate strips of brick-embossed styrene form the courses of bricks that stand proud of the surface.

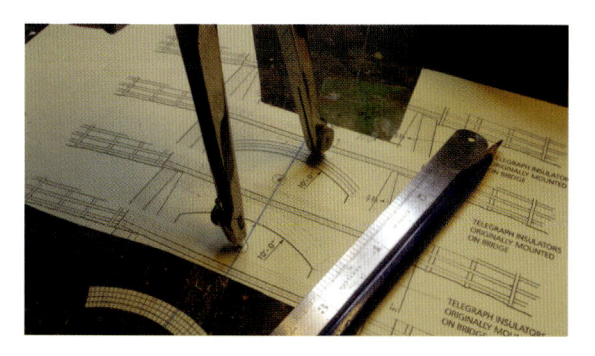

Each end of the brick arch is represented by a copy on thin card of the part in the drawing of the bridge, with the mortar courses embossed using a compass and pencil with 4H lead.

The overbridge before painting.

version, to check its fit within the model. Some 'adjustments' may be made during trial installation.

The off-white Marland bricks are represented using Humbrol 121 enamel, with a few bricks highlighted in various pale beige, brown and grey shades, and the arch and details in Humbrol 100. As the model is of the structure when it was brand new, no weathering needs to be applied, but a light grey acrylic wash highlights the mortar courses.

MILL LEAT UNDERBRIDGE (BRIDGE 7)

Details of this structure are inferred from drawings and photographs of similar bridges on the line, with a wooden deck on which the unballasted track was located.

An underbridge must be built and installed before track is finally laid over it, but the deck must be

The mill leat underbridge is constructed from a rectangle of 'planked' styrene sheet, with two styrene 'I-section' girders beneath. The handrails, soldered up from small brass angle and wire, are attached later to avoid accidental damage.

removable until the water of the mill leat has been completed.

The abutments are planked styrene, each with five 4mm-square wooden 'piles' and a cross-member supporting the bridge girders, and 3mm-square piles supporting the wooden retaining wall on each side.

MILL LEAT CULVERT UNDER THE LANE

The culvert carrying the stream beneath the lane consists of several layers of brick-embossed styrene, glued together with solvent and immediately bound tightly to a spray-paint can overnight. The abutments are balsa, faced with brick-embossed styrene.

The abutments are installed before the water is formed, and the ground is built up to the level of the lane after the arch is finally fixed in place.

ENGINE SHED AND WATER TANK

One photograph (see Chapter 3) shows this temporary engine shed, which consisted of two separate timber structures, end to end. Knowing the length of the three engines that may have been housed here, a drawing was produced, and a card space model built. A water tank for the engines was situated near the shed, next to the mill leat, and a platform carried a hand pump to refill the tank from the leat.

Clapboard-textured styrene sheet is used for the engine shed structure, with Wills window frames and a card/balsa roof. The water tank is built from planked styrene sheet, on a stripwood structure.

SCENERY: RALEIGH TUCKING MILL

Although only a background feature, this mill is historically interesting, and illustrates how a prototypical structure can be used to give context to a model.

A visit to Devon revealed that the mill structure survives, converted into four private houses. But what did the original mill look like? Internet searches revealed written descriptions of 'Raleigh Mill', but no old photographs. Some sources confuse the tucking mill, with its undershot wheel, with a larger mill on the hillside nearby, with several overshot wheels.

The obvious place for further research was Barnstaple Local Studies Library (which also holds material from the North Devon Athenaeum, an earlier private library). This revealed a 1970 book with contemporary line drawings of the remains of the building before modernization.

An enquiry to the library staff led to a website (www.artuk.org) giving free access to images of many publicly owned artworks. A nineteenth-century Barnstaple artist, Joseph Kennedy (c.1838–93), painted scenes of the area before the coming of the railway, including a painting of the tucking mill and another of the river nearby. References are as follows:

https://static.artuk.org/w944h944/DEV/DEV_BARN_PCF14.jpg
https://static.artuk.org/w944h944/DEV/DEV_BARN_1991_1484.jpg

These images, together with photographs from the site visit, allowed a drawing of the tucking mill to be prepared.

Space is limited in the background of the model for the mill, so it is built to a reduced scale (1:87, 3.5mm/1ft), which, together with H0 scale figures, helps to establish the perspective of the diorama.

Further research into undershot waterwheels led to a plausible arrangement for the sluice

LAYOUT CONSTRUCTION | 69

Drawing of the mill.

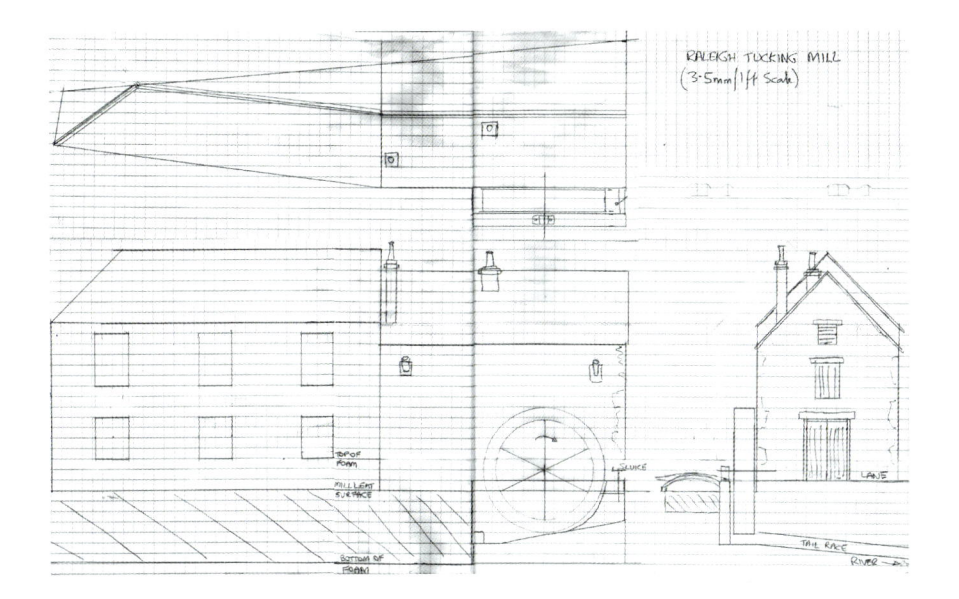

controlling water flow from the mill leat to the wheel, and the tailrace from the wheel passing under the mill into the river beyond.

The mill is built from plywood, balsa and card. The two phases of construction are emphasized by the use of different stone textures and roofing. Surface texture is less important on walls than on roofs, and the 'old' part is faced with stone paper created on the computer from photographs taken locally, whilst the 'new' section uses Noch stone-embossed card. The slate roof of the newer part uses Wills plastic roofing sheets, whilst the older part uses Slater's pantile-embossed styrene sheet. All surfaces are weathered using washes of dilute acrylic paint, to tone down the colours to blend into the landscape.

Time can be saved on a building in the background, so the mill windows are drawn on the computer and the design is printed on thin card, covered in Sellotape for a reflective finish, and glued inside the building shell.

The older part of the mill must be removable from the layout, in case the motor that drives the wheel fails. The wheel chamber is fixed into the foam block baseboard, leaving the building and wheel removable.

Raleigh Tucking Mill, showing the mill wheel fabricated from styrene sheet and angle.

The wheel is driven by a 4rpm, 12-volt, ac-geared synchronous motor with a series resistor, housed inside the mill.

PROJECT: SCENERY FOR RALEIGH WEIR

UNDERSTANDING THE GROUND CONTOURS

A scenic model requires an understanding of the ground contours that existed before the railway was built, so that the landscape looks convincing. The key features of the terrain for this model can be summarized as follows:

- The river obviously flows along the lowest point of the valley, so the ground must slope away towards the (off-stage) river at the right-hand end and back of the layout
- The weir (just off the right-hand end) raises the river level upstream to feed the town's mills via the mill leat, which is therefore higher than the river
- The man-made mill leat follows the contour of the higher ground at the front left of the layout to minimize the excavation work needed
- The railway has now been driven through this higher ground in a shallow cutting
- The lane has been raised on a new stone bank to cross the new bridge over the railway alongside the original lane alignment
- The engine shed and contractor's worksite are located on virtually flat meadows beside the river

THE MILL LEAT

The boarding and stakes that support the banks are represented by obechi stripwood, cocktail sticks, and (surprisingly) lengths of ribbon cable from an old desktop computer.

The stream bed is sealed at the baseboard edges and liberally painted with acrylic paints, then the baseboard is set up absolutely level and Woodland

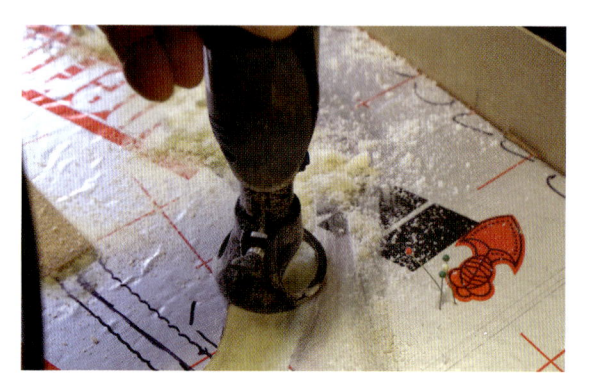

The mill leat is cut into the insulation block using a routing attachment on a Dremel multi-purpose power tool to create a trough of constant depth. Then the banks are sculpted with a craft knife with its blade extended.

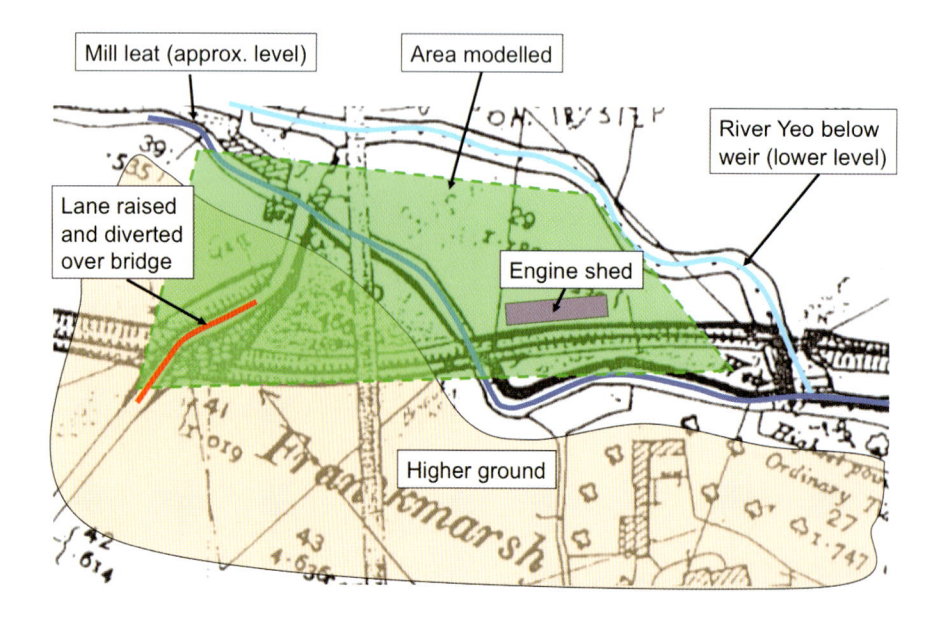

Key features of the terrain for Raleigh Weir.

LAYOUT CONSTRUCTION

Raised terrain is built up by gluing off-cuts of the foam block to the baseboard material, and the entire board surface is then carved using a craft knife with its blade fully extended – a messy task, but satisfying as the landscape gradually takes shape.

Scenics Realistic Water is poured in, in stages, over several days. Once the final layer of water is dry, it is given some surface texture by stippling on Woodland Scenics Water Ripples compound with a stiff brush.

THE HIGHER GROUND

The grassed areas of the scene are covered in pieces of felt, painted a base colour of dull green, and then scenic scatter is glued in place.

The raw embankments on each side of the overbridge are painted with a base colour of beige, and covered in Woodland Scenics Buff or Brown Medium Talus (loose rock) to represent substantial pieces of locally quarried rock. Brown Fine Talus is then sprinkled on top, worked into the cracks, and secured by drenching the entire slope in dilute PVA glue. Some topsoil may be added using finely ground talus material, with a hint of new undergrowth glued in place.

A similar approach is used for newly excavated cuttings, but the talus here is painted and covered with Fine Turf in soil and earth colours.

TREES

The small leafless trees and bushes bordering the river and the mill leat are represented by Sea Foam supplied as 'Forest in a Box' by Green Scene and others. The fragile dried twigs are shaped by breaking off lower branches and removing leaves from within each clump, before being sprayed (if necessary) with grey/brown dilute acrylic paint, and hardened with artists' matt spray varnish.

The bushes still in leaf – such as ground elder and holly – are represented by clumps of Woodland Scenics medium green foliage, and ivy is added to some larger trees.

SKY AND BACKSCENE

Dioramas need a backscene with distant hills and sky. The sky needs to be quite high to achieve a satisfactory appearance, but this makes a layout bulky to store. As an experiment for this layout, the backscene is limited to the low hills fringing the valley, the sky consisting of a thin fabric curtain draped behind the layout from the lighting frame. Therefore, 1.5mm plywood contours are cut to represent the hill profile, adjusted to fit together neatly, and glued in position on the layout.

Achieving a profile for the hills that is prototypical, and will also look right from normal viewing angles, can be difficult. Google Streetview can sometimes be used to help visualize the skyline from a nearby

---

ON-LINE VIEWING SERVICE

A free service is available on-line that allows a viewpoint location *and an elevation* anywhere in the world to be set, and an image of the view of the terrain from that point to be generated automatically from map data:

http://www.udeuschle.selfhost.pro/panoramas/makepanoramas_en.htm

To use this service, the viewing location, elevation and angular field of view are selected on the website, previewed and checked, and the panorama can be viewed immediately, or a link to a PNG image can be received by email.

location on a road, although recent tree growth often prevents the skyline being seen. The layout will be viewed from an angle, or angles, that may be impractical on the ground, a visitor at an exhibition perhaps viewing the layout from a higher eye level than the operator.

CURVED CORNERS ON BACKSCENES

These corners are essential on a backscene, but are tricky to achieve. Here they consist of two layers of thinner plywood, with the surface grain oriented vertically. Both layers are coated on one side with PVA glue, mated, and bound tightly to a cylindrical object of the required radius (a bottle in this case) using duct tape. After two or three days the tape is removed, and a rigid corner of the required radius results.

The hills are painted using acrylics, the colours being tailored to match the scenic scatter and foliage used on the scenic part of the layout. Distance is suggested by de-saturating the tones, so that further hills appear more 'washed out' than nearer ones.

DETAILING

CONSTRUCTION MATERIALS

Various materials are modelled at the trackside in the worksite area, including the following:

- Coal and ash near the engine shed
- Timber, ballast and rock
- Materials recovered from earlier contractors' track
- Materials for new track, awaiting laying
- Tools

LINESIDE FENCING

The L&B originally had stayed iron posts linked by seven wires, with three smaller, unstayed spacers between posts. The fences were presumably erected rapidly, before construction started, to separate the railway land from the farmers' fields.

A jig is used to solder up the stayed posts from 28-thou nickel silver wire, with 22-thou wire stays.

The fence wires are Berkshire Junction EZ Line 0.25mm elastic thread, from Model Scenery Supplies. This is stretched and superglued to the line of posts, and should tolerate accidental displacement. Four wires have been attached to this trial section so far, and some of the materials and the jig are seen.

After painting, the glued ends are simply pushed into the foam baseboard in the required location. Pieces of 22-thou wire glued into the baseboard between posts represent the spacers.

PEOPLE

A worksite needs a quantity of people to look convincing. Suitable period figures were found from the following sources:

- Langley Victorian/Edwardian working-class and upper-class figures (standing, and seated on the man-carrier wagon)
- Andrew Stadden Victorian/Edwardian figures
- Figures from old Airfix Rocket and Wild West Wagon Train kits, adapted as necessary
- Dapol Kitmaster C002 Railway Workmen
- Faller and Preiser H0 figures are used around the mill, to enhance the perspective

A horse and cart, with a man unloading crushed stone, suggests that the overbridge approaches are still incomplete.

LAYOUT CONSTRUCTION

PRESENTATION

At exhibitions, small 009 layouts are often shown without any form of 'staging' to add impact to the scene, exhibitors relying on the ambient lighting in the exhibition hall. Even at home, activities such as re-railing rolling stock and coupling/uncoupling, require a degree of care, and good lighting helps.

Traditionally, small fluorescent tubes behind a pelmet have been used for lighting layouts, but LED under-cupboard lights for kitchens now offer a more reliable alternative. For smaller 009 layouts it is possible to use rolls of inexpensive self-adhesive 12-volt LED tape to provide illumination.

PROJECT: PRESENTING THE RALEIGH WEIR LAYOUT

LED lighting is incorporated in a frame. Three rows of white, 12-volt, DC LED tape (600 LEDs per 5m roll, from www.directtrainspares-burnley.co.uk) are laid in parallel strips under each angle, warm white directly over the layout, and cool white in front of the layout. Each angle also carries a single rear-facing row of LEDs, to balance the illumination of the layout and the backscene. The LED tapes are wired to a connector on the frame, to connect a plug-type 12V DC 2A power supply.

The layout is viewed through a rectangular frame: two verticals of 25mm-square aluminium tube, joined across the top by two pieces of 30 × 30mm aluminium angle. The frame structure is here folded flat for transport/storage.

The 'sky' is very pale blue dress-lining fabric, its hem weighed down by chain. The fabric is suspended from an aluminium strip spaced behind the lighting angles. Further curtains conceal the non-scenic baseboards from view.

CHAPTER FIVE

LOCOMOTIVES

The biggest challenge for modellers attempting a prototypical layout in 009 scale is acquiring accurate models of the locomotives for a specific narrow gauge line. Even now that a few ready-to-run 009 locomotives are becoming available, it is unlikely that every locomotive needed for a realistic layout will ever be commercially produced.

This chapter identifies the key characteristics of narrow gauge locomotives, outlines the different ways of obtaining 009 model locomotives, and discusses the pros and cons of different approaches, including the main challenges of building 009 locomotives.

In Chapter 6 several locomotive projects are described, giving a sense of what is actually involved, and how modellers can learn to build locomotives by taking on a range of different projects.

A small inside-framed 2-4-0T locomotive with outside cylinders on the 2ft gauge Groudle Glen Railway in the Isle of Man.

A larger 0-6-0T locomotive on the Welshpool and Llanfair Railway. The outside frames, cylinders and valve gear can be clearly seen.

NARROW GAUGE LOCOMOTIVES

With the exception of small pleasure lines, industrial systems and some lines in Wales (for example Ffestiniog, Talyllyn and Corris) which ran loaded trains downhill to harbours or the main-line railway, most lines of 2ft to 2ft 6in gauge, especially common-carriers, used outside-framed locomotives.

The reason for this is that a line covering a significant distance probably adopts a narrow gauge because of difficult terrain, and therefore needs locomotives that will haul worthwhile loads round tight curves and up and down gradients. As a result, the locomotives need boiler, firebox and cylinders of sufficient size to provide the required power. The very limited space between inside frames of a 2ft to 2ft 6in gauge locomotive means that sufficiently large firebox and cylinders just will not fit.

Therefore outside cylinders are almost universal, and the firebox is always between axles, often behind the rear driving axle, to allow sufficient width for an efficient grate. But outside frames, outside cylinders and visible valve gear all make the 009 modeller's task more difficult.

Another powerful 2ft gauge locomotive, this outside-framed 0-4-0ST from the Darjeeling Himalaya Railway has its Walschaert's valve gear readily accessible.

MODELLING ISSUES

We now consider the various features of narrow gauge locomotives that designers of models must address, whether they are companies designing mass-produced ready-to-run models or kits, or individuals planning scratchbuilt models.

OUTSIDE FRAMES

Why are outside frames difficult? There are several possibilities for fitting wheels in a 009 outside-framed chassis:

- Permanently build wheelsets into rigid outside frames
- Drop wheelsets into slotted outside frames with slotted axle holes, and hold them in place by a keeper plate bearing on the axles (probably between the wheels)
- Fit wheelsets to inside frames, providing extended axles and cranks through thin dummy outside frames
- Drop wheelsets into slotted inside frames, and hold them in place by a keeper plate bearing on the axles

Once a chassis with wheels running in plain bearings has been assembled, the wheels cannot easily be removed or replaced. Small, delicate wheels could possibly develop a wobble, or a drive gear, wheel or wheel tyre could come loose. If this happened,

*The new-build Baldwin 2-4-2T locomotive **Lyn** has the Stephenson valve gear between the wheels. Because this arrangement makes assembly and access for maintenance difficult, outside valve gear is more common.* THE 762 CLUB

The valve gear on this 009 NGG16 Beyer-Garratt consists of many very small components.

76 LOCOMOTIVES

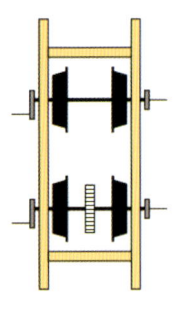

Wheelsets built into rigid outside frames

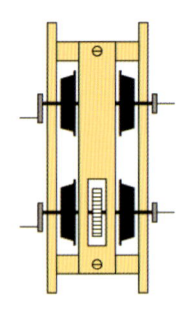

Wheelsets held in slotted outside frames by keeper plate

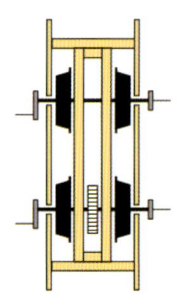

Wheelsets built into rigid inside frames, extended axles, dummy outside frames

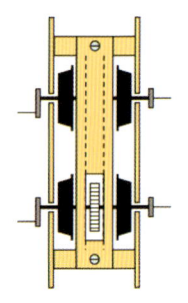

Wheelsets held in slotted inside frames by keeper plate, extended axles, dummy outside frames

The four main chassis options for 009 outside-framed locomotives.

Driving wheels suitable for 009 locomotives. Those on the left are intended for N gauge locomotives, the remainder are 4mm/1ft scale bogie/wagon wheels.

the chassis would have to be *completely* dismantled, which might be impossible.

It is more complicated to make the wheelsets removable from an outside-framed chassis. However, it is possible to build 009 outside-framed locomotives with an inside-framed chassis and extended axles to pass through slots in dummy outside frames to the outside cranks driving the coupling rods. When these cranks are outboard of the axle bearings, any play in the bearings will be amplified, and may lead to the coupling rods binding in operation. Some modellers overcome this by driving all axles, but again this complicates the design.

A 1970s-vintage L&B 2-6-2T chassis, showing wheelsets permanently fitted to rigid outside frames. This model has been re-motored.

LOCOMOTIVES

An inside-framed keeper-plate chassis with extended axles, this 1968 design also transfers part of the loco's weight to the leading and trailing trucks, in prototypical fashion. The design is complicated, and the loco's haulage abilities suffer as a result.

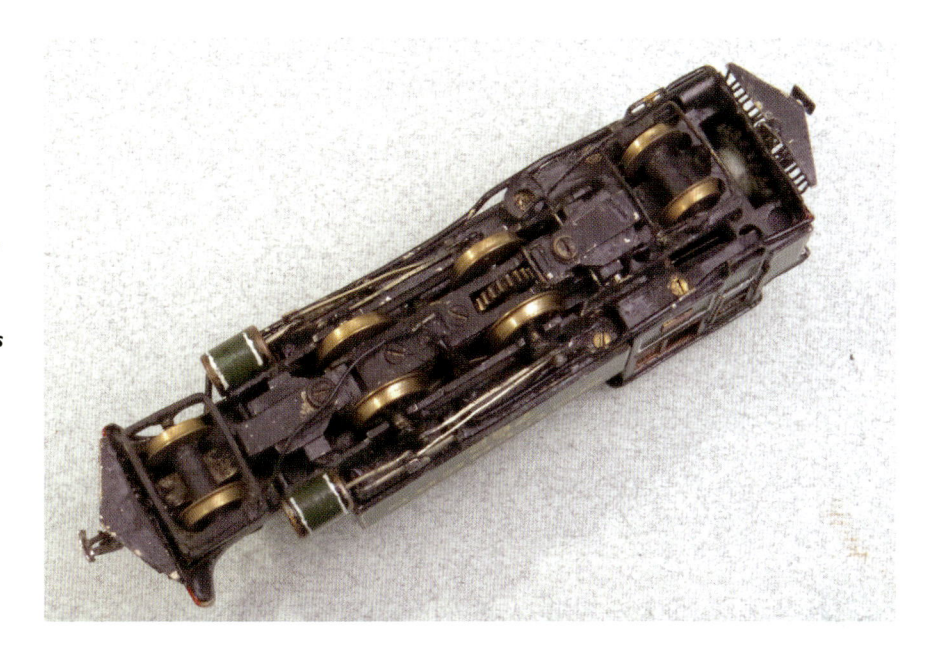

CURVING ABILITY

Flangeless centre driving wheels are rarely necessary in 009 for negotiating the sharpest curves of model layouts. It is preferable to provide the minimum of side play in the leading and trailing wheelsets to minimize lateral oscillation when running, and to provide a little side play on the centre axle(s). With this approach, most six-coupled 009 engines can negotiate 12in (30cm) radius curves.

The end overhang of many narrow gauge engines may look unrealistic on very tight curves such as this 9in radius track, even if it is within the capabilities of the locomotive. 12in radius track should be the absolute minimum for this type of stock.

GEAR RATIO

Narrow gauge trains run quite slowly, so we must ensure that model locomotives run well at low speeds.

A significant gear reduction ratio is needed to ensure slow running. It may be tempting for a motor with a worm gear to drive a pinion on one driving axle. However, with small wheels, the pinion size is limited (its overall diameter obviously must not be larger than the driving wheel diameter, or it will not pass over points!), so a high reduction is impossible, and such a loco may run unrealistically fast.

An 11mm-diameter driving wheel shown with a 24:1 worm gear set. This is clearly feasible.

LOCOMOTIVES

An 11mm driving wheel with a 38:1 worm gear set, illustrating the practical limit on worm gear ratio for 009. This might just work, but with any smaller wheels it would not.

Some typical M0.3 spur gears, suitable for 009 locomotives. Any smaller teeth than this would require very critical adjustment for correct meshing.

Experience shows that a gear ratio of about 60:1 is needed. This is not obtainable from a robust worm gear set with a small enough pinion, so double-reduction gearing is required – for example a 24:1 worm set plus 2:1 to 3:1 spur gears.

MOTORS

Motors have improved greatly over the years, but it is a good idea to buy the motor for a scratchbuilt model before planning the design, as continuity of supply can be an issue.

Many modellers will build end-to-end layouts, where locos do not run continuously for long periods, so extremely good long-term reliability should be obtained from most motor types. However, it may eventually be necessary to replace a failed motor, or one for which it is impossible to find replacement brushes.

Two motors suitable for 009 models. Their overall size is similar, but the right-hand one is more powerful, and better cooled thanks to its open construction.

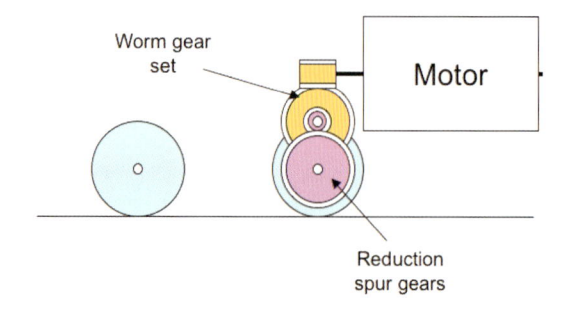

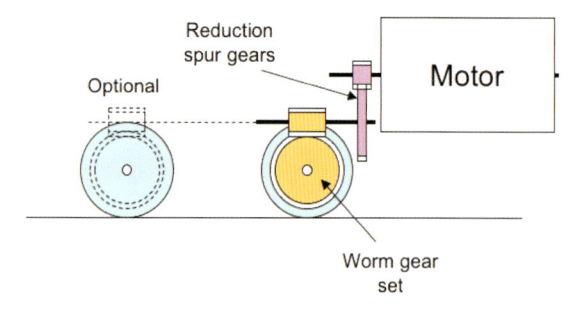

The two common drive configurations for 009 locomotives. Manufacturers often use the left-hand approach (sometimes with extra spur gears linking all the driving axles), while the right-hand configuration is probably easier for scratchbuilders.

LOCOMOTIVES

DRIVE TRAIN

A drive train that will give a sensible range of speed for the engine generally involves two-stage reduction gearing. There are two common configurations:

- The motor carries a worm gear, driving a pinion. This is followed by reduction spur gears to the driving axle
- The motor drives a layshaft by means of reduction spur gears. The layshaft carries a worm gear driving a pinion on the driving axle

Both these options are feasible, and examples of them are seen later.

The first approach is generally adopted for ready-to-run models (often with the spur gears driving all driving wheels) as well as by suppliers of gearboxes for models. The motor sits high above the wheels, which may allow a larger motor to be used (it does not have to fit between the wheels themselves). However, the spur gear on the driving axle is not accessible after assembly, and therefore should be a metal gear fixed to the axle, to prevent it working loose or becoming damaged during operation.

The second approach results in lower torque on the spur gears, allowing one or both to be made of plastic to reduce noise. They are also more accessible, allowing replacement during the life of the model if required. Worm gear sets generally have metal pinions, so can be fixed to the driving axle. Drive to all axles with this arrangement is possible using multiple worm gear sets.

Scratchbuilders seem to prefer the second approach, with the layshaft removable for maintenance, sometimes providing the means to adjust the meshing of the worm gear.

POWER PICKUP

Small locomotives running at low speeds can be susceptible to poor power pickup from the rails. This may be why 009 has sometimes been considered unreliable in the past.

There are two main approaches to power pickup: split-axle and insulated-wheel.

Split-axle Power Pickup

In this approach, non-insulated wheels with stub axles are fixed into insulating tube spacers. With an outside-framed loco, this can be quite straightforward, as the spacers can be of a large enough diameter to be robust (but of course the driven axle must also carry a gear).

The two frames are insulated from one another (and from a metal loco body), so that each frame collects power from the wheels on its side of the chassis – without the need for potentially unreliable wipers on each wheel. The two frames are simply connected to the motor terminals.

There are three potential problems with this approach:

Worm gears followed by spur gears to the axle.

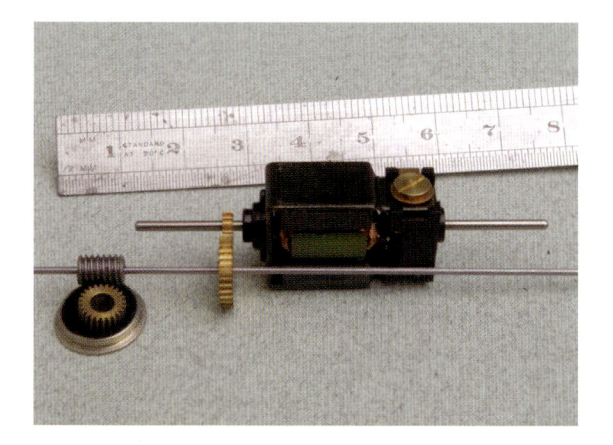

Spur gears followed by worm gears driving the axle.

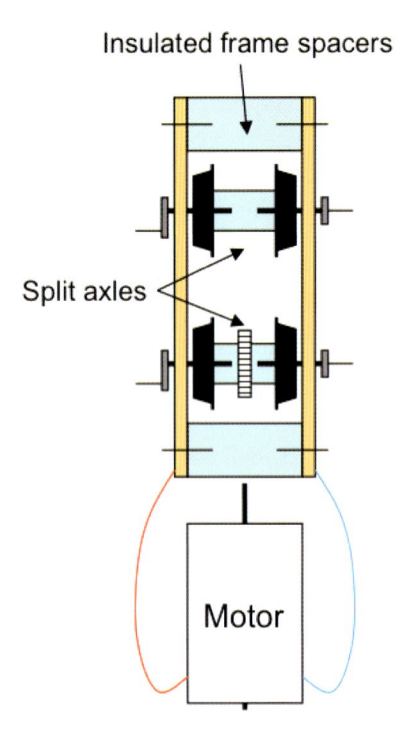

- The axle is in three parts (two stub axles and an insulating spacer). This leaves the risk that a part can work loose, leaving the wheelset out of gauge, and/or the cranks not correctly quartered. A major rebuild of the whole chassis is required if such a failure should occur
- In 009 scale, it is tricky to maintain electrical isolation between the frames, cylinders, valve-gear components and so on, and the locomotive's bodywork
- The need to use non-insulated wheels restricts the commercial products that can be used, although wheel tyres can in principle be connected to the hub or axle by a thin wire

Insulated-wheel Power Pickup

In this approach, the wheel tyres are electrically isolated from the axles, so the entire loco (frames, cylinders, valve gear, bodywork) needs no further electrical separation. Power is collected by wipers contacting each wheel, with the electrically isolated pickup assembly connected to the motor by wires.

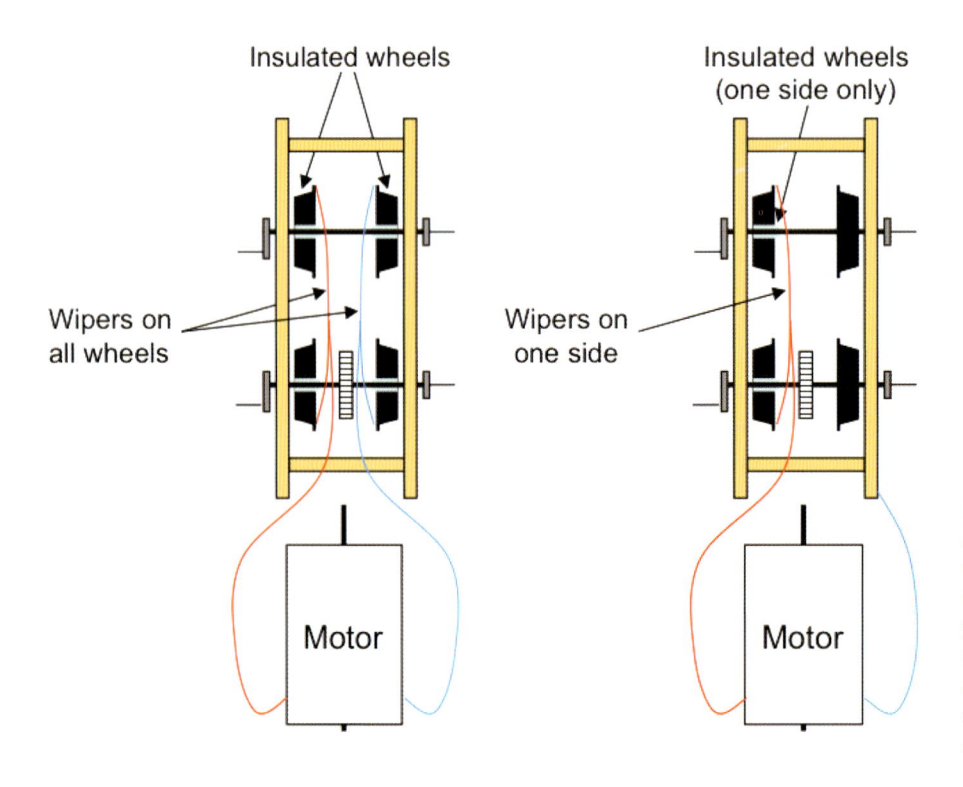

The key elements of a split-axle chassis.

The key elements of an insulated-wheel chassis. On the left, the frames are isolated, whereas on the right the frames are connected to one rail.

Most insulated driving wheels have metal tyres and centre bosses, connected by a plastic spoke moulding. The boss and tyre are keyed into the plastic to prevent them moving in use.

In a variant of the insulated-wheel approach, only the wheels on one side of the locomotive need to be insulated; the other side can be non-insulated, and connected to the metalwork of the loco. In this case, wipers are only required on one side of the locomotive, improving reliability.

There are two possible disadvantages:

- If locos can be turned to face either way, and double-headed trains are to be operated, the chassis of two locomotives could be connected to different rails, and short-circuit the power via the couplers
- If the metal of the loco body or frames comes into contact with one rail (for example, if cowcatchers touch the rails at an uneven track joint, or if leading/trailing wheels contact the loco frames on a sharp curve) a short circuit may occur

Achieving reliable power pickup is critical in 009, and the aim should be to collect power from all wheels of a locomotive, including leading/trailing wheels. It is also preferable not to build locos with a 'live chassis', for the reasons outlined above.

The power pickup assembly should be bolted in place, and easily removable to allow the wipers to be adjusted.

WEIGHT

The weight of a model locomotive, as well as determining its haulage ability, is a major factor in achieving reliable power pickup. The optimum approach to rolling-stock weight is as follows:

- All rolling stock needs to be weighted to achieve reliable running without derailments, even when being propelled by a loco
- Locomotives should be weighted as much as possible, to ensure reliable power pickup and the ability to haul the weighted rolling stock
- Locomotives should be fitted with the largest feasible motors, for robustness and to ensure plenty of power for the heaviest trains

DRIVING CRANKS

The driving cranks fitted to the axles of an outside-framed locomotive are a potential source of weakness in a 009 model. For a scratchbuilder, they can only realistically be soldered in place, and a failure of the soldered joint between crank and axle will lead to the coupling rods locking. Fortunately, resoldering a loose crank is usually straightforward, even if it requires the coupling rod to be removed.

The driving crankpins take a lot of stress, and need to be strong and firmly attached.

VALVE GEAR

There is no escaping the fact that 009 locomotive valve gear is tricky. With a gauge of 9mm rather than

A basic copper-clad power pickup assembly, with phosphor-bronze wiper wires. Note the screws used to remove the assembly for adjustment.

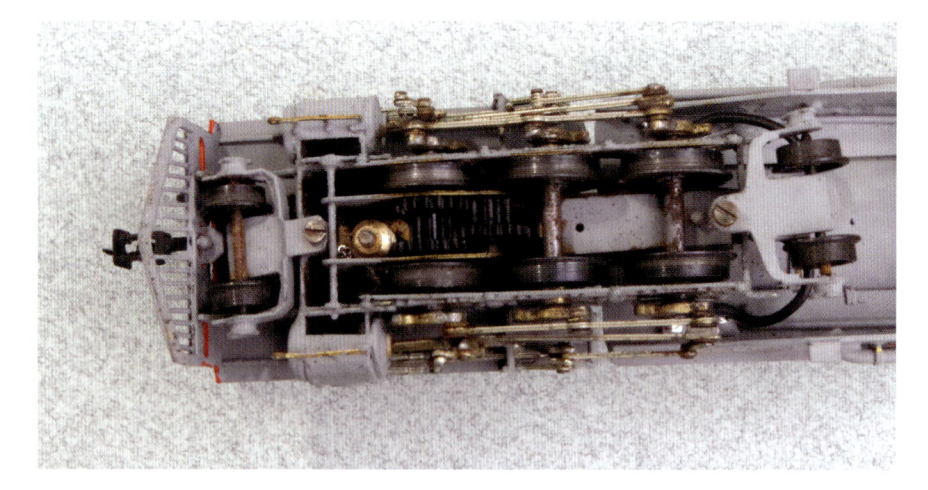

This view of a Garratt power unit shows the limited width available for the outside valve gear. Notice also the drive train, with the motor mounted vertically, and not one but two stages of reduction spur gearing.

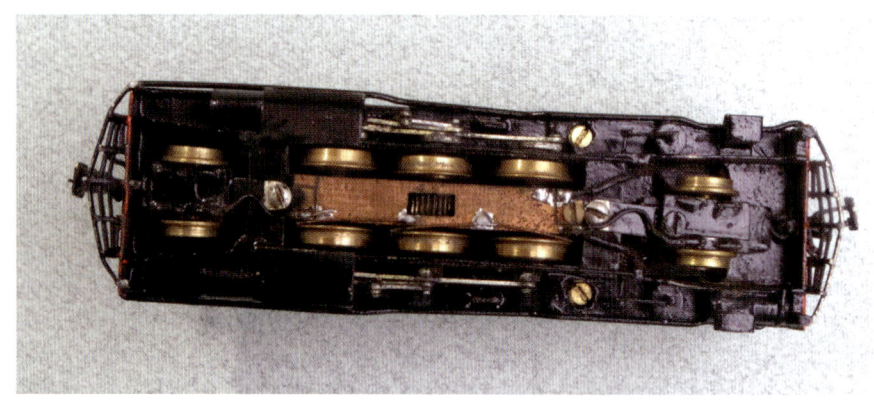

This underside view of a 009 L&B locomotive shows the tight clearances between valve gear components for (simplified) Joy's valve gear.

8mm, the frames of 2ft gauge locomotives modelled in 009 scale are wider apart than they should be.

Study of full-size 2ft gauge locos with outside valve gear shows that the clearances between components are extremely tight, perhaps $1/8$in or so in some cases. Models need much wider-than-scale tolerances to ensure operation without interference between rods. The challenge is to fix the various rods together so that they pivot freely without a lot of slack, which would lead to greater lateral movement, and therefore excessive width.

LEADING AND TRAILING WHEELS

Model layouts generally have sharper curves than the prototype, due to limited baseboard size. Longer locos with leading and/or trailing wheels can experience problems when running round tight curves.

The leading and trailing wheels may run in inside-framed trucks between the outside frames of the loco. This means that on curves these wheels must move laterally between the frames, and could contact the frames, derailing the engine and/or causing an electrical short circuit between the wheel and the loco frame.

Derailments must, of course, be avoided completely, by giving adequate sideways movement to these wheels, but occasional light physical contact between wheel and frame can be tolerated, provided electrical contact does not lead to a short circuit.

Different builders have found ingenious ways to increase the clearance on curves without unsightly frame 'cut-outs':

- Splay the outside frames past the leading/trailing wheels to give additional clearance

- Make the outside frames of thinner material than that used to support the driving wheels
- Use thinner tread width on the leading/trailing wheels
- Make cut-outs in the outside frames, and cover these frame sections with thin insulating material before painting the engine
- Provide flangeless 'dummy' leading/trailing wheels, with measures to ensure they remain above railhead level (for example, chamfered wheel tread)

The first three solutions can all be seen in the L&B locomotive photograph opposite.

There are also solutions that mitigate the risk of occasional short circuits between wheel and frame:

- Use insulated wheels on both sides of the locomotive to avoid 'live frames'
- Fit a thin insulating film inside the metal frames beside the leading/trailing wheels
- Use styrene sheet for the outside frames over the leading/trailing wheels
- Use plastic leading/trailing wheels (although these prevent power pickup from these wheels)

READY-TO-RUN 009 LOCOMOTIVES

Ready-to-run (r-t-r) 009 UK-outline locomotives are a recent development, so 009 modellers do not have long-term experience with them. However, most have long-term experience of using N gauge chassis, or have experience of modern standard gauge r-t-r models.

MANUFACTURING METHODS

The modern production methods used for models are truly amazing. A manufacturer who has decided (by market surveys, cost estimates and suchlike) to produce a particular ready-to-run locomotive goes through a number of design processes.

First, he creates a 3D computer-aided design (CAD) model of the complete locomotive, based on existing drawings, and perhaps a survey of a surviving locomotive. In some cases this involves scanning an actual locomotive with a 3D laser scanner.

Then he engineers (on the CAD system) all the component parts needed to build a working model that can be manufactured, and that correspond to

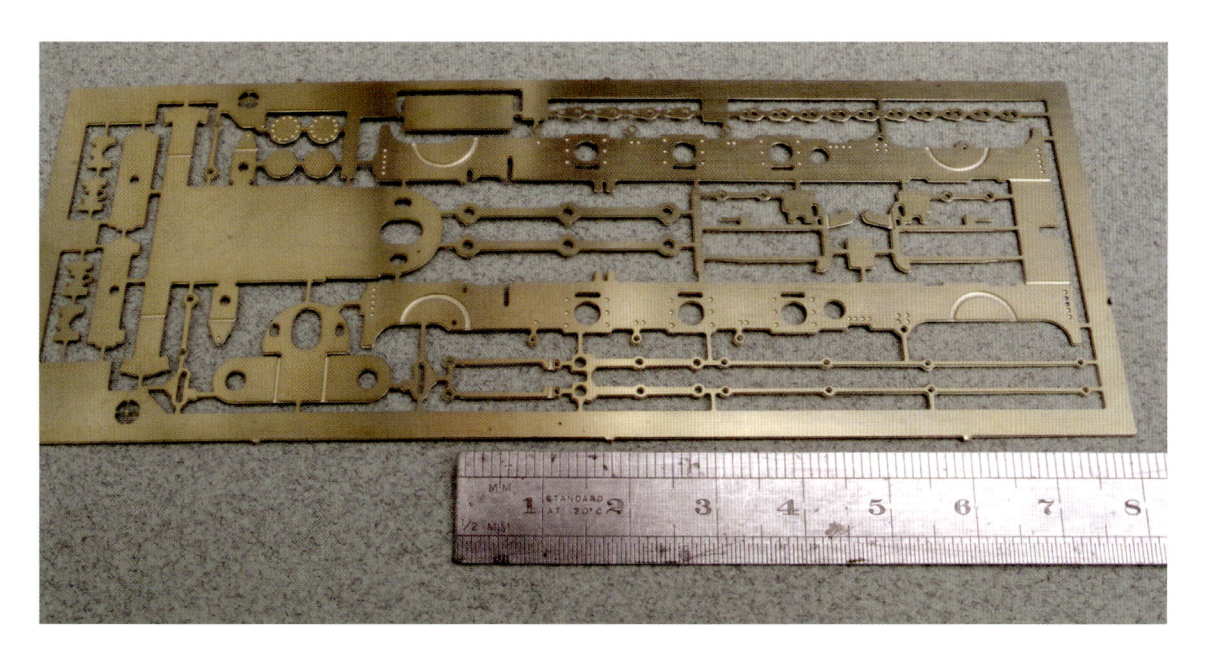

Typical frame etch for an outside-framed 2-6-2T kit. The semi-circles indicate the areas to be cut away to provide additional swing of leading and trailing trucks.

the CAD outline design. Choices are made at this stage about the individual parts that will form the final product. For example, this might mean making the cab moulding separate, if variants may require different cabs to achieve further sales in the future. This stage in the process relies on an established manufacturer's experience of how best to achieve reliability, and how to incorporate existing components into the new design.

Next he carries out extensive verification checking of the design, as rectifying mistakes later in the process is much more expensive. This verification may involve making 3D-printed trial parts from plastic, to check them and the assembly process.

Then he creates CAD models of the tooling required to make each part, and downloads these models to computer-controlled machines that (for example) electrically etch the shape of the part into metal tool blanks.

The various parts are then manufactured, first in trial quantities, later in production quantities, by fitting the tools into moulding machines (for plastic or metal), and literally watching the parts pile up in the output bin of the automatically controlled machine.

Assembly may be carried out before or after painting, depending on the design. The parts, or the complete models, are painted by spraying them with a base colour and then printing the detail in a giant version of an ink-jet printer, using UV-hardened paints rather than ink. The artwork for the printer is simply a layer in the CAD design for each face of the model.

MAKING CHANGES

It can be appreciated that some aspects of the design are easier than others to alter at a later stage. For example, the livery can be changed by modifying the artwork layer in the CAD model fed to the paint printer, so a different livery or loco number is easily achieved, at modest cost.

Parts originally designed to be separate can be replaced with different parts for a later batch of

Minitrains introduced this ready-to-run Bagnall tank to suit their H0e 0-4-0 chassis.

The long-awaited Heljan L&B Manning Wardle 2-6-2T. Here, 761 Taw is pictured running light through Chelfham station.
PETER AINLEY

LOCOMOTIVES

models. The CAD design, tooling design and the actual tool for the altered part must be produced, and the cost of this is small compared to the total design cost, but significantly higher than changing the livery. So in the example used earlier, a different cab design could be produced relatively easily for a later batch of models.

Other aspects of the design are potentially much more complex and costly to change.

3D-PRINTED LOCOMOTIVES

Anyone with a CAD facility and the skills to use it can produce a 3D CAD model of a complete locomotive body (in effect the first step in the sequence outlined above). With very little additional effort – involving selecting a commercially produced mechanism (perhaps an N gauge one in the case of 009) and designing the locomotive body to fit that – a single 3D-printed plastic loco bodyshell can be produced on demand for a modest cost by anyone with a suitable 3D printer (for example, a local design facility, or an on-line 3D-printing bureau).

As a result, small suppliers can offer ready-to-run 3D-printed 009 locomotives.

The railways serving the World War I trenches are popular with modellers. Also, several of these Baldwin 4-6-0T locomotives afterwards ran on UK narrow gauge lines. This may have led Bachmann to choose this prototype. The Ashover Light Railway's Hummy, *heavily weathered, is seen here.*

Fourdees produce a range of hand-finished and painted ready-to-run 009 locomotives, with 3D-printed bodies (some with etched brass overlays) on N gauge chassis. The North Wales Narrow Gauge Railway 0-6-4T Beddgelert *is seen here.*

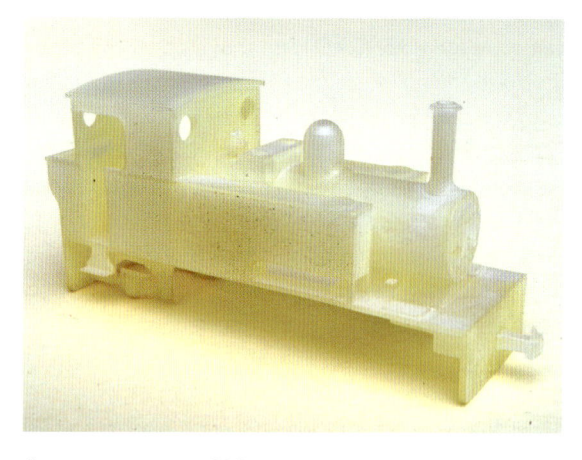

A growing range of 3D-printed bodyshells is available for 009 locomotives. This one is for Bagnall 0-4-2T Isaac. It will fit an inside-framed N gauge chassis, but an outside-framed chassis would be more authentic.

Spare-time CAD designers create 3D models of locos and other 009 equipment, which can be ordered via on-line 3D-printing bureaux. The accuracy and quality of the model are unknown to the prospective purchaser, but the price is usually low enough to warrant taking a chance.

COMPROMISES

It is a huge benefit for a modeller when a reputable supplier introduces a ready-to-run model of a prototype that suits their layout. It saves a lot of time and effort, and a reliable engine can be confidently anticipated.

However, there is a price to pay for this benefit, because no model, scratchbuilt or commercially produced, is ever perfect. When scratchbuilding, one of the tricks is to understand what will be 'good enough' to produce a convincing model that satisfies the builder, and stop there.

Commercial suppliers have a different priority. They must limit the money they spend developing the design, engineer it for efficient production, and then sell as many as possible from the same tooling. As most buyers will not be perfectionists, but are cost-conscious, a model may have to include compromises that simplify the design and/or keep the price to a reasonable level.

Even so, ready-to-run models sold in the quantities likely for 009 (perhaps a few thousand) will be quite costly to develop, and therefore to buy. But they will still be only a fraction of the cost of paying a professional to assemble a kit.

Where a ready-to-run model becomes available, it should be assessed as follows:

- Will it run on my layout – that is, fit through my overbridges, clear my platforms and negotiate my curves?
- Does it capture the essence of the prototype?
- Could I do any better if I scratchbuilt a similar loco?
- If I could, have I got the time?
- Could I make a few easy improvements to overcome any shortcomings I perceive with the model?

It is very easy nowadays to jump into print to criticise. It must be dispiriting for the designers, and for the manufacturer who has invested a lot of money in a new product, when people who would never contemplate scratchbuilding a locomotive post over-critical comments in on-line discussion groups, purely to try to show how much they know. It is also counterproductive, because if such criticism adversely affects sales, the manufacturer will not invest in other designs in the future. Praise a model if you want to, but if not, unless it is so bad that people need to be warned about it, say nothing and don't buy it.

Of course, when using a ready-to-run locomotive, the modeller lacks the sense of achievement that comes from having built the model oneself…

DETAILS

Today's ready-to-run locos are very finely detailed, and often come with a bag of parts (mostly small plastic mouldings) that can be attached to the model for greater realism.

Generally, crew (driver and fireman) are details that the buyer must add to a ready-to-run loco.

The small details on modern models are very fragile, and are extremely vulnerable to accidental

LOCOMOTIVES

damage in use over a period of time. This is a particular risk at exhibitions, where models may be handled by less experienced operators.

LIVERY

One of the attractions of a ready-to-run model is the beautifully-printed livery, whose quality exceeds what could be achieved by an amateur modeller. But this is a two-edged sword, as it means that a repaint (or even a small change to the livery) will worsen the model, as it is impossible to match the colour and finish of the original precisely.

Also, the ready-to-run model livery may highlight im-perfections in other models on the layout…

READY-TO-RUN CHASSIS

It is attractive for a 009 modeller to buy a ready-to-run N gauge or H0e locomotive, discard the body and use the chassis for a 009 model.

There are few N gauge models of outside-framed locomotives, an exception being the Graham Farish Class 08 diesel shunter. This has a short wheelbase (12+12mm) and small wheels (about 8mm), and although some modellers (and suppliers of 3D-printed bodyshells) use it, it may not suit scale modellers of the larger narrow gauge engines.

There are outside-framed H0e locomotives (from Roco and Minitrains, for example). Here, the 1:87 scale means that both the wheel diameter and the wheelbase are generally too small for scale models of any except the smallest British narrow gauge engines in 1:76 (009) scale.

BUILDING 009 LOCOMOTIVES

The principal methods by which a 009 modeller can build a particular type of locomotive are as follows:

- 3D-printed body on ready-to-run (usually N gauge) chassis
- Whitemetal body kit on ready-to-run (usually N gauge) chassis
- Modifying a (009, H0e or N gauge) ready-to-run locomotive
- Etched brass kit (usually body and chassis)
- Scratchbuilding (body and/or chassis)

The N gauge Grafar Class 08 chassis and a Roco H0e chassis can be useful to 009 modellers.

The differences in wheel diameter and wheelbase are apparent here, as a Roco H0e 0-6-0 chassis is compared to a 009 L&B loco.

These methods involve some of the more specialized skills outlined in Chapter 2.

Some information and guidance on each approach is included in the following sections.

WHITEMETAL KITS

The parts should be laid out on a tray and identified against the list in the instruction sheet. Then study how all the parts are designed to fit together. For the main structural components (sides, ends, footplate, cab), each one should fit neatly against a ledge on the inside of the mating part, the outside of mating parts matching neatly at corners, to ensure the joins are invisible on the finished model.

Usually, small amounts of whitemetal (known as 'flash') need to be cleaned off the edges of components, and the feed holes in the moulds used to make the part. Use old, fairly coarse files for this as the whitemetal will quickly clog a fine needle file. Similarly, holes in the castings to receive spigots on parts such as the chimney may need clearing, or even in extreme cases drilling out, to suit the mating part.

Especially in older kit designs, the cast panels may be quite thick. This gives strength, and prevents them distorting during manufacture or during use, but can mean that visible edges of panels (for example around cab side openings) look too coarse.

A key decision to be made before starting assembly is whether to assemble a whitemetal kit using low melting point (LMP) solder, or glue. This is discussed in the section 'Whitemetal Kits: Glue or Solder?' at the end of Chapter 2.

ETCHED BRASS KITS

Etched brass locomotive kits, available from several suppliers, are not for the absolute beginner, as a level of skill is required to make the chassis run well.

Unopened or unbuilt etched brass 009 kits appear from time to time on on-line auction sites, and probably many people who buy such kits never

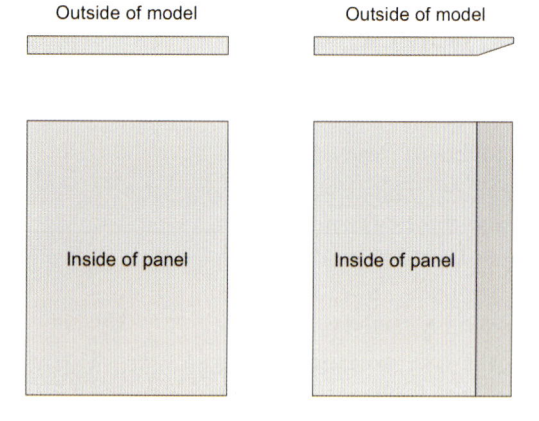

*ABOVE: **The appearance of whitemetal locomotives can be considerably improved by chamfering the inside of panel edges. Double-check first which is the inside.***

The contents of an etched brass and nickel silver 009 locomotive kit.

build them. Some modellers pay professionals to build these kits (or the chassis at least).

Some etched brass kits prove to be easier to assemble than others. Such kits involve complex CAD designs, and there may be residual errors in the dimensions of the etches. So the builder must be prepared to make changes (or even replace parts) to address any such problems found during assembly.

Before beginning any work, it is worth spending some time studying the (usually comprehensive) instructions, which contain hints on how to assemble the tricky bits.

Curving Ability

Kits often make provision for the builder to cut semi-circles out of the front and rear frames, to give clearance for the leading/trailing wheels on sharp curves. Some ways to avoid the need for this were described earlier.

Motor and Drive Train

The motors provided in brass kits are rather small, leaving a concern that the loco will have inadequate haulage capability. Generally a small nylon spur gear on the trailing axle is driven by a motor with an attached gearbox of nylon gears. There is a possibility of trouble from such a drive train if the nylon gear becomes loose on the axle, or is damaged. Changing the drive train would involve major redesign, so it must be accepted, but the engine should be made very free running to minimize the load on the motor and gears.

There is often a degree of flexibility in the motor mounting plate, which could result in one of the fragile nylon gears being stripped, but the plate can be strengthened before installation.

Two tiny fixing screws are all that holds the motor, gearbox and chassis in alignment (that is, controls the meshing of all the gears).

Power Pickup

The wheels in some kits lead to a 'live chassis' engine, so care must be taken during assembly to insert the wheelsets in the outside frames the correct way round.

Both inside- and outside-framed front/rear trucks can be modified to assist with power pickup. We will see an example of how to do this for outside-framed trucks later, but the technique for inside-framed trucks is slightly different. The live-chassis variant is described for simplicity.

1. Remove the metal tyres of the disc wheels in the kit from their plastic wheel centres. Turn

Standard 8mm 009 wheels, showing one metal tyre removed.

View of an inside-framed split-axle truck made by the method described.

The same truck seen from underneath.

new wheel centres from brass bar, each having an integral hollow half-axle. Solder the tyres to the new centres.
2. Thread one half-wheelset on to a plastic-coated steel axle (such as florist's wire), securing with epoxy. Add a fibre washer or a sliver of paper to insulate the half-axle from its neighbour.
3. Open out the axle holes in the truck frame to accept the half-axles (with clearance to ensure free running). Drill and tap at least two holes in the brass truck frame. Bolt a small piece of $1/32$in fibreglass (for example, copper-clad board with the copper filed off – a useful strong insulating material) to the truck, then remove it again.
4. Saw the 'insulated wheel' side axle bearing and its tapped hole(s) from the remainder of the truck frame, and reassemble, giving the frame a touch of epoxy to secure everything. Check that the two side frames are isolated from each other.
5. Feed the wheel + axle through the frame, and fix the other wheel in place with epoxy, setting and checking the back-to-back dimension after assembly.
6. Solder a thin flexible wire to the 'insulated' side sub-frame to carry current to the main current collector assembly, current from the 'live' side passing via the truck pivot bolt. Fix a lead weight on an over-length bolt on the 'live' side of the truck, carefully filing the lead to shape to maintain clearance from the 'non-earthed' side of the truck and its wheel, and solder in place.

Robustness

Most kits contain a thicker nickel silver etch for the frames, coupling rods, valve gear, and other critical parts. The resulting frames are rather insubstantial, so to improve rigidity it is a good idea to fit additional $1/32$in brass strengthening plates.

Rivet detail

The parts often have dips etched on the rear, to be pressed through to form rivet heads on the front of the part. To do this, place the etch on a piece of thick writing paper on a Formica surface (for example a kitchen chopping board, not the worktop!), and then press down a scriber firmly on each dip. A test soon establishes the pressure needed.

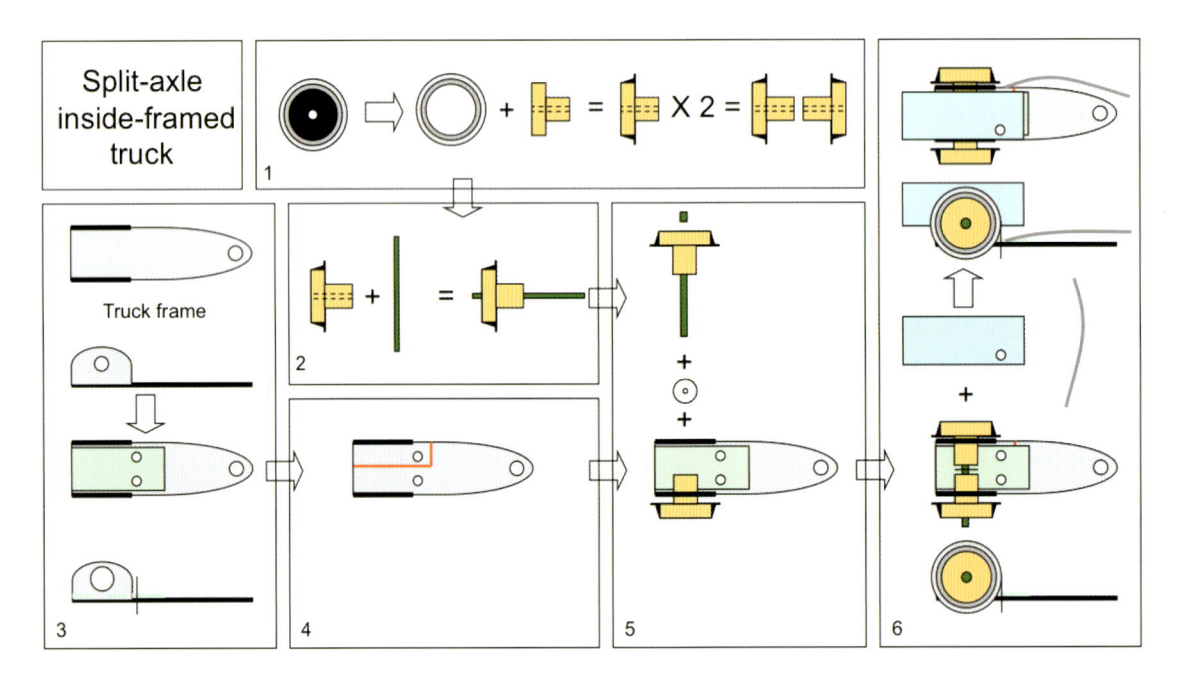

The process for making an inside-framed split-axle truck.

Boiler fittings

Items such as chimney and dome are supplied as either lost-wax brass or whitemetal castings. For engines with polished chimney cap and dome, it is worth replacing these with turned and polished copper or brass ones.

Assembly

Assembly is straightforward, although often fiddly, using a 15W soldering iron, liquid flux and (preferably) lead/tin solder, rather than lead-free. A possible approach is to use the thin flux-cored lead/tin solder which is still sold for repairing old electrical equipment. A larger iron may be needed for major sub-assemblies. It is important to clean the mating surfaces well, both before and after assembly.

In spite of reservations about certain design aspects of brass kits, they can be made to work well, and they certainly make up into beautiful models.

SCRATCHBUILDING LOCOMOTIVE CHASSIS

Although some modellers favour inside frames with extended cranks or keeper plates, the most certain path to a successful 009 chassis is simplicity – pre-assembled and checked wheelsets permanently built into a very strong chassis with rigid outside frames.

Wheelsets

When building the wheels permanently into a chassis, it is essential to spend time on the driving wheelsets – wheels and axles (and gear on the driven axle) – to ensure that they remain reliable in service over many years.

The wheelset assembly procedure is as follows:

1. Turn brass sleeves to fit snugly on the axles. The sleeves are 7.5mm long (less the thickness of any wheel bosses). Solder these sleeves to the centre of overlength axles. The sleeve for the driven axle must accept the brass worm set pinion (bored out if necessary), which is soldered centrally on the sleeve. Clean off any excess solder.
2. Press the first wheel on to the axle. Using flat-faced bored mandrels with clearance holes for the axle, press the wheel between the flat jaws of a good machine vice, or between the tailstock and the chuck of a lathe, ensuring that everything remains in perfect alignment. Pressure must be applied to the wheel boss, and the wheel must remain perpendicular to the axle throughout.
3. Repeat the above for the second wheel.
4. Check that the wheelsets run absolutely true, by rolling them in turn down a length of 9mm gauge track. Then work a small amount of epoxy between the base of the spokes and the sleeve on the axle, as an extra measure to secure them in place.

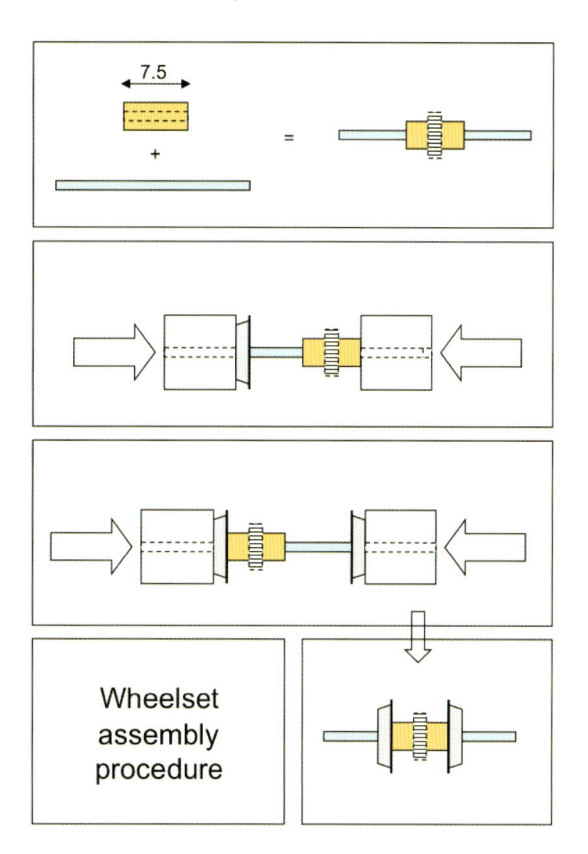

The method for assembling driving wheelsets.

Frames

A chassis should be very strong, with frames and spacers soldered up from $1/32$in brass or nickel silver strip. As described earlier, the front and back ends of the outside frames can be splayed to give clearance for the leading and trailing wheels. Alternatively they can be made separately from thinner material, the solid frames only needing to include the driving wheels.

The frames are simple rectangles, cut square at the front of the cylinders and in front of the eventual trailing wheel location. Two oversize frames are cut out, and soldered together. The pair of coupling rod blanks should also be made and soldered together at this stage.

The detail is then carefully marked out using a sharp scriber. A blue or black thick-tipped spirit-based marker provides a good substitute for old-fashioned marking blue, allowing the scriber marks to be seen more clearly. The ink is cleaned off when polishing the part later.

To hold everything square during assembly, turned brass or aluminium temporary spacers are bolted between the frames, front and rear. At the front end, the temporary spacer can often be fitted where the cylinders will be, but at the rear

Frame spacers used for chassis construction.

the frames can be artificially lengthened purely to accommodate the spacer, and then shortened after the chassis is soldered up.

The pair of frames is then placed on a substantial steel plate (or the top of a machine vice), and the holes are marked with a sharp centre punch hit with a pin hammer. Double- and triple-check that critical holes are punched in exactly the correct place. A lot depends on this.

The pair of frames can now be drilled. First, make a small pilot hole (of a size no bigger than the planned crankpins) in each marked position. Before opening up these holes, clamp the coupling rod blanks to the frames and drill through them, using the frames as

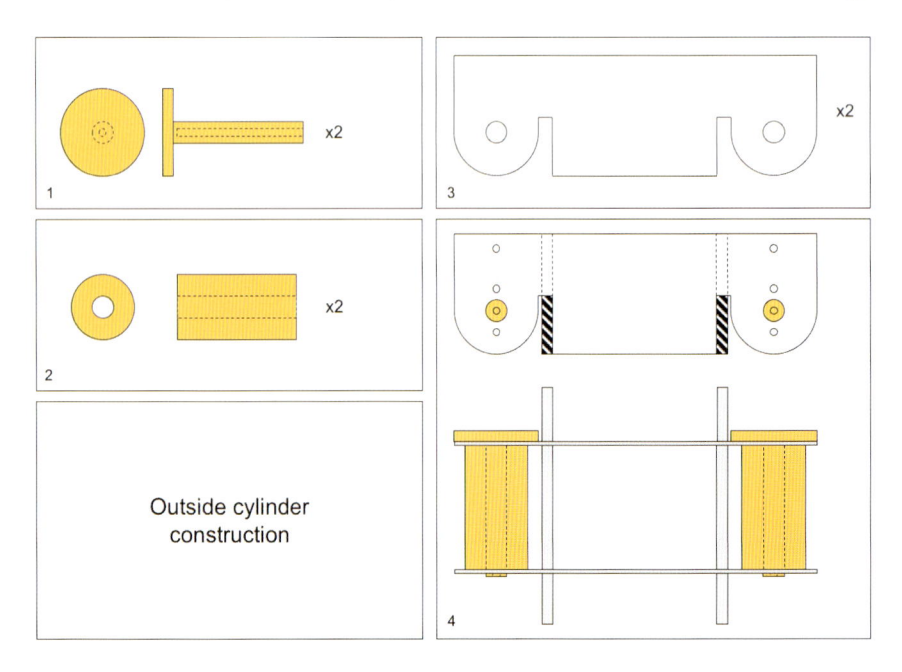

Outside cylinder construction

The method of outside cylinder construction.

a jig. Then mark the front end of the coupling rod blanks with a centre punch mark.

Next, open up the axle holes in the frames in stages until the final required size is reached. This minimizes the risk of the drill wandering. This drilling is best accomplished using a vertical drill stand, or a lathe. If doing it 'freehand', make a jig to keep the drill vertical at all times. A simple support block could be made from stripwood, and used to hold a minidrill during this operation.

Cylinders

Cylinders and motion covers can be made as follows:

1. The cylinder front covers are turned on the lathe, and are drilled for the pistons.
2. Spacers are turned to separate the cylinder end-plates.
3. Make two identical cylinder end-plates from thin nickel silver. Motion covers (if required) are made similarly.
4. The cylinder assembly (with the front motion cover soldered to the cylinder rear, if appropriate) is located in two slots cut across the frames, after removal of the temporary frame spacer. A rear motion cover is similarly attached.

The cladding for cylinders and motion covers is formed from oversized pieces of thin nickel silver sheet, soldered in place before the excess is trimmed.

Driving-Wheel Cranks

The driving-wheel cranks are marked out on $1/32$in nickel silver sheet, undersize axle holes drilled, and then the crankpin holes are drilled using a steel master as a jig, to ensure that the throw of all the cranks is absolutely identical. The cranks are then cut out from the sheet, and carefully filed to shape. The crank pins are steel dressmaking pins.

The cranks need to be a tight push-fit on the axle ends, and the outside faces should be countersunk slightly to allow a solder fillet to fix them in place. Also countersink the rear of the crankpin holes to accommodate the heads of the crankpins, which are then soldered in place (ensuring they are perpendicular to the cranks).

All the cranks can then be carefully pushed on to the overlength axles, with washers to prevent the cranks fouling the frames, and soldered in place on one side of the chassis. Each crank must be soldered very quickly, with a large iron, to minimize the risk of the heat reaching the nylon wheel spokes. Some say that the wheels should be wetted to dissipate the heat better. The excess axle end can then be sawn off.

Quartering the Cranks

One coupling rod is put in position on the soldered crank side, and turned experimentally to check its operation (individual holes may need to be eased slightly, if required). After a few small adjustments, it should be possible to turn all the wheels together,

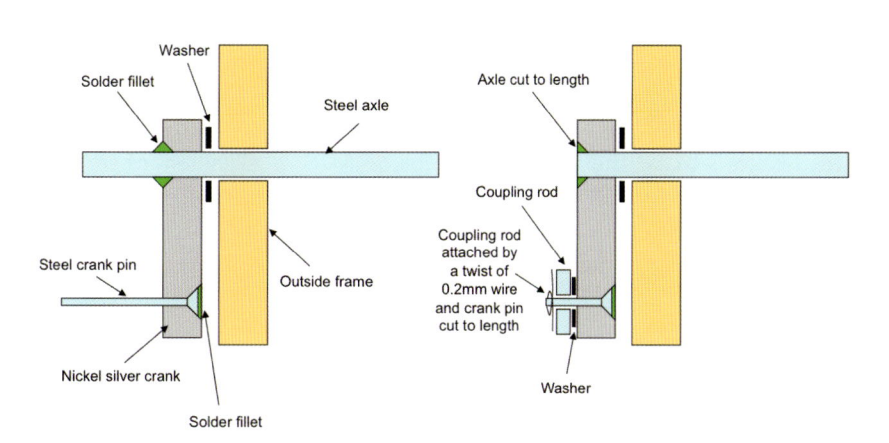

The steps involved in fitting and fixing a driving crank on an outside-framed locomotive.

using fingers, without feeling any binding at the front or back dead-centre positions. Push a short piece of PVC wire insulation over the crankpins, to keep the rod in position. The rod should be marked to ensure it remains in the same orientation on the same side of the engine.

Next, the coupling rod is moved to front or back dead-centre position, and one of the cranks on the other side is quartered by eye to top or bottom dead centre (for example 'right-hand side leads'), and soldered in place.

Then the other two cranks can be aligned using the second coupling rod, adjusted as necessary, and soldered. After shortening the axle ends, the coupling rods can then be re-checked.

If there is any tightness when turning the wheels by hand, recheck the quartering, and then ease the holes in one coupling rod slightly. Once working smoothly the coupling rods can be fixed in place, a loop of fine wire being soldered round the outer axle crankpins over a temporary paper spacer, to hold them in place.

SCRATCHBUILDING LOCOMOTIVE BODIES

When discussing scratchbuilding 009 locomotives, we should consider the techniques for both the body and chassis of a locomotive. However, having built a chassis, the body for the chosen locomotive is likely to prove straightforward.

It is, of course, possible to build locomotive bodies from styrene sheet, strip and tube, and some modellers do this very successfully. However, metal locomotive bodies have the advantages of robustness and weight.

It is very satisfying to work with nickel silver sheet, which is by far the best material for bodywork. It can be sawn easily with a piercing saw, and filed quickly to shape with a variety of needle files. It is easily drilled and soldered.

Some guiding principles for scratchbuilding locomotive bodies are as follows:

- Spend time planning how to construct the body. Once you have assembled kits, it is easy to understand the sort of parts breakdown that works. Remember that brass kits have a half-etched line as an aid to making neat bends, but when working with sheet metal, this is not available. So it may be better to fabricate (say) a cab from flat pieces, rather than trying to bend it from a single sheet of metal
- Have various thicknesses of nickel silver sheet available, and choose the best one for each part. When planning you need to have identified which parts must be more rigid, which ones must be bent neatly, and so on
- Solder two oversize pieces of nickel silver together for any parts that are identical (for example the cab sides). Mark out one side of the two sheets, check the measurements carefully, and drill, cut and file both together, separating them by heating them to melt the solder only when finished. That way, they will be absolutely identical. Make the boiler and smokebox using brass tubes of the appropriate diameter. Alternatively they can be turned from brass bar, which gives the model extra weight. Be flexible in selecting materials, but be aware of their limitations. If (say) a plastic tube seems easier than metal, build it into a removable sub-assembly to be fitted to the engine after all the soldering is complete
- Boiler fittings (chimney, dome, safety valves) are best turned from brass on the lathe, although some modellers have built them up from plastic tube, rotating them in a power drill, and filing them carefully to shape
- Spend half an hour making a softwood jig to provide a level base from which to assemble the body. Use an engineer's square to check the alignment of vertical components relative to this base. Dressmaking pins are useful to hold components in place on balsa jigs
- As with a kit, build the basic bodyshell first, and then progressively add smaller details. It is necessary to identify which components should not be fitted until late in the assembly (for example, a polished brass dome may best be fixed in place with epoxy at a late stage)

LOCOMOTIVES

- Don't be afraid to discard a first attempt at a part. It takes a short time to rework it, and once you know the pitfalls it is easier to do a better job the second time

Weight

Scratchbuilt locomotives built in this way are largely metal, and so are quite heavy. With metal locomotive bodies (fabricated from brass or nickel silver, or assembled from whitemetal castings), pack the available spaces over the coupled wheels with lead weights, and they will then achieve good performance.

The otherwise excellent 3D-printed plastic bodies can be a simple solution for modellers, but they may result in a loco with insufficient weight to haul a long train.

Take steps to minimize excess weight *outside* the coupled wheelbase, especially since many NG locos have significant rear overhang, and too much weight here could lead to instability when running. So, for example, a whitemetal cab roof could be replaced with a lightweight plastic or nickel silver sheet one.

> **TABLE OF LOCO WEIGHTS**
>
> In the next chapter we will study the construction of six 009 locomotives, but it is instructive to correlate their weights with their form of construction:
>
> | | |
> |---|---|
> | *Heddon Hall:* | 3D-printed, 59g (2oz) (weighted) |
> | *Dennis:* | Whitemetal, 107g (3.8oz) |
> | *Axe:* | Whitemetal, 68g (2.4oz) |
> | *Excelsior:* | Plastic, 51g (1.8oz) (as modified) |
> | *Lyn:* | Brass, 169g (6oz) (weighted, compared with 189g (6.7oz) for my scratchbuilt *Lyn*) |
> | *Exe:* | Whitemetal, 179g (6.3oz) (cf 144g (5oz) for a weighted brass kit for an identical loco) |
>
> *Exe*'s body weighs 124g (4.4oz), as compared to 11g for a (slightly smaller) 3D-printed body. A much larger etched brass NGG16 2-6-2 + 2-6-2 Garratt only weighs 189g (6.7oz).

A 009 locomotive with its cab removed. The bodyshell on this Baldwin engine was easier to make as a number of separate parts.

CHAPTER SIX

EXAMPLE LOCOMOTIVE PROJECTS

In this chapter we will look at six 009 locomotive building projects, which between them illustrate the various approaches explained in the previous chapter. These projects are arranged in increasing level of difficulty:

Heddon Hall: Fitting a 3D-printed loco body to an N gauge chassis.

Dennis: Building a whitemetal body kit with an N gauge chassis.

Axe: Building and adapting a whitemetal body kit with an N gauge chassis.

Excelsior: Modifying a ready-to-run 009 locomotive to represent a specific engine.

Lyn: Building a locomotive from an etched brass kit.

Exe: Building a locomotive from a whitemetal body kit and a scratchbuilt chassis.

Many 009 modellers say they would never attempt to scratchbuild a loco, whilst demonstrating a very high standard of workmanship when adapting a ready-to-run model, or building a kit. So more modellers should 'have a go', and work their way through locomotive projects of progressively greater difficulty. They may be pleasantly surprised…

PROJECT: *HEDDON HALL*, A MODERN-ERA LYNTON & BARNSTAPLE HUNSLET DIESEL WITH A 3D-PRINTED BODYSHELL

THE MODEL

CAD designer Chris Ward designed a bodyshell for the 60hp Hunslet, for production by 3D printing. One of these is used for the model of *Heddon Hall*.

The body comes as a single part, unfinished, in translucent white plastic. The surfaces have a

The six example projects (left to right): Heddon Hall, Dennis, Axe, Excelsior, Lyn, Exe.

EXAMPLE LOCOMOTIVE PROJECTS | 97

The restored L&B has two 1960s Hunslet 60hp diesel locomotives, used on engineering trains. **Heddon Hall** *is seen here at Woody Bay.* TONY NICHOLSON

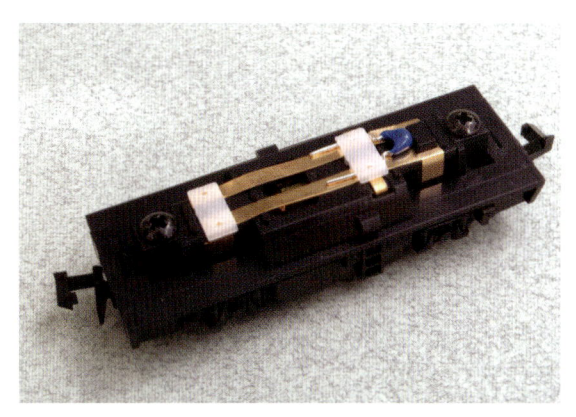

The body takes an inexpensive Japanese Kato 11-103 four-wheeled chassis, so the body and chassis together produce a cheap 009 locomotive.

slightly rough texture – the buffer beams particularly so. The body detail is good, but the spacing of the dummy axleboxes is increased to match the Japanese chassis.

> **MATERIALS AND TOOLS NEEDED**
>
> 3D-printed bodyshell
> Kato 11-103 chassis
> Scrap of lead sheet
> Glazing material and styrene sheet off-cuts
> Basic hand tools
> Glue
> Paint

ASSEMBLY

No assembly is required for the body – the 3D-printed bodyshell is complete as purchased, even including standard 009 couplers.

The bodyshell fits straight on to the chassis, needing a shim of styrene sheet at one end to make sure the chassis stays in place when the loco is picked up. The body weighs next to nothing, so lead sheet is folded up to fit within the bonnet, and fixed in place with a layer of thin card (which also prevents it short-circuiting the mechanism).

No more work than that is needed to have a working 009 loco, although *Heddon Hall* has a driver's door and window fitted in the open cab side. The plastic is quite brittle, so care is needed, as an edge can easily be chipped off (but can be re-attached with superglue).

The body should be painted with several thin coats of grey primer (which tends to soak into the plastic material) before the final livery (black in this

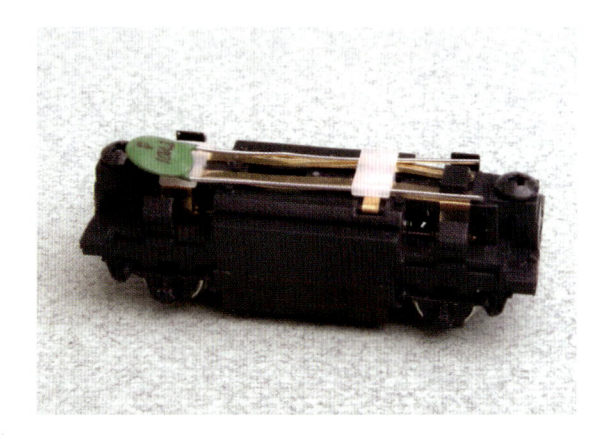

The ends of the chassis block must be shortened. This is simply achieved in a couple of minutes – straight cuts with a piercing saw through the whitemetal and plastic, and a touch with a file to remove any burrs on the corners.

Heddon Hall *complete.*

case) is applied. Experts say that throughout the priming process, the body panels should be carefully rubbed down with wet-and-dry paper between coats, to remove surface roughness. This is difficult to do on such small surfaces as this, without also rubbing off the fine details. The model pictured probably does not have as good a finish as could be achieved with more patience.

The engine is painted black, with a white cab roof, red buffer beams and Indian red frames. As a quick solution for the lining, thin red lines are printed on to paper with an ink-jet printer, and then with a very sharp craft knife these are cut into strips with red on one edge and white on the other. The strips are then glued to the locomotive to form the lining, and the paint is touched up as necessary at the corners. The same computer-printing approach is used for the nameplates, the L&B crests, and the Hunslet badge on the radiator.

The most difficult part of the build process is perhaps the final one – fitting tiny pieces of plastic glazing into the cramped cab.

The Japanese chassis allows the loco to run extremely fast, but it does also run well at low speeds.

PROJECT: *DENNIS*, A GLYN VALLEY TRAMWAY LOCOMOTIVE FROM A WHITEMETAL BODY KIT

THE PROTOTYPE

The Beyer Peacock locomotives for the Glyn Valley Tramway in North Wales were compact outside-framed 0-4-2Ts, but – critically for 009 modellers – side plates enclosed the cylinders and motion.

Heddon Hall *in pieces, showing the lead weight.*

Dennis *at Chirk in 1932.* H.C. CASSERLEY

THE KIT

In the early days of 009, Peco (who encouraged the popularity of the scale by producing a 009 flexible track system) released three simple whitemetal body kits designed to fit on N gauge 0-6-0 locomotive chassis. Two were for generic side- and saddle-tank engines, which purists might argue are not particularly realistic for 2ft gauge, having inside frames and inside cylinders. The third kit was for a scale model of one of the three Glyn Valley Tramway locomotives.

As a locomotive building project for a newcomer to 009, this kit is ideal. It is extremely simple and straightforward to assemble, and the result is a heavy and reliable engine capable of hauling long trains.

This prototype offered Peco advantages: there were three very similar locomotives for modellers to build (increasing Peco's potential sales), and the side plates would effectively hide a sturdy and reliable Grafar N gauge 94xx pannier tank 0-6-0 mechanism.

> **MATERIALS AND TOOLS NEEDED**
>
> Peco kit GL-6 *Dennis* 0-6-0T tram engine body kit
> Graham Farish 1109 chassis, checking that the chassis of modern Grafar (now Bachmann) engines is compatible
> Etched brass name- and maker's plates
> Basic hand tools
> Glue and/or low melting-point solder
> Paint

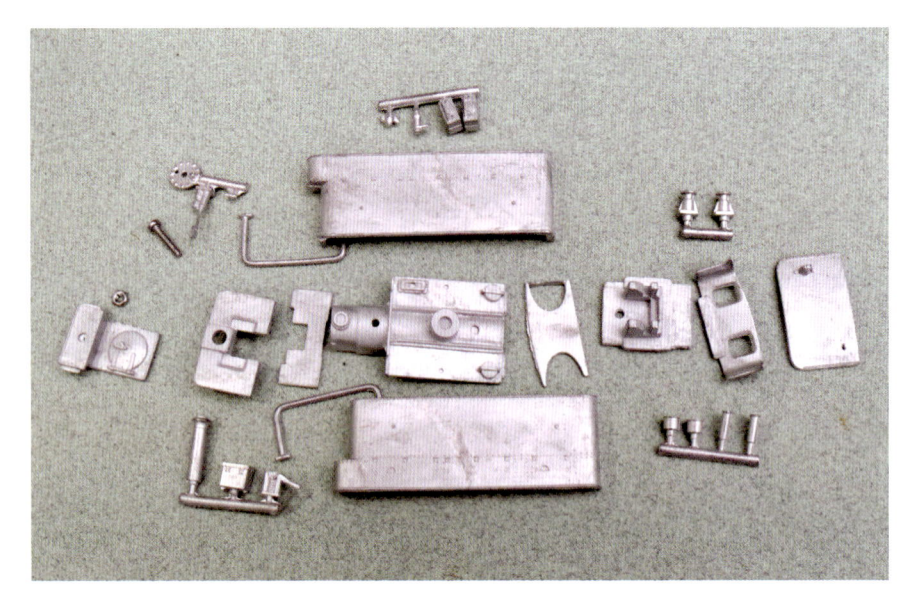

On opening the kit, it is apparent that the main structure of the locomotive is built from only ten whitemetal parts, with another sixteen smaller parts providing the detailing.

PREPARATION

The third of these locomotives, *Glyn*, was different from the other two, being longer with a somewhat different cab. The kit makes the first two engines in as-built condition, and the small changes that occurred during their life are easily made. A little extra work is required to model *Glyn*.

We will initially make the second engine, *Dennis*, in later condition.

KIT ASSEMBLY

The instructions describe clearly how to fit the locomotive ends to the chassis. Small sections must be filed from each end of the chassis, after protecting the motor and gears by covering them with adhesive tape. The chassis is bolted to the front (chimney) end casting after lugs on the rear of the chassis have been slotted into pockets on the cab end casting.

Little needs to be added to the instructions supplied. Usually it is best to assemble one corner of a main structure (for example the side, end and floor) with LMP solder, and then add other sections to this. However, Peco suggest fitting the front footplate casting and rear casting to the actual N gauge mechanism. With these in place, the two body sides are positioned, and the assembly can be held

Dennis *complete.*

together by elastic bands ready for soldering. This method certainly works.

If gluing, the glue must obviously be applied to the parts first, then they are assembled and finally held together with elastic bands whilst the glue hardens.

The remainder of the assembly follows the instructions, adding the larger parts and then the small details.

CUSTOMIZING THE MODEL

Sir Theodore and *Dennis* were identical, but during their lives, the condensing apparatus was removed, and removable cab front sheets were provided for

EXAMPLE LOCOMOTIVE PROJECTS

The set of three GVT engines (left to right): **Sir Theodore** *in lined green, built as per the kit,* **Dennis** *in later black livery with the cab front panel fitted, the doors open and the condensing gear omitted, and* **Glyn** *also in black.*

bad weather – perhaps much of the time in North Wales…

Generally, it is best to choose one photograph of the engine at the period to be modelled, and use that to determine its condition. That way, no one can legitimately complain that the model is wrong…

The variations between the engines, and the changes made during their lives, can be included as the kit is built, but some small touches help greatly to improve the realism of the model. For example, the cabs were fitted with hinged doors, modelled closed in the kit. Photographs of the line show that these doors were often left open, so it is possible to cut round the door panels carefully with a piercing saw before assembly, and after cleaning up the opening and the door itself, solder the removed door back, but partly opened. There were similar doors ahead of the tanks to gain access to the motion, and these were often left open as well.

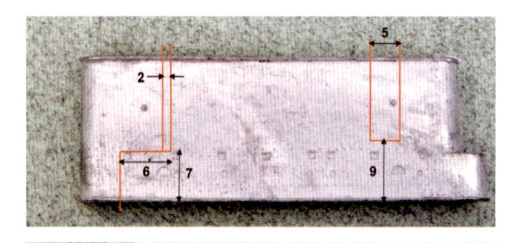

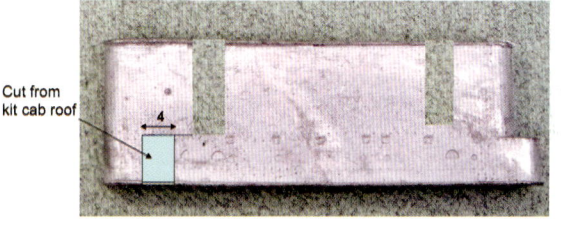

To model **Glyn**, *the cab and bunker must be extended. This can be done by reusing the cab door panels to form the longer bunker sides, filling in the equivalent gap in the side plates using whitemetal from the cast cab roof.*

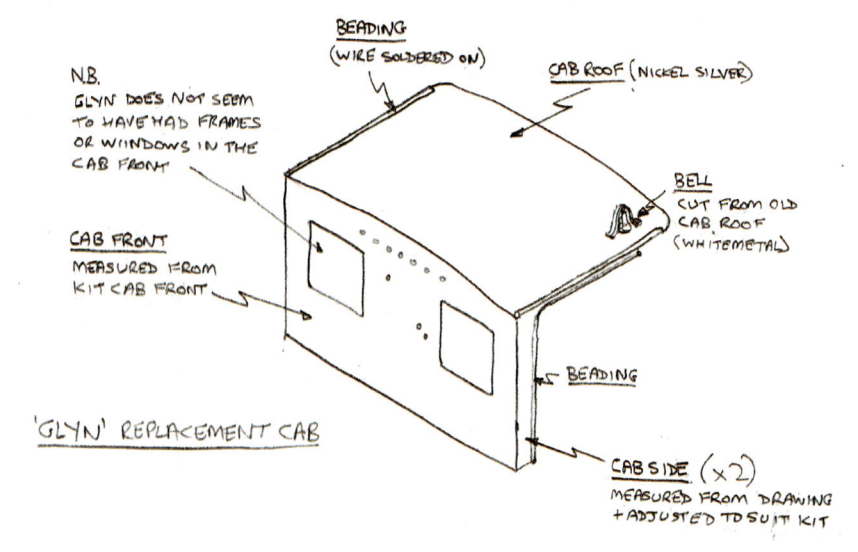

Sketch of **Glyn's** *replacement cab. A new sub-assembly (sides, front and longer roof) is made from nickel silver sheet and wire.*

102 EXAMPLE LOCOMOTIVE PROJECTS

Having opened the cab doors, it is necessary to add a cab floor each side of the mechanism for the crew to stand on, and pieces of balsa are cut to size and glued in place. The driver should face backwards, as the engines usually ran cab first.

PROJECT: *AXE*, A KERR STUART JOFFRE CLASS 0-6-0T

THE PROTOTYPE

> **MATERIALS AND TOOLS NEEDED**
>
> Five79 Kerr Stuart 'Joffre' class whitemetal body kit
> Roco N gauge BR80 0-6-0T chassis
> Nickel silver or brass sheet/strip
> Basic hand tools
> Glue and/or low melting-point solder
> Paint

In 2008, the revived Lynton & Barnstaple Railway unveiled the rebuilt Kerr Stuart Joffre Class 0-6-0T Axe at Woody Bay station in North Devon.

THE MODEL

Five79 (formerly Chivers Finelines) produce a whitemetal body kit for a 009 Kerr Stuart Joffre class. To complete the kit requires the chassis from an N gauge Roco BR80 0-6-0T, which can be purchased on-line.

The model was built very quickly, but has been modified to follow some of the changes made to the engine in Devon.

THE KIT

As a first impression, the kit contains few components, and they are tiny compared to the parts for a larger 009 locomotive.

ASSEMBLY

The body goes together very easily, and the basic model can be built in a weekend. With the weight of the cast body, it runs well – from the lowest speed up to a very high speed.

The prominent air pump was added to the tank front. Etched brass nameplates and works plates can be bought and fitted, but this model has plates produced from a photograph of the locomotive in Devon, printed on thin card using an inkjet printer.

EXAMPLE LOCOMOTIVE PROJECTS | 103

Because Roco took over another supplier's range, they had two different BR80 models. Labelled as a Roco model, the chassis purchased for this model was from the other company's tooling. Some careful sawing and filing was needed to get the chassis to fit in the whitemetal body.

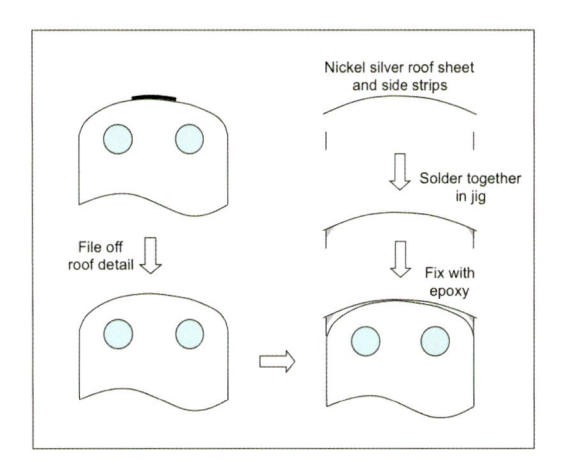

The cab profile of the L&B loco was achieved by filing the cab top smooth, and attaching a sheet-metal cab roof, which overhangs the curved edges of the whitemetal cab. The gaps between the old and new roof profiles are filled with thin brass strip, soldered to the sheet-metal roof before it is fixed in place with epoxy.

The finished model. It has become out of date, as the air pump has been removed, and the engine has been repainted in a different shade of green and lined. Modelling a working locomotive involves ongoing work, if it is to be kept up to date.

EXAMPLE LOCOMOTIVE PROJECTS

PROJECT: *EXCELSIOR*, A BAGNALL 0-4-2T FROM A MINITRAINS R-T-R LOCOMOTIVE

Late in 2016, the German manufacturer Minitrains introduced its first British-outline 009 locomotive, using its proven H0e 0-4-0 steam loco mechanism. Due to delays in the introduction of other promised 009 locomotives, this little model was the first UK 009 ready-to-run loco produced by a mainstream supplier.

The Minitrains model as purchased.

Photographs of Excelsior *on the L&B show that it was the Kerry engine, extended at the rear by a rather ugly cab extension containing an additional water tank (perhaps a reflection of the length of journeys on the 19-mile (30km) L&B).* L&BR TRUST

THE PROTOTYPE

In 1888, W.G. Bagnall Ltd of Stafford supplied an 0-4-0 under-slung saddle tank for the Kerry forestry estate in mid-Wales, where it ran until the railway was dismantled in 1895. One photograph has been discovered in mid-Wales of such an engine, named *Excelsior*.

Edmund Nuttall of Manchester was awarded the contract to build the Lynton & Barnstaple Railway in Devon in 1895, and construction took place between 1896 and 1898 when the line opened. Nuttall used three 2ft gauge engines in the construction, one of which was a Bagnall 0-4-2T called *Excelsior*.

After the L&B contract, the engine worked on a quarry line in Portland, Dorset.

THE SOURCE MODEL

At first sight, the model does not look much like the *Excelsior* that worked on the L&B, due primarily to the flat sides beneath the boiler, the longer coupled wheelbase, and the level (rather than inclined) cylinders of the mechanism.

In fact a conversion is quite straightforward, and forms an example of the common 009 modellers' practice of adapting a ready-to-run model to look more like their desired prototype. Care is needed to plan how to carry out the modifications, and the task is best spread over a period of several weeks, although the total time involved is quite modest.

It is best to use a small lathe for a few tasks. Everything else uses common materials and hand tools, and much of the work on the project could be undertaken on a tray in front of the TV, or even in a hotel room during the evenings of business trips away from home.

THE REBUILD PROJECT

Feasibility Study

Before starting a modification like this, it is worth conducting a small exercise to determine whether the adaptation is feasible:

- Download the drawing of the engine, usefully provided on the Minitrains website

EXAMPLE LOCOMOTIVE PROJECTS

> **MATERIALS AND TOOLS NEEDED**
>
> Minitrains Bagnall Wingtank 2011 or 2012
> Pair of 4mm-diameter wheels
> Brass sheet and tube
> Styrene sheet (various thicknesses)
> Styrene tube and rod (various sizes)
> Scrap of $^1/_{32}$in copper-clad board
> Brass or nickel silver wire (various sizes)
> 8BA bolt
> Springside loco lamps
> 00 scale bucket
> (Optionally, brass bar, lathe)
> Basic hand tools, minidrill
> Glue
> Etched brass nameplates and works plates
> Paint

- Print this drawing to scale alongside the best drawings available of *Excelsior* from the *L&B Magazine* and from *Narrow Gauge & Industrial Railway Modelling Magazine (NG&IRM)*
- Combine the two drawings on the computer, to superimpose the changed features from the *NG&IRM* drawing over the relevant parts of the Minitrains drawing. In this way, an idea is obtained in an hour or so of the appearance of the finished model

In most respects the bodywork aligns fairly well, apart from the fact that the engine was rebuilt as an 0-4-2T before working in Devon. On the basis of this assessment, the project could be taken forward, and a Minitrains model was purchased. It ran beautifully, its flywheel giving extremely smooth performance.

The *NG&IRM* drawings were produced from the few known photographs that have been published, so the photographs (rather than the drawings) should be believed if the two appear to differ. This was the case with a few small details.

Convert the Engine?

The next task is to decide exactly how to convert the engine into its L&B form. The key question is whether or not to dismantle it and attempt to modify the cylinders and slide bars to the correct inclined position, and also to cut away the panels below the boiler to improve the appearance.

Several attempts to remove the body proved unsuccessful. Enquiries among 009 Society friends locally, and other modellers on their web forum, suggested that it could be done, but that it was difficult and required considerable force. The decision was therefore made not to risk it...

Planning

Examination of how the model is constructed revealed that the body is in fact assembled from a number of separate plastic mouldings – footplate and cab, boiler and tanks, cab floor, tank fillers, and so on.

In addition to the composite drawing already produced, a freehand isometric view is drawn of the changes to be made to the superstructure. Then, as the work proceeds, this sketch is kept up to date. This makes it easier to visualize the shape of each item to be made and added, and gives the chance to consider how it will finally be assembled.

Surgical Procedure

The most invasive surgery was to saw off the cab rear sheet under the edge of the roof, using a fine-bladed piercing saw held at an angle, taking great care not to damage the cab side sheets. This allows much

With the cab back separate, all the 'add-on' parts can be added, and then the whole sub-assembly refitted towards the end of the process.

of the work to proceed away from the mechanism, whilst leaving the option of removing the body later.

KEY CHANGES MADE TO THE MINITRAINS MODEL

Rear Extension

Find or buy some small trailing wheels (most modellers have a 'bits box' which may supply such items), and make a small brass plate-and-tube sub-assembly for the wheels to run in. This is bolted loosely in place to the rear frame extension so that it can 'float' vertically. The brass provides extra weight to keep the wheels on the rails and rotating, and the vertical float allows these wheels to follow undulations in the track. The overall wheelbase is so short that minimal lateral movement of the axle is necessary.

A small piece of $1/32$in copper-clad board inside the cab roof has brass wire handrails soldered to it.

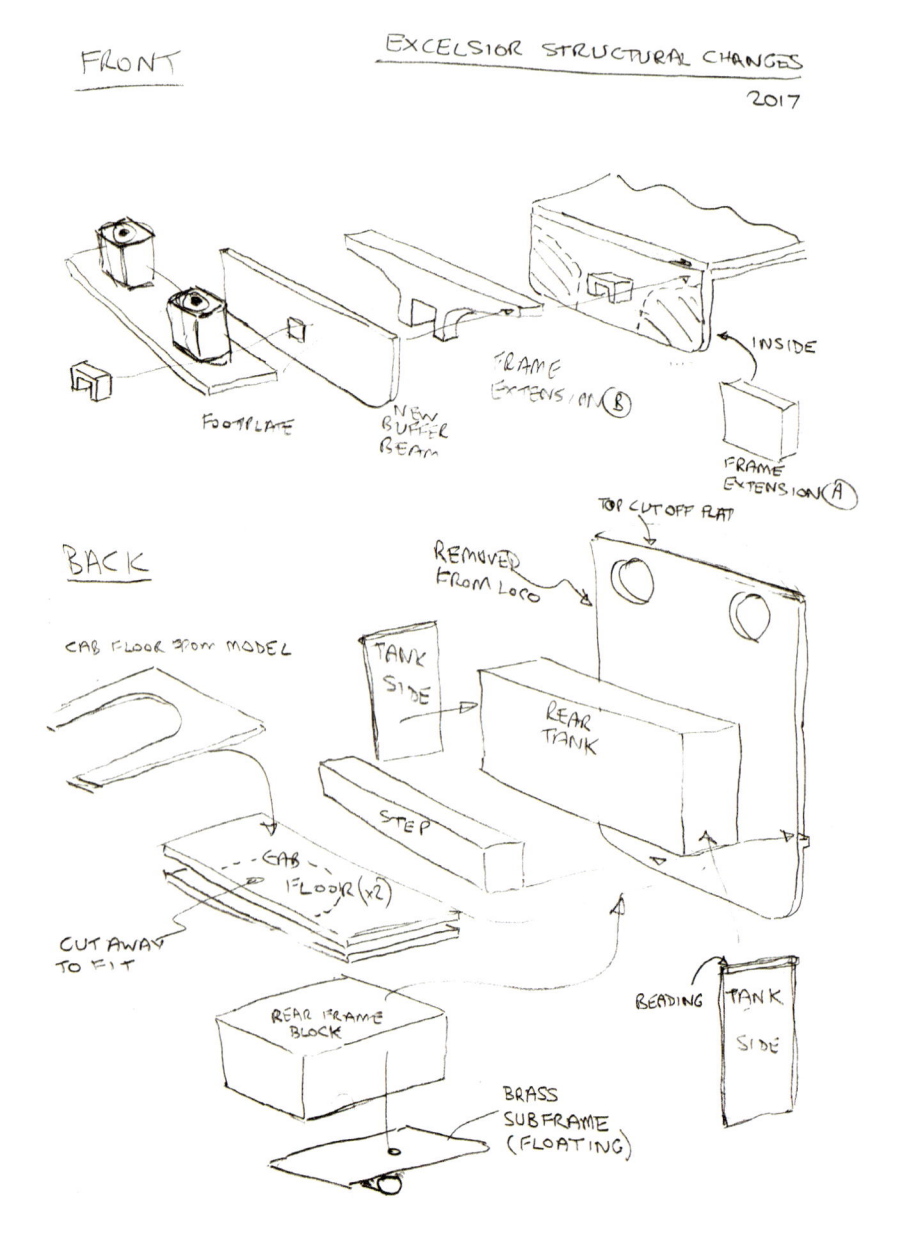

The rear extension is built from styrene sheet and strip of various thicknesses. The roof of the cab extension was lower than the original cab roof, and appears to have had a flat top.

EXAMPLE LOCOMOTIVE PROJECTS

As work progresses, it must be decided how the rear extension will be fixed to the main body. In fact the (separate) cab floor was removed from the loco, and reattached to the rear extension, and a strip of styrene was glued under the loco cab roof to locate under the roof of the rear extension.

The front footplate of the model is too short, and the look of the model was improved by extending it. The original buffer beam was reshaped to be less visible from the side, and a new buffer beam/coupler pocket unit was fixed to the front of it.

Modified Boiler Fittings

An important change is to fit a new larger dome over the moulded plastic one: the associated Salter safety valves fit into two holes drilled in the top of the boiler.

A spark-arresting chimney was turned from brass, leaving the original to be used as an alternative (during its time on the L&B, the spark-arresting chimney fell apart and was replaced by a straight one). The chimney base is cut from 10-thou styrene, and formed to the boiler diameter by being taped to a suitable diameter twist drill and immersed in boiling water for a couple of minutes.

The whistle should also be added to the cab front sheet. The whistle is a tiny piece of fine brass tube soldered to a length of wire, the top then being filed carefully to a hemispherical shape. *NG&IRM* says the whistle was mounted off-centre, but study

The whole sub-assembly fits together neatly during trial assembly, and is finally attached to the loco very easily.

Extended Front Footplate

The two square sandboxes on the front footplate either side of the smokebox door were a distinctive feature of the original loco.

The sandboxes are short lengths of square plastic tube, with styrene sheet tops, and lids crudely made out of dressmaking pins threaded over small washers.

108   EXAMPLE LOCOMOTIVE PROJECTS

The various parts of the loco before assembly.

Another view of the parts.

of the photographs seems to disprove this. This may be a case where careful study of the best photographs now available may prove earlier research slightly wrong.

Lack of Daylight under the Boiler

By not removing the loco body, its appearance is still marred by the flat panels below the boiler; however, these can be disguised somewhat by adding details in this area.

The reverser rod is added on the left-hand side footplate, and the rectangular toolbox on the right-hand side. The toolbox is made from a couple of layers of thick styrene sheet, glued together and then filed to shape, with a lid made from a piece of thinner sheet.

Side Tanks

The tank fillers visible in photographs are distinctive tall ones, so the existing ones, which are separate

EXAMPLE LOCOMOTIVE PROJECTS   109

Leaf springs (or half springs, in fact) cut from the solebar of a 009 coach kit are fitted on both sides to mitigate the starkness of these panels.

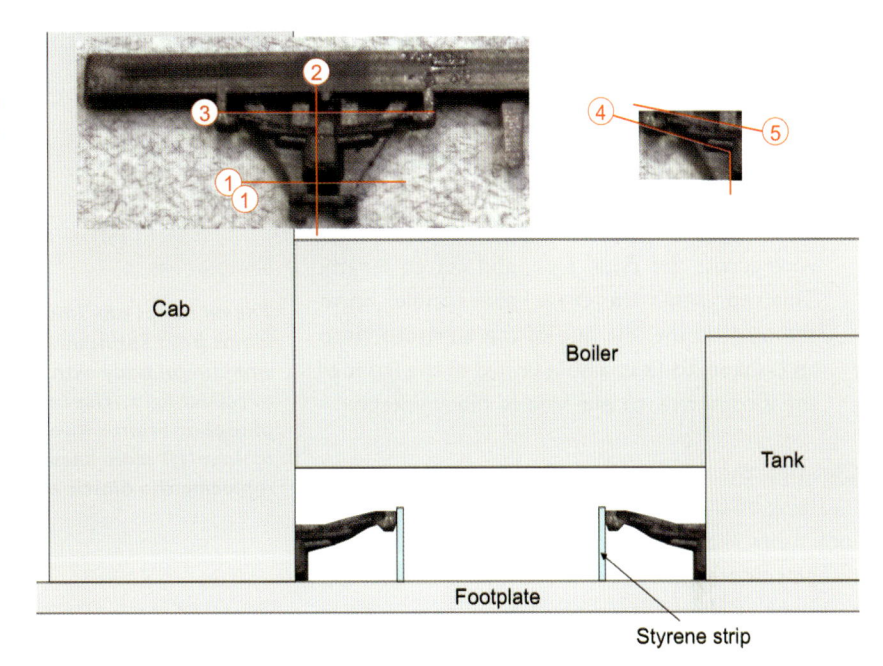

plastic mouldings and easily removed, are replaced. The replacement fillers are turned from brass rod, but plastic could be used.

When working on the L&B, the engine had a prominent Roscoe displacement lubricator fitted to the front of the left-hand side tank. This lubricator illustrates the approach needed when striving to create an accurate model. A little research into the item will give an understanding that enables it to be created in model form.

Few modellers would have detailed knowledge of these components, but (as is usually the case nowadays) a Google search easily produces a diagram showing how one works, plus many photographs of very similar lubricators – full-sized ones, and also versions for live-steam models. From these sources, a dimensioned sketch can be made.

The steps towards building this lubricator are as follows:

1. Solder a small nickel silver pin (representing the oil-filler valve on the top of the lubricator) into one end of a short length of fine brass tube (the body of the lubricator), and a piece of wire into the other end of the tube, to represent the water drain pipe.

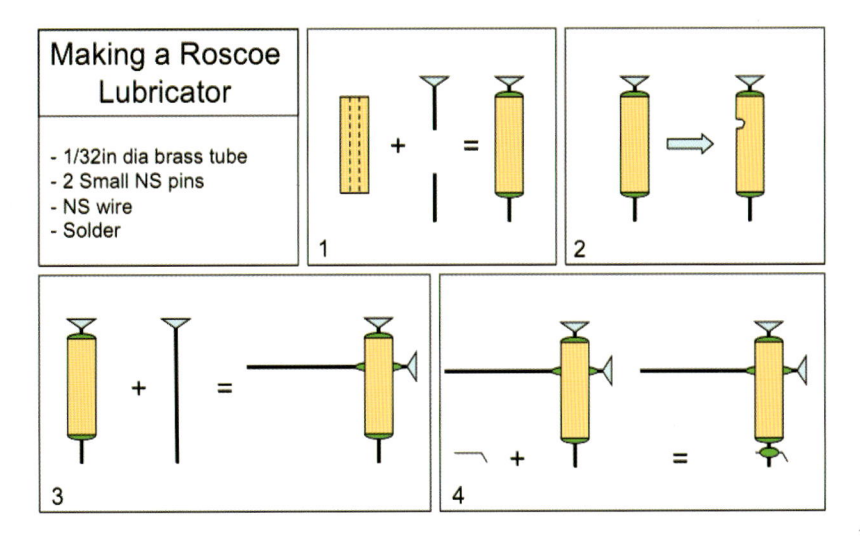

Making a Roscoe Lubricator

- 1/32in dia brass tube
- 2 Small NS pins
- NS wire
- Solder

The method for making a Roscoe lubricator.

2. File a slot across the back of the lubricator body, near its top end.
3. Solder a second pin across this slot, to represent the valve on the right side of the body and the pipe on the left side.
4. Solder a pre-formed, L-shaped piece of thin wire across the drain pipe, and cut to length. This represents the drain valve handle. Form the pipe on the left side of the lubricator into an L-shape, to fit in a hole drilled in the front of the locomotive, to one side of the smokebox.

Clean up the solder with a fine knife-edge needle file, filing off the domed tops of the pins so that they look more like handwheels.

The soldering may take more than one attempt, as attaching the later, smaller pieces risks melting the earlier joints.

The finished Roscoe lubricator.

The oil lamps are 7mm/1ft scale GWR locomotive lamps from Springside Models, consisting of a whitemetal body with a 'brilliant' on the front to reflect light. The cast handles are replaced by phosphor-bronze wire. The bucket is from a set of 4mm/1ft scale lineside figures, a wire handle replacing the plastic one.

Lamps

In contrast to the earlier photo of *Excelsior* on the Kerry Tramway, and the later photo in Portland, oil lamps front and rear were a feature when the engine worked on the L&B – works trains ran after dark when Nuttall's were working hard to complete the line…

Lamp irons made from pieces of flattened nickel silver wire are superglued into holes drilled in the body front and rear to carry the lamps and the bucket (of sand?) always seen in photos hanging from the front lamp iron.

Pipework

Various other small details were fitted, such as clack valves on the boiler sides, and a pipe from the cab to the right side of the smokebox, as seen in the photographs. These can each be bent from brass wire and pins of suitable thickness, and attached with superglue into holes drilled in the plastic body.

It appeared that a similar pipe ran along the left-hand side of the boiler, but what is visible in photos was in fact a re-railing bar, and was always carried when on the L&B.

Brakes

The screw and crank for the handbrake are bent from wire and added below the right-hand side of the cab.

The wooden brake blocks are made by filing the surface of a narrow strip of 1/16in copper-clad board hollow, to match the wheel tread diameter, and then cutting 1mm-wide slivers from the end of this, forming tiny, non-conducting brake blocks, which are soldered to 1.5 × 0.3mm brass strip hangers.

EXAMPLE LOCOMOTIVE PROJECTS

Pairs of brake hangers are soldered to wires using a jig (see above) to space them apart. After painting they are glued in position under the chassis, taking care that they do not interfere with the free running of the wheels, and that the top ends do not short out the current collectors.

Nameplates

The name and works plates were obtained from Narrow Planet, who already had artwork for this engine in their range, but the length was altered slightly to fit on the Minitrains tanks. They are fixed in place with superglue.

Livery

The livery that *Excelsior* carried when working on the L&B is not known. In contrast to the contractor's other two engines, which appear plain black in photographs, it appears to have been a lighter colour, and lined. The *NG&IRM* drawing shows it in lined green, but this is speculative.

The model is finished in unlined mid-green (Humbrol 80). On such a small engine, lining might look too strident, but can be added later.

Before and after.

Trial run after assembly of the main parts.

EXAMPLE LOCOMOTIVE PROJECTS

PROJECT: *LYN*, THE L&B BALDWIN 2-4-2T FROM AN ETCHED BRASS KIT

There are three options to making a Baldwin *Lyn* to accompany the very nice Peco coaches and freight stock in L&B livery:

- Scratchbuild a complete loco, as I did for my SR-livery model of *Lyn*
- Scratchbuild an outside-framed chassis to accompany a Langley whitemetal body kit. Study of the contents of the Langley kit suggested that a lot of work would be needed to bring it to a satisfactory level of accuracy
- Assemble a Backwoods etched brass kit (always a challenge)

I settled on the Backwoods kit approach, accepting that I might have to redesign parts of the engine to make it work well.

THE PROTOTYPE

Before the L&B opened, its directors realized that the three locomotives they had ordered would be insufficient. They therefore placed an order with the Baldwin Locomotive Works in Philadelphia, USA, pioneers of modern production methods, who could design and build a locomotive quickly from standard parts.

RESEARCH

Few of the Backwoods *Lyn* kits seem to have been assembled, but an on-line search revealed two detailed descriptions of the assembly process, both reporting the work of professional model builders, who had each chosen to make substantial modifications to the kit design.

A few clear photographs of the original engine, at around the time intended for the model (1910–20 in this case), were selected to act as sources for detailing.

THE KIT

Inspection of the kit reveals a mixture of very nice etched brass and nickel silver parts with plenty of rivet detail, along with some whitemetal components (smokebox, boiler top and boiler fittings).

Significant modifications are needed, as the etched nickel silver frames are so insubstantial that it would be impractical to rely solely on their strength for a working model. They are intended to incorporate a compensated leading driving axle, running on inside bearings, to ensure good power pickup from only four wheels. But as both professionals had abandoned this, it seemed wise to follow suit, preferring

Baldwin supplied an elegant 2-4-2T, dismantled, packed in crates, and accompanied by people to supervise reassembly in Devon.
W.G. TILLING

EXAMPLE LOCOMOTIVE PROJECTS

BACKWOODS *LYN* – CHASSIS ISSUES

When modifying a design, it is helpful to split the problem into separate questions:

Q. What are the options for a rigid 4-wheel mechanism instead of an equalized one?
- Outside or inside driving-axle bearings? A. Outside, from experience.
- Plain bearings or a keeper plate between the wheels? A. Plain bearings because gear mesh depends on fit of keeper plate, and fine gears need accurate alignment.

Q. Will the flimsy bar frame etches be sufficiently rigid? A. Yes, if a thick plate is fitted under the entire 4-wheel chassis.

Q. Rebuild the drive train with the spur gears between the motor and the worm? A. No, because:
- It would be more robust, but a worm gear set with a brass pinion would have to be substituted, to solder to the axle.
- It would prevent the motor fitting within the firebox and the backhead detail would be lost.

Q. Splay the front and rear frames to give clearance on curves? A. Probably not, because:
- It looks difficult to achieve on this engine.
- Do some tests to decide if it is essential.

Q. Can the leading/trailing wheel insulation be bypassed, for split-axles? A. Probably, because:
- Wires could be fitted between tyres and stub axles.
- The wheels are a standard size, so can be replaced if one is damaged.
- Try adding wire to a similar wheel beforehand, to check feasibility.

Q. What are the options for modifying the truck frames for split-axle power pickup?
- Use thin copper-clad stretchers separating brass frames? A. No, too difficult.
- Fit insulated bearings inside widened truck frames? A. Yes.
- Will wider split-frame trucks fit, and pivot on curves? A. Should do.

Q. Will the motor supplied (lacking in power on other models) be OK? A. Hopefully.

---

to collect current from all eight wheels and adopt a rigid chassis on the model. (Note: One amateur builder has since come to light who built the kit as designed, and had no trouble with the equalization.)

The driving wheels supplied in the kit have steel tyres, so wheel cleaning could be an ongoing problem, although opinion on-line suggests that the steel tyres cause no problems, needing just a light clean to prepare the loco for use.

BUILDING THE KIT

After analysing the various problems to be solved, work can begin. Some modellers find it helpful to report their progress with construction from time to time on a relevant on-line discussion group (in this case the L&B modelling e-group), as others may be able to offer useful advice and encouragement.

First, consider how to strengthen the thin nickel silver etched frames to make a rigid outside-framed

EXAMPLE LOCOMOTIVE PROJECTS

> **MATERIALS AND TOOLS NEEDED**
>
> Backwoods *Lyn* kit
> Couplings
> Brass and nickel silver sheet and strip
> $1/32$in copper-clad board
> Perspex block
> Styrene sheet
> 8BA and 10BA bolts
> Fine flexible wire
> Glue
> Basic hand tools
> Paint

Top view of the part-complete running chassis.

chassis. This model is built with outside bearings for both axles. The approach used is to design a $1/32$in brass plate to form a solid base for the chassis, to keep it square, soldering it into place between the frames after fitting the wheelsets. The shape of this plate is complex, so a template is made out of 30-thou styrene, drilling, cutting and filing it until it fits within the kit frame with the wheelsets in place. The shape is then copied to brass sheet.

In designing the chassis base plate, the leading and trailing truck pivots are moved nearer to the driving axles, to improve the chassis geometry on curves. The plate also needs holes for the $1/32$in copper-clad collector sub-assembly, so that it is removable for pickup wire adjustment.

The driving cranks and coupling rods can then be fitted to the engine. Quartering of the cranks is easier for a four-coupled engine. Leave the connecting rods off at this stage.

The design of this kit makes it difficult to splay the front and rear frames to give extra clearance for the leading and trailing wheels on curves, so tests were carried out to see whether extra clearance was needed for the nominal 18in (46cm) minimum radius curves (probably 15in (38cm) in places) on the layout. There seemed to be adequate clearance without any splaying.

Whilst contemplating the next stages of chassis assembly, relax by building the various body sub-assemblies: the cab/bunker, the two side tanks, the smokebox, and the boiler/dome/sandboxes. These are generally straightforward and satisfying to put together.

The side tanks consist of a substantial folded brass box, overlaid by fine brass etches carrying the rivet detail. It is tricky to solder the outer etches on to the tank boxes without distorting them, as they are very thin. The kit instructions suggest filling the tanks with lead before closing the boxes completely. Following this advice, it proved impossible to solder any small details to the very heavy tank units, due to the mass of metal. So items such as steps have to be attached with cyanoacrylate adhesive.

The front footplate and buffer beam can be assembled according to the instructions.

EXAMPLE LOCOMOTIVE PROJECTS | 115

Trial assembly.

It is a good idea to fit additional locating strips to the underside of the cab roof, so that it can be fitted easily after final painting.

TRIAL ASSEMBLY

A trial assembly of the cab, smokebox and tanks on to the chassis, aided by BluTack and adhesive tape, showed that very little holds these sub-assemblies together: they are difficult to align and hold accurately for assembly, and would be fragile thereafter. The smokebox is designed to be fixed to the chassis, but it may be more securely attached to the boiler/tank assembly.

PERMANENT ASSEMBLY

The solution for attaching the tank/boiler/smoke-

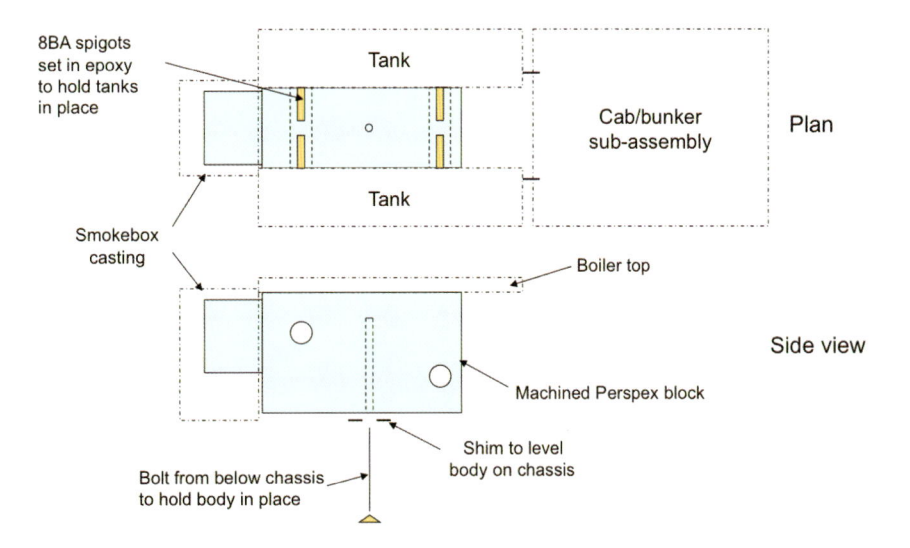

Attaching the tank/boiler/smokebox unit to the chassis.

box unit to the chassis is to use a block of Perspex. The machined block of Perspex achieves the following functions:

- It spaces the tanks the correct distance apart
- A turned spigot on the front end of the block fits within the whitemetal smokebox, and locates it
- A hole tapped vertically through the block allows a bolt to be inserted through the chassis base plate to hold the superstructure in place
- Shims under the block allow the superstructure to be levelled during assembly
- The whitemetal boiler top can be levelled and firmly seated on to the machined top face of the block, and then fixed in place with epoxy

The result is a very solid unit held to the chassis by a single screw, and aligned by means of the spigot on the base of the cast smokebox.

To attach the tanks, 8BA bolt off-cuts are soldered into tapped holes on the inner face of each tank, and the Perspex block is drilled with oversize holes to accommodate these. With a liberal application of epoxy, the tanks, boiler top and smokebox can then be carefully assembled, aligned and clamped overnight whilst the epoxy hardens.

Running the engine to and fro on the layout for some time allows the bearings to bed in. It is tested propelling a couple of coaches (it has no couplings yet!) to check the adhesion, the steel tyres providing better adhesion than nickel silver tyres. The engine should also ride steadily.

CYLINDERS

The Backwoods design includes cylinders of rather insubstantial construction – whitemetal cylinders fixed with LMP solder to flimsy brass support frames previously soldered on to the outsides of the chassis. The whitemetal steam chests can then be fixed in on top using epoxy.

The cylinder castings must be carefully drilled before assembly:

- Gently grip the cylinder casting in the headstock of the lathe
- Put the drill in a chuck on the tailstock
- Drill a small distance at a time, clearing the whitemetal from the drill frequently

Now the engine is a very heavy 0-4-0 held together without the help of adhesive tape. The kit's firebox is unprototypically extended backwards inside the cab to accommodate the motor. Whilst this could lead to the motor overheating, the backhead detail is very good, so this feature is worth retaining.

EXAMPLE LOCOMOTIVE PROJECTS

- Carefully measure the hole depth to reach almost to the front cylinder cover – this is important, because otherwise the piston may need to be cut too short, and may drop out of the cylinder at back dead centre

The connecting rods, slide bars and cross-heads/pistons are assembled next. Recheck that the engine runs smoothly before fixing the connecting rods in place on the crankpins.

FRONT AND REAR TRUCKS

It is actually quite challenging to achieve split-axle pickup on the tiny leading and trailing trucks (see box).

MAKING A SPLIT-AXLE OUTSIDE-FRAMED TRUCK

This locomotive has an isolated chassis.
1. Fit two (to ensure reliability) 0.2mm wires on the outside of each insulated wheel between nicks in the (steel) tyre and the axle. A fiddly job, but the wires can follow the spokes to be less visible.
2. Cut a back-to-back length of brass tube and fill it with epoxy. When hardened, face up the ends and bore it out on the lathe to form an insulating sleeve. Drill a small hole across its mid-point.
3. Cut the axle in two and then glue the wheel/stub axle assemblies into the tube, checking the isolation between wheels.
4. Cut tiny slivers of $1/32$in double-sided copper-clad sheet to fit inside the truck outer frames. Drill a hole in each, and solder a tinier sliver of brass shim over the hole, then press on this with a centre punch to form a pinpoint bearing.
5. Solder by its outer face or glue the copper-clad into the truck frames and align the bearings with the centre of the frames. Solder a thin insulated wire to each piece of copper-clad bearing, and glue to the truck frame to prevent it breaking in service.
6. Assemble the wheelset into the frame, and solder up the frame.

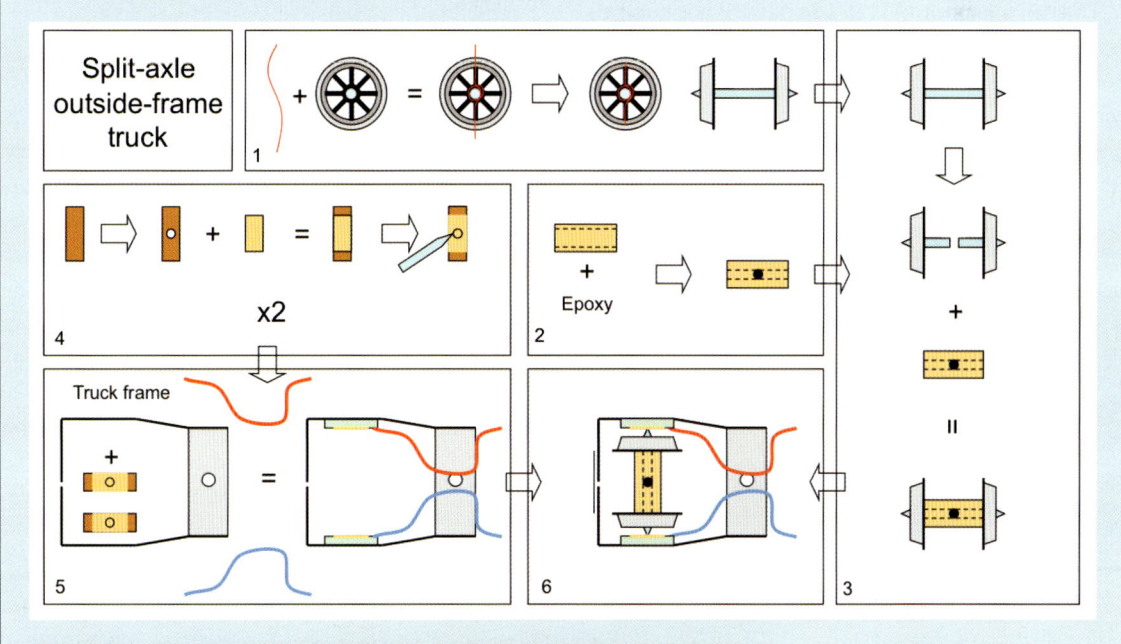

The method of making a split-axle outside-framed truck.

118 EXAMPLE LOCOMOTIVE PROJECTS

Trial assembly with trucks fitted (but not wired).

The trucks can be fitted to the loco, and it should run successfully over all pointwork and curves on the layout – this time as a 2-4-2T.

The couplers were initially attached to both trucks, and inevitably slightly impeded the trucks' movement on curves and over bumps. However, it is perfectly normal for problems to be experienced initially with an item such as this, and some adjustment may be needed. The model now has the front coupler attached to the inside of the buffer beam, whilst the rear coupler remains attached to the trailing truck. Both trucks are weighted with small pieces of lead.

The remaining work is to add details. It is good to try to maintain the open appearance of the chassis between the wheels, and fit dummy inside-valve gear, but the chassis baseplate precludes fitting the brake hangers, as much of them would be cut away to clear it.

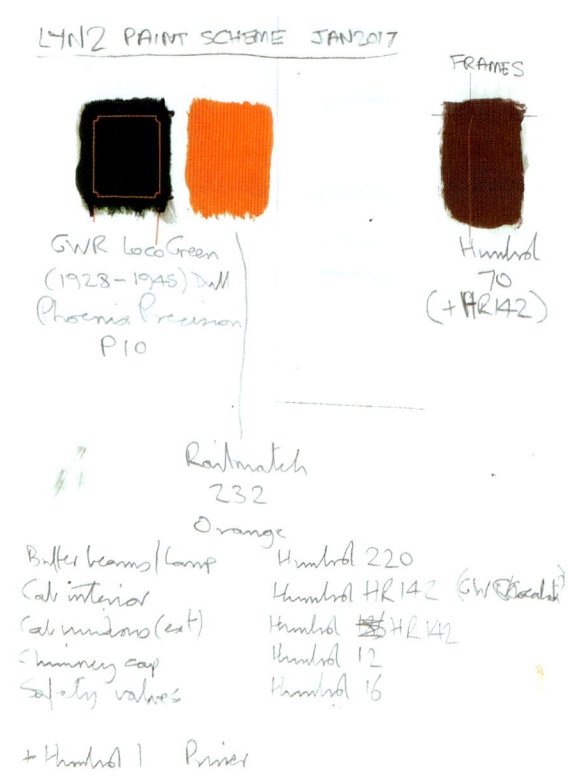

Paint samples for **Lyn**. *Here, the lining has also been tried out on the sample.*

PAINTING

Some primer is needed on brass, to help paint adhere to it, so after cleaning the model thoroughly, it is given two or more coats of either a two-part etch primer (for example as produced by Precision Paints), or a simpler approach using diluted Humbrol No.1 grey primer.

The paint used for the 'holly green' of the original is Precision GWR 1928–1945 green, which looks quite like the colour of holly leaves, while the red/brown frames are a custom-mixed colour intended to look similar to that in photos of pre-production Heljan locos.

Lyn *almost finished.*

LINING A MODEL

The easiest way to line a model is to use lining transfers. However, this livery has very broad black bands around the panels, filling the inward-curved corners of the orange lining, so the black lining is done using dilute matt black enamel paint and a bow-spring drawing pen, drawing out the inner edge of the black areas, and then painting up to the corners of the bodywork with the same paint on a fine brush.

The orange lining is from Fox Transfers, and is an overscale 0.35mm width. It is very difficult to get long lines, such as the horizontals on the tanks, to look straight with the more accurate 0.15mm lining, no matter how much they are pushed around with a fine brush laden with gluey water (as recommended by the supplier). Another factor is that Fox only supply curved corners in the 0.35mm width. The 0.15mm lining is used round the cab side and door panels, but it is quite tricky to apply, even though those lengths are shorter.

As an option, a real copper cap can be made for the elegant Baldwin chimney, rather than just painting the whitemetal copper colour.

Lyn *in a cradle to support it during lining.*

Lyn *complete.*

EXAMPLE LOCOMOTIVE PROJECTS

FOR COMPARISON: LANGLEY MODELS *LYN* KIT

The contents of a Langley Models Lyn kit, simpler than the Backwoods version, and with a greater proportion of whitemetal parts.

A finished Langley Lyn with a Grafar N gauge chassis, seen here waiting to leave Barnstaple Town. DAVID PRIME

PROJECT: *EXE* PART 1: A LYNTON & BARNSTAPLE LOCOMOTIVE FROM A WHITEMETAL BODY KIT

Having always modelled the L&B in the Southern Railway (SR) period, my Chelfham diorama was convertible between the independent and SR periods, the former to use scratchbuilt and Peco rolling stock in L&B livery. Therefore I needed L&B locos in pre-1923 livery. I found a Rodney Stenning whitemetal Manning Wardle body kit, plus the frame plates and wheelsets for a scratchbuilt chassis I had begun some years before, but had never finished. I decided to use this as the basis of *Exe* in L&B livery.

Part 1 of this example project describes the assembly and modification of the whitemetal body kit, and Part 2 covers the scratchbuilding of the chassis.

THE KIT

Sources of information and kit standards have improved a lot in recent years, but running a ruler over the whitemetal bodyshell parts confirmed their accuracy. They also looked right alongside scratchbuilt and Backwoods engines. The least satisfactory feature of the Stenning kit is that the tank tops are formed from a single flat casting, a lump down the middle representing the boiler. This is quite unlike the view of a real Manning Wardle from above, where the long thin boiler sits between the side tanks.

A contemporary postcard showing Exe *in L&B livery at Lynton.*
LOCOMOTIVE PUBLISHING COMPANY

EXAMPLE LOCOMOTIVE PROJECTS

MATERIALS AND TOOLS NEEDED

Rodney Stenning L&B 2-6-2T kit
Brass and nickel silver strip and sheet, various sizes
Brass bar, various sizes
Styrene strip and sheet, various sizes
8BA and 10BA taps
Styrene solvent, epoxy and cyanoacrylate adhesives
Basic hand tools
Small lathe
Soldering equipment (including LMP)
Etched brass nameplates and works plates (spares from a Backwoods kit)
Paint

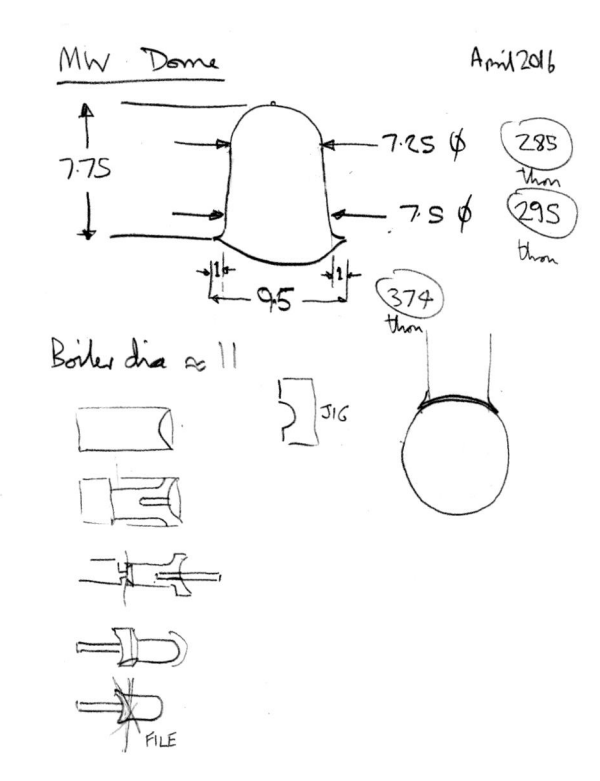

Example component sketch – a Manning Wardle dome.

CHANGES TO THE KIT DESIGN

The biggest change that can be made to the whitemetal body is to modify the tank tops, boiler and sandboxes, so that it looks significantly more realistic. The procedure is as follows:

- Cut along each side of the raised 'boiler' section of the original tank/boiler casting
- File the edges of the boiler piece into a better curve
- Finally, reassemble the three pieces. Use a jig to align them to the correct width to fit in the body, and fix them together by soldering the two sandboxes in place with LMP solder to strengthen the sub-assembly

This is simple to do, but the resulting improvement in appearance is significant.

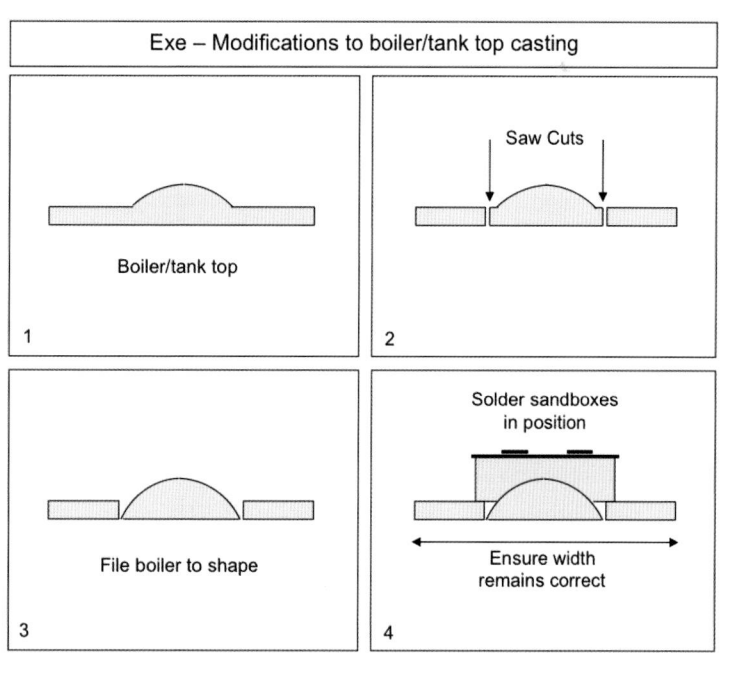

The biggest change made to the whitemetal body was to modify the tank tops, boiler and sandboxes, so as to look significantly more realistic.

EXAMPLE LOCOMOTIVE PROJECTS

1. Turn bar oversize and drill for spigot	5. Solder spigot into dome
2. Mill/file to dia. of boiler	6. File dome to shape using template to check
3. Turn down to correct dia.	7. Shape base carefully with round file in stationary lathe
4. Bevel top and part off	Turning a dome From brass bar

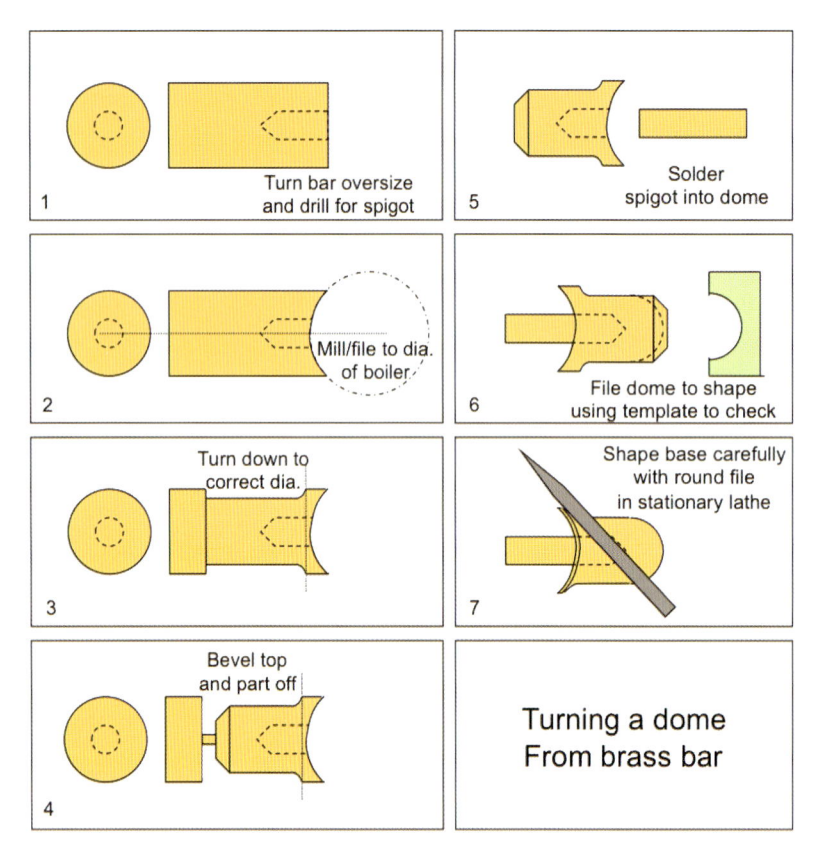

Turning a dome from brass bar.

A part-completed brass dome, with a whitemetal dome for comparison.

To further improve the appearance, a polished turned brass dome replaces the diecast one in the kit: the diagrams and photo show how to turn a dome from brass.

Replace the whitemetal cab roof with one made from a layer of styrene sheet, which is taped to a curved former and immersed in a pan of hot water for a few minutes to form it to the radius and leave it permanently curved after cooling. This roof helps to reduce the weight of the engine's rear end, and improves the engine's balance.

The whitemetal chimney provided in the kit could beneficially be modified to add the distinctive brass cap, to be left unpainted and polished.

PREPARATION

Before assembly, clean up each of the parts, and file down all the visible edges of the whitemetal cab sides to reduce their thickness and improve the final appearance.

BODY ASSEMBLY

The remainder of the bodyshell is built more or less according to the instructions, but including the improved tank/boiler-top unit.

As this model was not to use the N gauge chassis that the kit was designed for, the scratchbuilt chassis

EXAMPLE LOCOMOTIVE PROJECTS   123

A cab floor/underframe unit was fabricated from styrene sheet to minimize weight, and the rear frames were 'splayed' to give additional clearance for the rear truck on curves, the plastic effectively preventing short circuits.

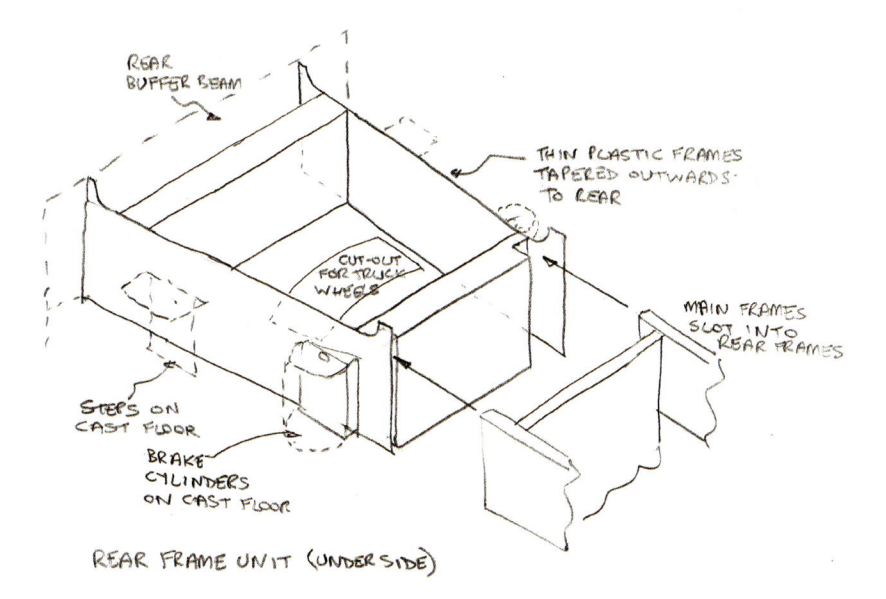

should ideally have been designed and built before assembling the bodyshell, so that the area to accommodate the motor can be cut out of the cab floor. But without having built the body, it was unclear what space would be available for the motor, so in the event, the body was built first.

Later, as the chassis was taking shape, most of the whitemetal cab floor was cut away (a good idea anyway, as it reduces the tail-end weight). The rear underframe of this model forms part of the body assembly. The motor, which projects unsupported from the rear of the chassis, is inserted into the cab as the chassis and body are brought together.

DETAILING

After assembly, the cab back sheet is drilled for a tiny button magnet to be glued in place, to allow a removable steel loco lamp to be attached to the rear of the engine when running cab first.

Brass surrounds to the cab spectacle windows can be fitted by cutting short slices of brass tube of the correct diameter, and opening out the holes in the whitemetal spectacle plates to accept them. The brass tube slices can then be superglued in place, projecting slightly from the spectacle plate.

Pipework is made from brass or nickel silver wire, bent to shape and superglued into holes in the whitemetal body (it is too risky to try to solder

The many small details shown on drawings and in photographs, which make the model locomotive reasonably accurate, are added progressively.

The whole of the tank/boiler space can be filled with lead, to weigh down the front. Even with the plastic cab roof, and with the whitemetal cab floor removed, there is still a lot of whitemetal (and the weight of the motor) at the back end.

details to large existing assemblies, as the whole lot might melt). Vacuum pipes should be added to the buffer beams, having been made from a piece of nickel silver wire with 0.2mm copper wire (a strand from 7/0.2mm low-voltage electrical wire) wound round it to represent the internal structure of the flexible pipe.

Unused *Exe* and *Manning Wardle* maker's plates from a Backwoods kit were used to finish off the model.

PROJECT – *EXE* PART 2: SCRATCHBUILDING AN OUTSIDE-FRAMED 2-6-2T CHASSIS

Having very rapidly adapted a body kit for my new L&B Manning Wardle 2-6-2T, I had to scratchbuild the chassis. Taking a very deep breath, I set about the challenging task of building a new outside-framed chassis.

MATERIALS AND TOOLS NEEDED

10.5 or 11mm-diameter driving wheels
8mm-diameter truck wheels
Mashima 1024 motor
M0.3 spur gears (30T and 10T)
24:1 worm gear set
Langley Miniatures L&B Manning Wardle cowcatchers
Brass and nickel silver strip and sheet, various sizes
Brass bar, various sizes
Steel shafting, various sizes
1/32in copper-clad board
8BA, 10BA and 12BA nuts, bolts, washers, taps and dies
Epoxy and cyanoacrylate adhesives
Basic hand tools
Small lathe
Soldering equipment (including LMP)
Paint
A lot of patience…

WHEELSETS

Suitable wheels are available from Markits and other suppliers (often 3mm/1ft or 4mm/1ft scale bogie/tender wheels are the correct diameter for 009 models). In this case, old Beaver Products N gauge 5ft 6in locomotive driving wheels were used (11mm diameter in 2mm/1ft scale – correct for the 2ft 9in diameter of a 4mm/1ft scale L&B loco).

The metal tyres of this type of wheel can sometimes turn relative to the nylon wheel centres, so each tyre was pinned to its wheel centre. This was done by drilling in through the tyre and gluing a tiny pin in place alongside a spoke, then trimming the excess length off the pin on the outside of the tyre.

In case the wheels had not been tortured enough, every other spoke was carefully cut out with a fine-bladed craft knife, to improve the appearance of the 2mm/1ft scale wheels for a 4mm/1ft scale engine.

The wheels should be painted at this stage, as it is difficult to do after the chassis is complete.

FRAMES

A large-scale sketch of the chassis is used to determine the layout of the drive train and frame spacers.

A Mashima 1024 motor (24mm long, 10 × 15mm cross-section, open frame) drives a layshaft via 3:1 reduction M0.3 spur gears (bought on-line from Poland). The layshaft carries the worm gear that drives the centre axle (in this case a Beaver Products 24:1 set).

An L&B Manning Wardle has a short-coupled wheelbase, so the driving-wheel flanges virtually touch one another, and it is difficult to fit a substantial plate beneath the chassis to strengthen it (as was done with *Lyn*). Instead, a vertical 1/32in brass spacer at each end of the frames, and short baseplates fore and aft of the coupled wheels, hold the frames together. The bottom plates each have two tapped holes in them, one for the truck pivot, and the other to fix the current collector sub-assembly in place later.

To simplify assembly, the rear vertical frame-spacer is extended upwards to include both a bearing for the longitudinal layshaft, and the location and fixing holes for the Mashima motor.

EXAMPLE LOCOMOTIVE PROJECTS

This front layshaft bearing is fitted in another small frame-spacer. This spacer is made early on so that trial assembly can be carried out, but only soldered in position later. It is tapped 8BA, to take a bored-out piece of 8BA bolt, so that the longitudinal play in the layshaft can be adjusted, and the bearing can be unscrewed to remove the layshaft for servicing.

COUPLING RODS

Next, the pre-drilled pair of coupling rod blanks is carefully marked out and shaped, using a bench magnifier/light for close work such as this. The coupling rods must be made from quite substantial nickel silver sheet, as they should not flex under the forces involved in turning the non-driven wheels. The plain rod sections can be filed down in thickness, to leave a raised boss around the crankpin holes, to avoid the need for washers between the rod and the crank.

On an outside-cylindered engine, the front coupling rod boss should be filed down in thickness before assembly, to give an extra few thou of width for the motion to be fitted later!

PICKUPS

Pickups of the traditional type are reliable – thin phosphor-bronze wire soldered to a strip of $1/32$in copper-clad sheet, bolted in place between the front and rear frame-spacers.

VALVE GEAR

After two weeks of work, the chassis was running, but without the connecting rods and valve gear.

The first attempt at assembling the valve gear was a failure as it wouldn't fit within the whitemetal motion covers! The following week was spent trying to solve this, with a few false starts… After making sketches of several alternative solutions, valve gear sub-assemblies that would (just) fit behind the motion covers were made.

The Stenning cast front footplate, cylinders and motion covers can be used as supplied (with a Langley etched brass cowcatcher added). A nickel silver cylinder backplate and flattened nickel silver

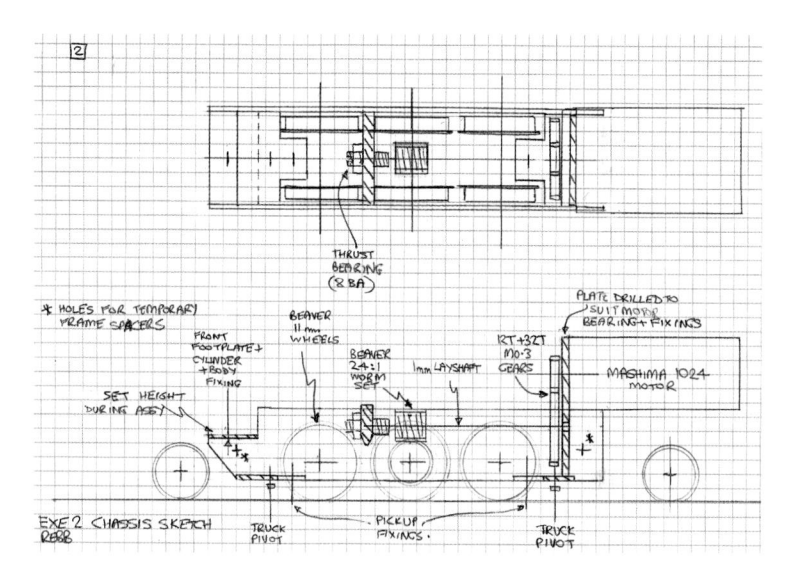

Chassis sketch for **Exe**.

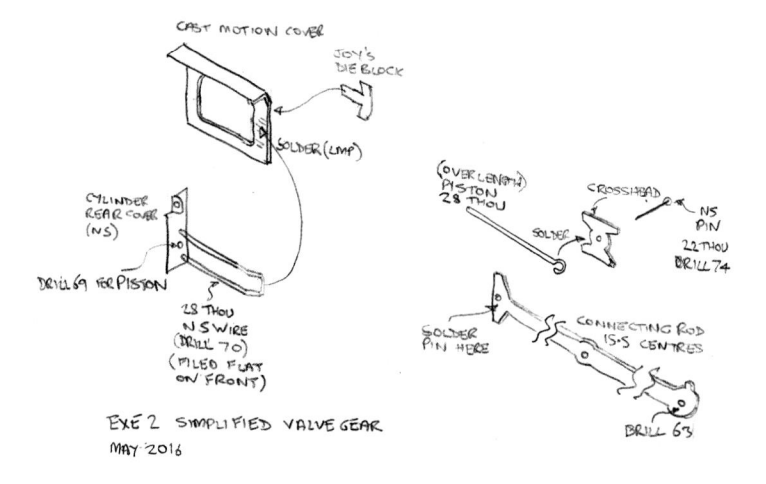

Sketch of **Exe** *valve gear assembly.*

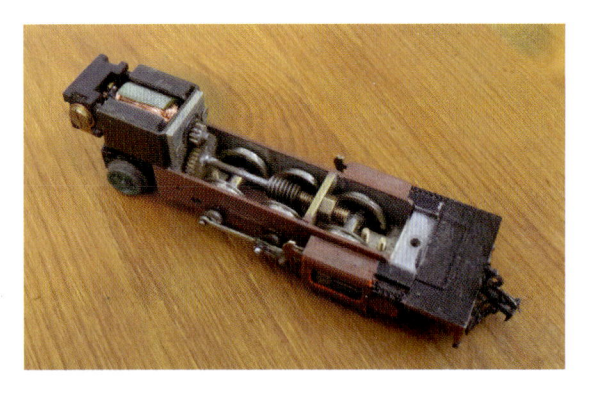

The final stage of the functional chassis construction (apart from detailing) is to fit the motor, and apply a tiny drop of sewing-machine oil to each bearing with the smallest flat-bladed jeweller's screwdriver.

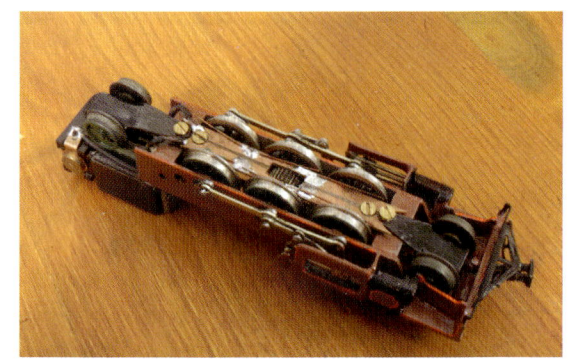

The underside of Exe's chassis.

wire slide bars are fixed with LMP solder within the whitemetal motion cover on each side. Each connecting rod has a T-shaped 'little-end' to hold the cross-head in place on the slide bars whilst minimizing the thickness.

Simplified motion is fitted (the tiny return cranks are non-functional). Some experimentation is needed to get everything to fit within the available width. The cross-head must sit in ahead of the leading crankpin, and the length of the piston is absolutely critical – or, even with the cylinder drilled almost to the front cover, the piston will fall out of the cylinder at back dead centre.

The leading and trailing trucks are bent from nickel silver sheet, loaded up with as much lead as will fit within the chassis, and Dundas Models 8mm disc wheels are fitted. Split-axle current collection on the leading and trailing trucks, using the method outlined earlier, will be added to this loco later.

The body and chassis come together.

Once the chassis and all its valve gear is running freely, the layshaft front bearing frame-spacer may be fitted. The drilled-out 8BA bolt bearing (held in place by a locknut) and the layshaft are fitted in position. Then, ensuring a tiny amount of clearance between the worm and its pinion, the bearing stretcher is soldered in place in the frames.

The chassis should then be run on the bench for an hour or so in each direction. The speed will gradually increase, and it is a good idea to turn the voltage down periodically, to avoid over-stressing the motor. The final test should be to turn the controller down to see just how slowly the chassis will run. The builder can feel really proud of a scratch-built loco when it creeps steadily along at less than a scale walking pace.

Exe *in operation.*

CHAPTER SEVEN

ROLLING STOCK

The acquisition of narrow gauge rolling stock for a 009 layout is easier than acquiring the locomotive fleet, since a selection of ready-to-run UK 009 stock is currently available, and a wider range of simple plastic, whitemetal and etched brass kits is available. Even where no kit exists, there are considerably fewer challenges for scratchbuilders of rolling stock, as a motorized chassis is not needed.

THE OPTIONS AVAILABLE

READY-TO-RUN

Peco and Bachmann currently produce ready-to-run 009 passenger and freight rolling stock, notably for the Lynton & Barnstaple Railway, the Glyn Valley Tramway, and the War Department Light Railways.

Bachmann ready-to-run WDLR ambulance van and D Class bogie open wagon.

German and Japanese suppliers offer ready-to-run H0e stock based on local prototypes, much of which can be used or adapted for freelance UK-themed 009 layouts, or modified to represent specific prototypes.

MODIFIED READY-TO-RUN

As with locomotives, commercially produced, ready-to-run rolling stock can benefit from simple enhancements. Alternatively, a commercial model may be used as the basis for a more radical conversion into another type of vehicle to suit the chosen layout.

KITS

009 rolling stock kits are available from several specialist suppliers. For example:

- Etched brass kits from Langley Models or, to aid scratchbuilders, time-saving brass etches from Worsley Works
- Plastic kits from Dundas Models, Ninelines, Meridian Models, the 009 Society, and others
- The Shapeways 3D-printing service advertises a large variety of 3D-printed 009 and H0e rolling stock, from many different designers. Other suppliers also market their own 3D-printed rolling stock

The plastic kits are straightforward to assemble, usually with comparatively few parts. The finished model will always benefit from care taken to ensure that the chassis is flat, and that the parts are fitted together accurately.

The brass kits require knowledge of folding the etched parts, embossing rivets, and soldering and fitting the very small details. These skills were all discussed in the chapters on locomotives.

The 3D-printed models are usually complete, or consist of a few sub-assemblies.

Kits can also be adapted to suit the requirements of a particular layout, just as ready-to-run models can.

SCRATCHBUILDING

The creation of a prototypical 009 layout is likely to require some items of rolling stock that are not available commercially, and cannot easily be converted from a commercial model or kit. However, it is quite straightforward to build such items from scratch.

The remainder of this chapter illustrates these different approaches by means of examples.

PROJECT: DETAILING A PECO L&B COACH

The Peco Lynton & Barnstaple coaches are fine representations of the prototypes – especially those carrying the independent-era livery. However, the practicalities of running this stock, and a study of prototype drawings and photographs, reveal a few small improvements that can easily be made, even by less experienced modellers.

RUNNING IMPROVEMENTS

The plastic wheelsets fitted by Peco may easily be replaced with metal-tyred 6.2mm disc wheels, available from Dundas Models, Grafar or N-train.

Dismantle the coach by removing the roof, carefully pulling out the seating unit, and then compressing the pivot pins to remove the bogies. Removing the keeper/pivot moulding from each bogie allows the wheelsets to be replaced.

A touch of sewing-machine oil on each bearing will prevent the coach squeaking while running.

With the coach in pieces, some modellers may wish to add small pieces of lead sheet in the cavities provided in the coach floor, and to detail and paint the interior (see below).

Some may also wish to replace the bulky couplers and their support beams. Many 009 modellers use the neater Greenwich couplers, which plug into the NEM pockets and operate with the Peco couplers.

To be totally accurate, the couplers should be headstock-mounted chopper type, which require the support beams to be cut off the bogies, and the cut-outs in the moulded headstocks to be filled in and repainted.

IMPROVING THE APPEARANCE

Unpainted plastic surfaces such as the footsteps, roof and underframe can be weathered with matt paints. The end steps and handrails can be carefully picked out in black paint.

The edges of the white plastic roof may be painted with the body colour, to represent the painted wooden moulding that edged the roof of the prototype. A good match for the L&B red/brown colour is obtained by mixing equal amounts of Humbrol 73 and 160.

The lamp tops and bungs on the original Peco roofs are slightly undersize, but painting the upper parts of the lamps black makes them stand out more. For greater accuracy, or on later Peco coaches supplied with the oversize black lamps, these and the associated bungs can be carefully filed off the roof moulding, and replaced by scale ones. Langley Models produce whitemetal items, or accurate items can be purchased via the 3D-printing bureau Shapeways.

If the plastic roof is being modified, the moulded handrails at each end can also be replaced with wire ones. The roof should be weathered if desired to represent the discolouration of white lead paint as a result of the effects of sunlight, steam and oil.

INTERIOR IMPROVEMENTS

The interior details in the coaches are hard to see from the outside, but they can be improved with a small amount of work. Comparison with drawings shows some errors in the interior layouts, which

A Peco bogie during replacement of its wheels.

ROLLING STOCK

An 'improved' interior for a Peco coach.

can be corrected by inserting balsa seats with styrene sheet backs and partitions. The modified seats and the 3rd class interior sides can be painted with Humbrol 119. Alternatively, paper overlays can be printed on the computer to represent the various surfaces.

The interior partitions and inside the coach ends are white above the seat backs on restored stock, but originally they were varnished wood, and later 'scumbled' (painted with brown wood-grain effect paint).

1st class seats may be painted to represent the blue velvet (non-smoking) or dark red leather (smoking) of the originals, and 1st class compartment partitions can be painted or have printed paper overlays attached, to represent the white surface and framed photographs.

Drawings and photographs identify in which compartments smoking was permitted, and it is possible to add 'smoking' and 'no smoking' signs on the glazing.

A few seated passengers can be added, toning down brightly coloured modern clothes to more sombre shades.

Curtains were visible at many L&B coach windows, to provide protection for passengers against the summer sun. They can be modelled by gluing tiny scraps of off-white tissue paper into the coach interior.

PROJECT: MODIFYING H0e WAGONS

The Raleigh Weir layout needs models of the various wagons known to have been used by the contractor, and this section describes how they can be provided.

BOGIE WAGONS

Scratchbuilding realistic wagon bogies is tricky, so it is worth finding suitable 'donor' r-t-r wagons or kits to provide them.

Two bogie wagons are seen in photographs of the construction work on the L&B.

One was the short bogie open wagon on skip-chassis bogies, for which a drawing was created from a photograph in Chapter 3, in the Section 'Example: Create a Drawing of an L&B Contractor's Wagon'.

The other was a longer, more sophisticated bogie bolster wagon on sprung bogies. This was fitted with sockets for holding stakes to support timber and other loads.

After finishing the L&B construction work, this second wagon was modified and taken into L&B stock as wagon No. 19, so its dimensions are known.

A pack of two Minitrains H0e bogie stake wagons (Ref 5122) was bought cheaply at the 009 Society stand at a local show, as they looked promising candidates for being modified to represent the contractor's wagons. They seemed to have suitable bogies, and the wheelbase corresponded to that of the bogie bolster wagon.

The bogie bolster wagon, seen here with longitudinal benches fitted. This wagon transported visitors to view progress with the construction works. MAJOR, DARKER & LORAINE

ROLLING STOCK

The 'donor' wagons as purchased.

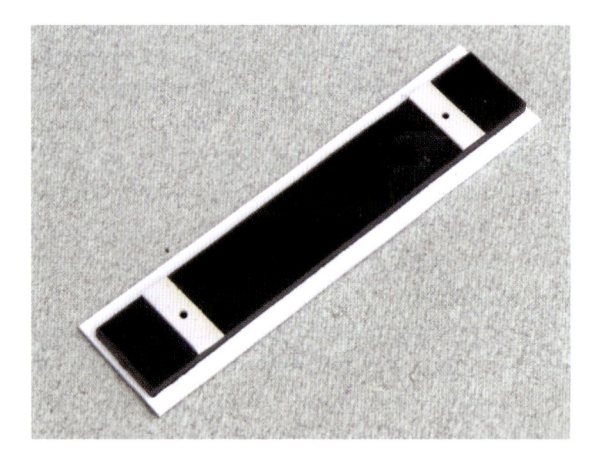

A new flat platform is fabricated from styrene sheet.

The stakes themselves are reused, being attached to the new floor in the correct positions.

Comparison of the model wagons with the drawings revealed a choice that is common when modifying an r-t-r item: re-use and compromise, or rebuild to achieve greater accuracy.

Re-using one of the Minitrains wagon bodies for the flat wagon would have left the stakes in the wrong positions, so a new platform was constructed.

Tiny pieces of 12BA bolts are superglued either side of each axlebox to represent the springs.

The bogies require extended couplers, so Greenwich couplers are superglued to the bogie frames.

The drawing showed that the open wagon was much shorter than the Minitrains model, so planked styrene sheet sides and ends are fitted to a new platform, and small details are added based on photographic evidence. This gives a plausible-looking wagon with the minimum of effort.

The wagons are painted grey (Humbrol 64), with floors dark brown (Humbrol 98) and weathered. The man-carrier superstructure (presumed to be new softwood) is fabricated from styrene strip and painted with Humbrol 110 (Natural Wood).

FOUR-WHEELED WAGONS

These wagons are easier to source than bogie wagons, as most of those needed for this layout were common V-tipper skips or trestle wagons, which can be obtained either ready-to-run or in kit form from several suppliers.

Another picture shows a skip chassis with a timber bed fitted, carrying sleepers. This is easily constructed with a skip chassis and planked styrene sheet.

ROLLING STOCK | 131

Several Roco packs of two skips (Ref 34498) are used. The H0e skips seem to best represent those seen in photographs. Only weathering and a supply of removable loads of stone, spoil and so on are needed to make an adaptable fleet for the layout.

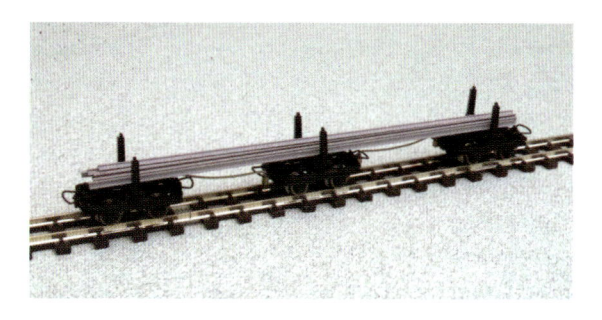

Timber and rails were transported on four-wheeled trestle wagons, roped together within trains. To permit propelling moves, the skips are 'roped' together with nickel silver wire, the outer wagons coupling to other stock normally.

Skips with transverse V-tipper bodies were used to tip ballast on to newly laid track ahead of a works train. Those seen here (before painting) are made by gluing one Roco skip (minus wheels and axleboxes) transversely across another skip chassis.

WAGON LOADS

The removable loads for the wagons on the layout include the following:

Bogie bolster wagon: With temporary seating for workmen, the press and VIPs. Each of these is an assembly of suitable painted figures glued to strips of glazing material.

Bogie open wagon: This carries a portable toilet shed and sleepers from temporary track (as seen in the photograph), and various construction tools and materials (bricks, timber, wheelbarrows). Each load is constructed from scraps of styrene or balsa wood.

Trestle wagons (roped together): These carry 30ft (9m) rails (Code 55 rail, painted), and timber telegraph poles (cut from wire coat-hangers).

Skips: These carry stone for structures along the line, spoil from cuttings, and ballast. To form each of these loads, wood is shaped to fit in a Roco skip, a steel M3 bolt is glued into a hole drilled through it (for weight, and to allow removal using a magnet), and Woodland Scenics material is glued to the top.

End tippers: These carry ballast (as provided by Woodland Scenics).

A variety of part-finished wagon loads, and some loaded wagons.

PROJECT: SCRATCHBUILDING L&B COACH NO. 2

The inspection trains seen in several photographs carrying the L&B's directors, and planned for the Raleigh Weir layout, often used a single coach, one of the 1st class saloon composite brake coaches (No. 1 or No. 2).

Inspecting progress with the construction from the 1st class saloon. MAJOR, DARKER & LORAINE

Coach No. 2, displayed unrestored in the National Railway Museum in York, is not currently produced by Peco, so is used as an example of how to build an apparently complex panelled vehicle using quite simple methods.

DRAWINGS

Drawings of these coaches have been published several times, the best-known being the following:

- R. E. Tustin, *Model Railway Constructor*, 1950s, and reproduced several times in other publications (these include some significant errors)
- SR official diagrams, *The Lynton & Barnstaple Railway*, Brown, Prideaux and Radcliffe (Atlantic)
- Stephen Phillips, *The Lynton & Barnstaple Railway Measured and Drawn* (prepared from a detailed survey of the NRM coach)

The model in this project is based on Stephen Phillips' drawings.

SIDES

The panelled sides of the coach are a good place to start, as initially they appear daunting. The task is simplified because they are flat-sided, rather than bowed.

A pair of sides is cut from 30-thou styrene sheet, leaving them slightly over-height and with at least 15mm (½in) of scrap at either end. The pair of sides is glued together with a small amount of liquid poly applied sparingly to the scrap area at each end (too much and it runs between the wanted areas, fixing them together permanently!).

Attempts to cut out the windows with a craft knife will result in cuts that weaken the narrow dividing pillars. However, there are two simple ways to make each window aperture:

1. A hole can be drilled through the pair of sides within each window, and most of the unwanted material cut out with a piercing saw. Once all apertures are roughly cut, the tops and bottoms are finished by clamping a straight edge (for example, a metal strip) along the required edge, and filing up to it with a small needle file. The process can be repeated for each vertical edge, to align the sides of the windows and top lights.
2. If several coaches are to be built, it may be worth making a jig consisting of two steel plates with locating dowels. This may include each

ROLLING STOCK

The window positions are marked on the pair of sides, or alternatively a 4mm/1ft scale copy of the drawing is temporarily attached with Pritt paper glue.

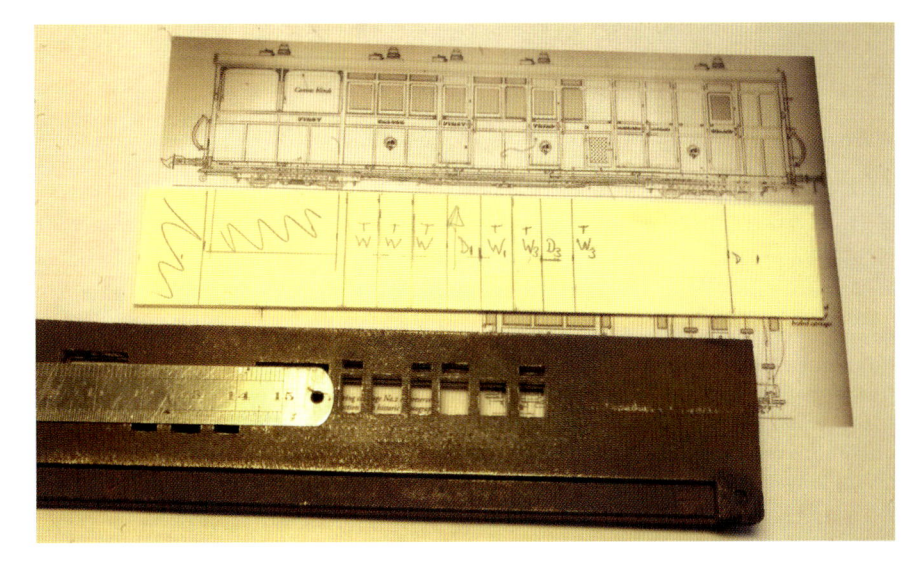

size of compartment window, or whole compartment layouts. Clamping the pair of sides between the two steel plates, the windows are drilled, roughed out and finished one at a time.

If an error does occur, it is quick to make replacement sides. Once correct, the pair of sides will be ready for panelling.

It is worth sticking each of the sides down on two prints of the drawing (one reversed, of course), so that the panelling pattern can be copied without mistakes and so that a left-hand and a right-hand side are produced.

Coach sides in the window jig.

Cutting the scrap from each end allows the sides to be separated, but the extra material is left along the top edge for the moment. Replicating the rounded upper corners of the windows is not really necessary in 009 scale.

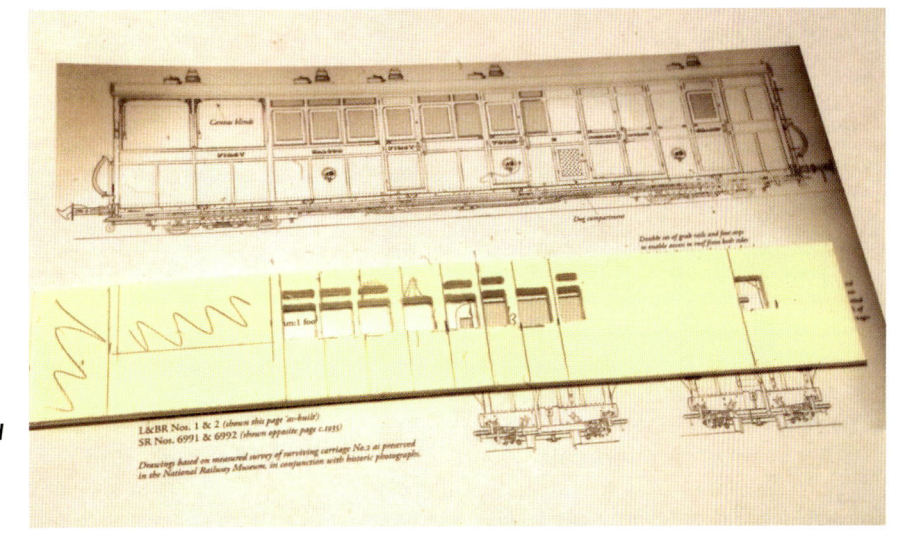

Few tools and materials are needed for panelling, so this can be done away from the workbench, or even from home (for example on holidays or business trips). Panelling is mostly 10-thou × 30-thou styrene, and an Evergreen pack of ten strips about 300mm (12in) long is plenty for a coach.

fully on the coach side, hold it in place and apply a drop of liquid poly from a tiny paintbrush. Then add the vertical framing of door openings, leaving a tiny gap between this and the door vertical.

The sequence for adding the strips is as follows:

1. Verticals either side of door windows, the full height of the coach side. Align the strip care-

2. Horizontals above and below windows, cutting each piece to fit between adjacent verticals, and securing it with a touch of liquid poly. Care is needed to ensure each section aligns with the preceding one, forming a straight line along the entire side. Then add horizontals below waist panels and above toplights. Horizontals are not needed across the top of doors, as this makes it easier to accommodate the ventilator louvres.
3. Remaining verticals to complete the panelling.
4. 50-thou width horizontal across the bottom of all doors. Also ventilator louvres above each door.

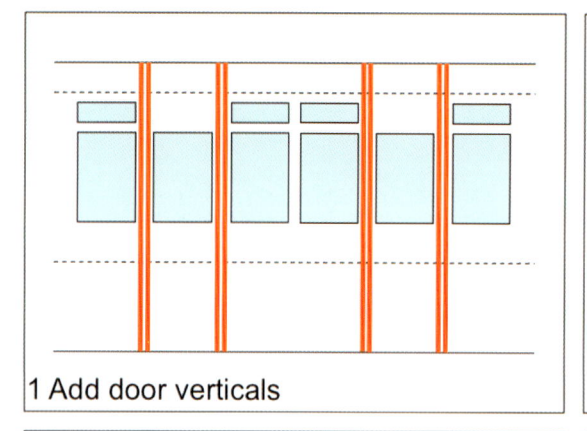

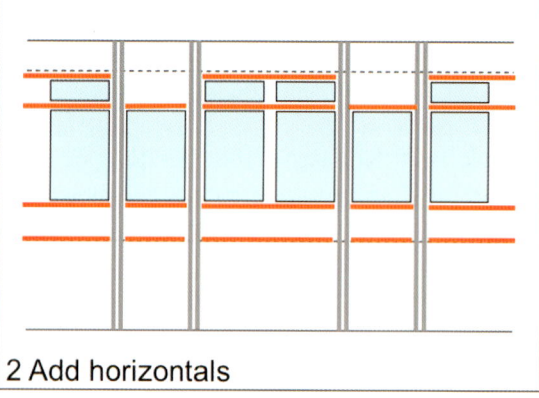

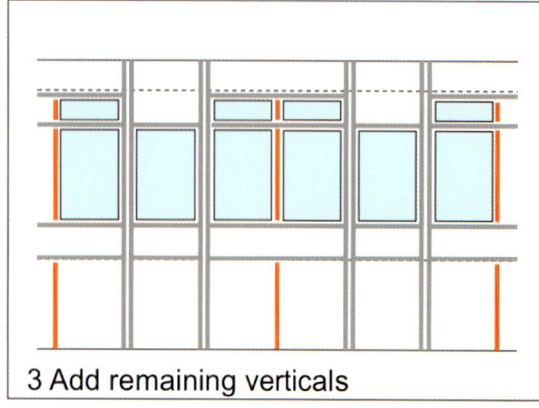

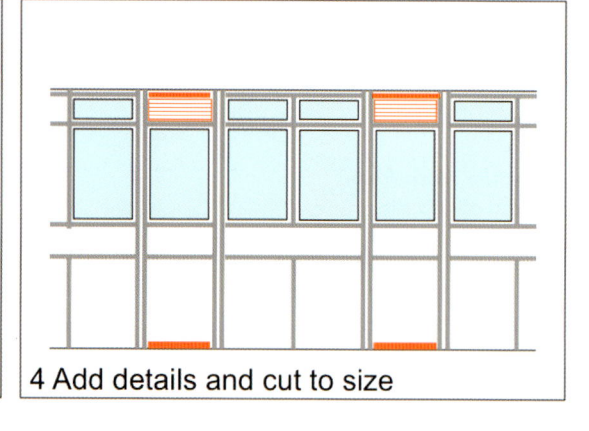

1 Add door verticals

2 Add horizontals

3 Add remaining verticals

4 Add details and cut to size

The sequence for panelling a coach side.

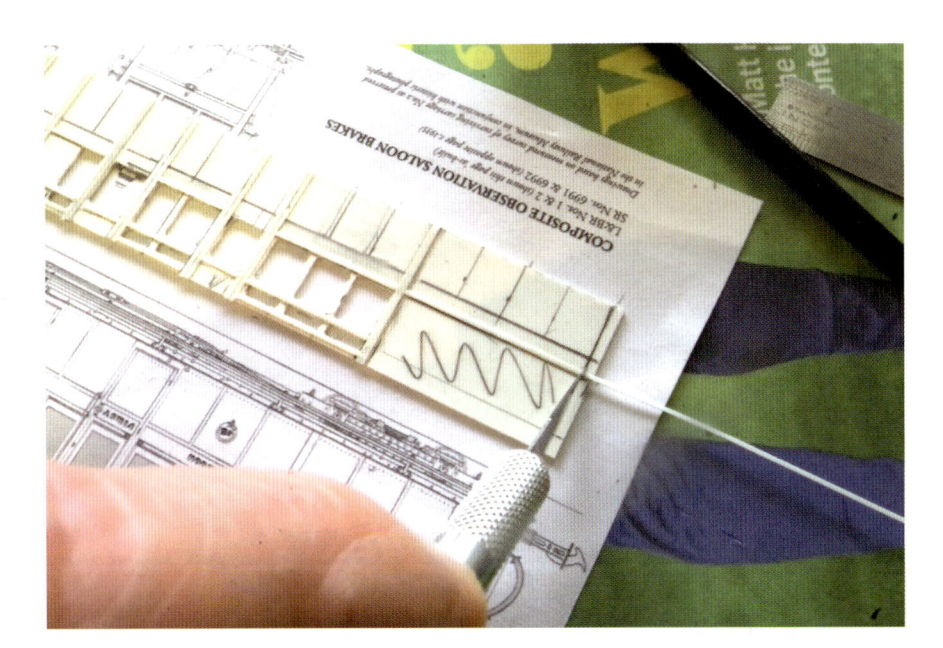

Panelling work in progress.

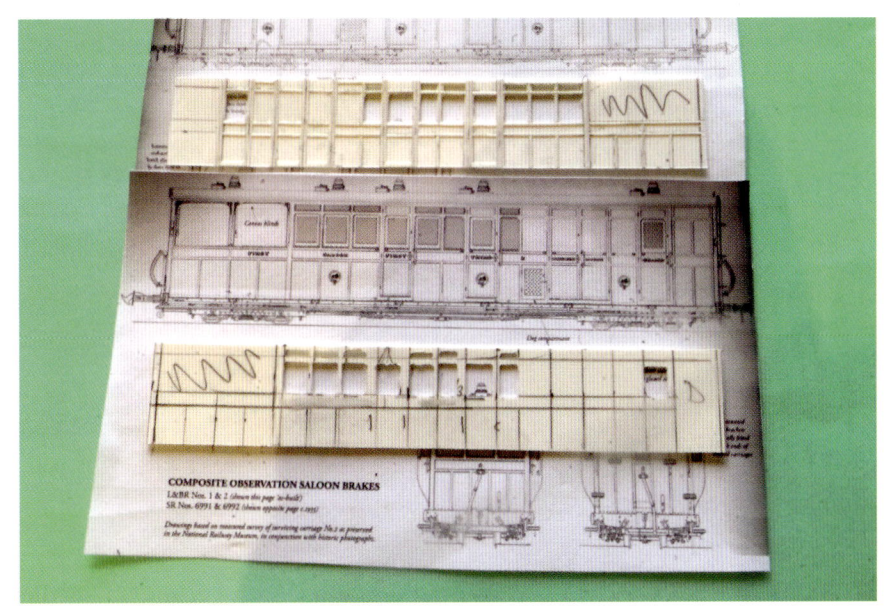

One panelled side complete. The guard's ducket sections are not panelled.

The ventilator louvre at the top of each door is a short strip of Evergreen Clapboard material (Item No. 4031, 40-thou styrene with 30-thou planking). A three-planks-wide strip of this material is cut into lengths, the ends shaped, and each piece fixed in place with solvent.

The sides are left overnight for the cement to harden fully. Then a further touch with a needle file can be used to square up the windows parallel to the panelling where needed, and to remove any burrs from the edges.

The top of each side is now cut to height, with multiple light passes with the craft knife to avoid the blade distorting the plastic over the top lights.

FLOOR

The floor is cut from 2.5mm spruce, and edged with 30-thou plasticard to form solebars, and to form an inner strengthening layer for the lower part of the sides, about 8mm above the floor.

ENDS AND SEATS

Each end, complete with headstock, is marked out on styrene sheet. A pilot hole, to be opened up later, is drilled for the coupler, and any windows are cut out.

When making the observation saloon end, scrap material is initially left either side of the component to strengthen the narrow pillars. The corners of each window are drilled, before cutting out the aperture with a fine piercing saw and finishing it carefully with a needle file.

The rear of the plastic is then recessed around the window area with a dental burr in a minidrill, to accommodate the glazing later. The observation end overlaps the coach sides for extra strength of the corner pillars, and the brake end beyond the guard's ducket is made similarly, although normal saloon coach ends would be made from 40-thou plastic and would fit between the sides.

Intermediate partitions (between compartments, and leading into the saloon) are made from 30-thou plastic, as are seat backs within open saloons.

Seats are cut from balsa strip, and glued to seat-

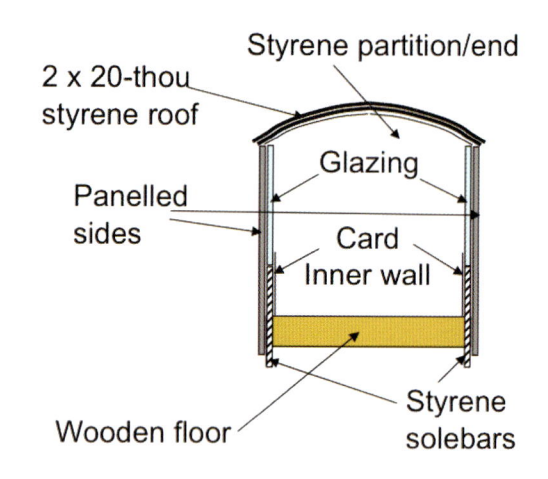

Method of coach construction.

backs as appropriate. After assembly, they are sawn and filed to represent the seat profile more accurately, and arms are added to 1st class seats. It is easier to paint the seats before their installation in the coach.

BOGIES AND RUNNING GEAR

Coach bogies can be made from 30-thou brass strip, with frames drilled for the pinpoint axles of

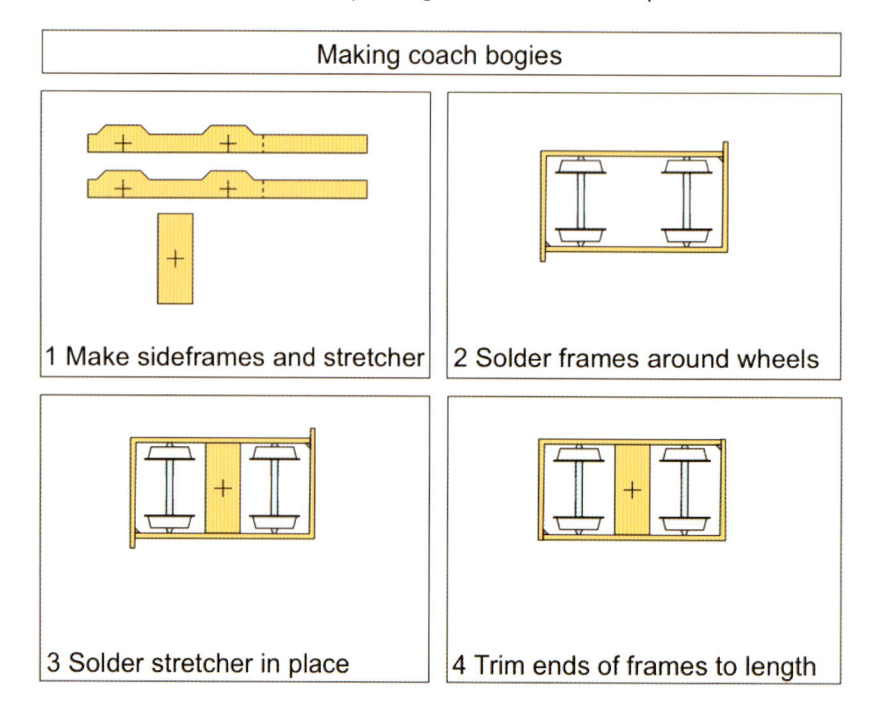

Making coach bogies.

6.2mm disc wheelsets. Each side/end frame is bent, and the two are soldered together, sandwiching the wheels in place. After checking that the bogie is square and flat, the cross-stretcher is soldered in the centre.

For this model, Peco coach bogies (Part No. GR-104) are used, the plastic wheels being replaced by metal ones. The floor must incorporate 3.75mm holes in a 1.5mm plastic stretcher to permit the bogies to clip in place.

Peco coach bogies (Part No. GR-104) are used for this model.

GUARD'S DUCKETS

The curved-sided duckets consist of two full-width 'partitions', made into a box using styrene spacers. The sides are faced with pre-curved oversize pieces of 10-thou styrene, and the excess is cut away from the edges once the solvent has hardened. The whole sub-assembly can be slotted into the coach structure, the sides having been cut away to facilitate this.

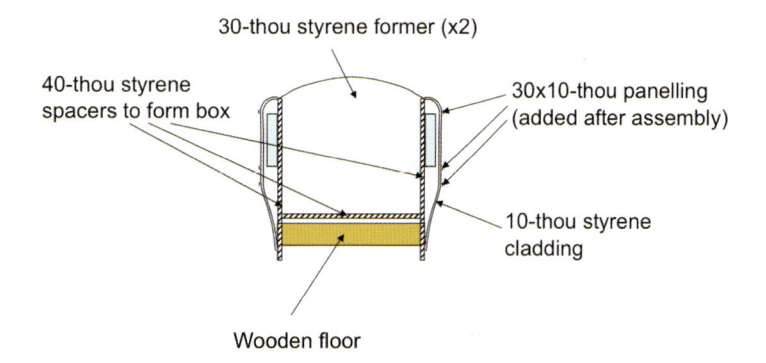

The curved-sided duckets consist of two full-width 'partitions'.

ASSEMBLY

The sides are carefully aligned with the floor, and fixed in place with liquid poly. The ends and intermediate partitions are then glued in place.

If body-mounted Peco or Greenwich couplers are to be used, NEM coupler pockets are glued in place behind each headstock.

Finally the panelling can be added to the ends and to the duckets, exactly as for the coach sides. The ends must be panelled after assembly to cover the join between the sides and ends to represent the corner posts, and the duckets can

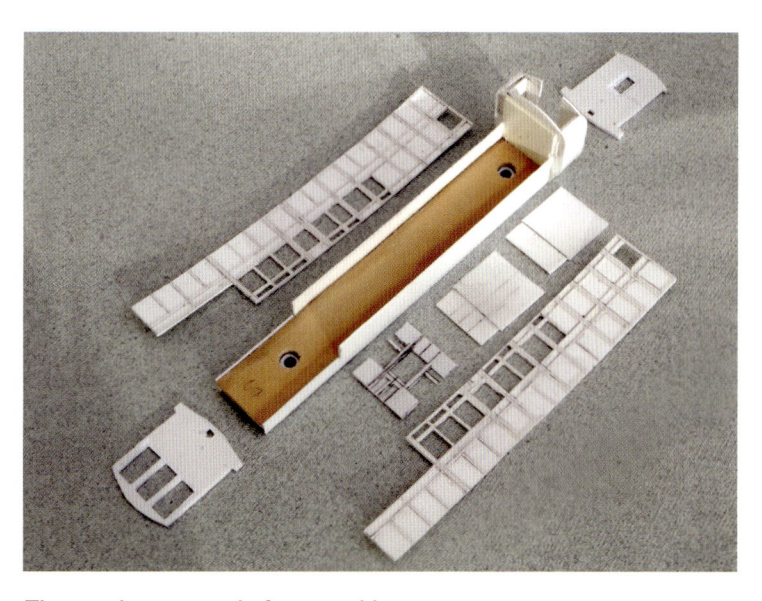

The coach parts ready for assembly.

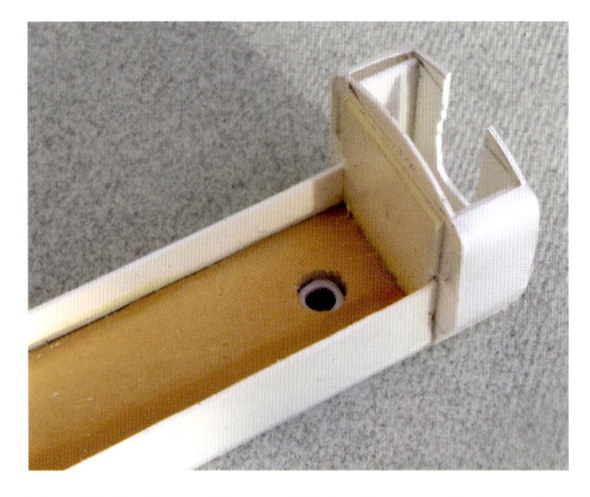

Guard's ducket sub-assembly in place on the coach.

only be panelled now to ensure that the horizontals align with those on the coach sides. Use a minimum amount of liquid poly to attach the ducket panelling, to avoid softening the thin styrene sheet.

INTERIOR DETAIL

Computer artwork is used to produce the coach interiors, although in fact little detail is visible after assembly.

On thin card (160g/m^2):
Internal lower sides (3rd class varnished horizontal planking, 1st class upholstered panels, both with window straps).

On paper (80g/m^2):
3rd class partitions (vertical planking, varnished originally or white on restored carriages).
1st class partitions (white walls above wooden panelling, with pictures).
3rd class seating (varnished planking).
3rd class ceiling (longitudinal white planking with cross-framing).
1st class ceiling (geometric pattern, white).

PAINTING

The original L&B livery (before about 1905) was referred to as terracotta and flesh/salmon, and is represented as follows:

- Upper panels: flesh/salmon – Humbrol 148 + 73 + 186
- Lower panels, framing, ends, solebars, headstocks: terracotta – Humbrol 100 + 186 + 113
- Interior of luggage compartment: light grey – Humbrol 64

The two-tone livery is painted over several days, in the following sequence:

1. The upper panels are given two coats, which are both allowed to dry thoroughly.
2. The lower panels are painted.
3. The upper framing is carefully picked out in the lower bodyside colour, as appropriate, using a very fine brush. Inevitably some irregularity occurs along the edges of the framing.
4. Once this colour is dry, the upper panels are carefully retouched using the fine brush.
5. The last two steps are repeated until the appearance of the coach is satisfactory.

Commercial transfers are rarely available for narrow gauge stock, but this need not prevent the model being completed.

For this coach the shaded lettering is designed as a slide in Microsoft Powerpoint (or CAD software could be used), with multiple photographs of the L&B crests added. A background approximating to the livery is provided behind the lettering. By experiment, the image is scaled so that it prints at the required size for the model, for example by printing the slide in 'handout (six slides per page) layout', to obtain a large reduction in size.

The required areas are carefully cut out with fine scissors from a print on thin paper (80g/m^2), as close as possible to the outline of the crest or the letters. These tiny items are held in tweezers and glued in place on the coach sides, and then background colour paint is teased up to the edges of the paper, to disguise them. The result, after varnishing, looks tolerable from viewing distance.

WINDOWS

Strips of 20-thou glazing material are cut to fit in

ROLLING STOCK 139

Marking the position of the window openings on the glazing.

1 Scribe round closed droplights

2 Scribe round lowered droplights

3 Paint droplight frames on scribed lines

4 Glue glazing into bodyshell
Glue glazing behind door vents

each compartment. They fit into the slot between the card inner side and the plastic outer side.

A scriber run lightly round the window openings marks their position on the glazing. Cut-aways in some windows represent part-open droplights. Droplight frames are drawn on the glazing in brown paint with a drawing pen.

The glazing in each compartment is held in place by a spot of glue behind the ventilator at the top of each door.

DOOR HANDLES

Door handles and grab rails are 15-thou brass wire bent round brass rod and strip, filed to the required

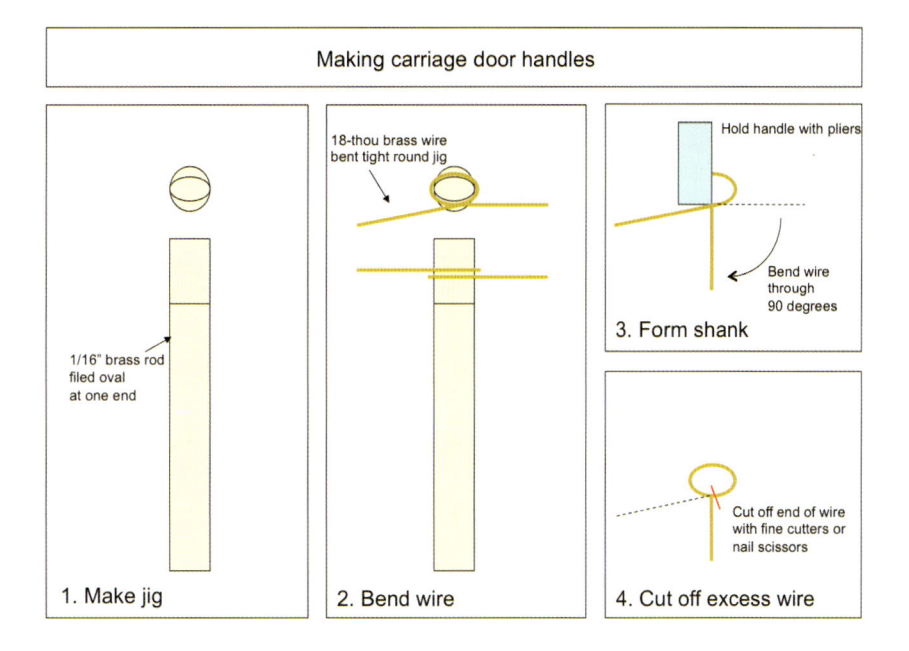

Making carriage door handles

1. Make jig
1/16" brass rod filed oval at one end

2. Bend wire
18-thou brass wire bent tight round jig

3. Form shank
Hold handle with pliers
Bend wire through 90 degrees

4. Cut off excess wire
Cut off end of wire with fine cutters or nail scissors

Making carriage door handles.

140 ROLLING STOCK

Making carriage door handrails.

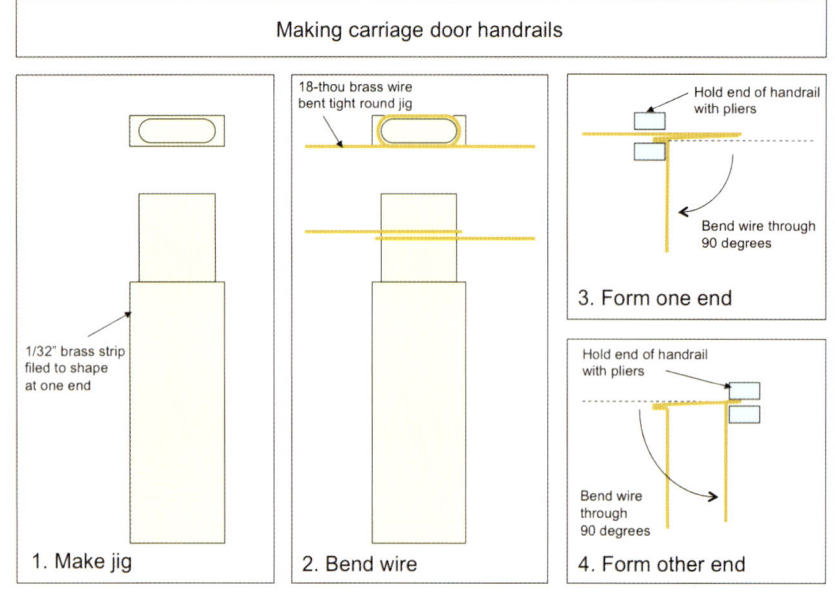

Making carriage door handrails.

Door handles and grab rails.

shapes. The ends of the wire are then cut and bent to shape, and the items are glued into holes drilled in the coach sides.

ROOF

Two oversize pieces of 20-thou styrene are shaped to the correct radius using a wooden former. The plastic is placed on this former, covered in a piece of scrap card, and bound as tightly as possible using many turns of string. The whole thing is then placed (curved side up) on the shelf in a pre-heated oven at Gas Mark 3 (350°F, 175°C) for about five minutes, by which time it should have become nearly too hot to hold comfortably.

On removal from the oven it is left to cool down completely before the string is removed. The resulting plastic remains curved to the correct radius for the coach roof.

The two layers of plastic are then cut to size, the upper one slightly larger than the lower one,

ROLLING STOCK | 141

The coach with the ends panelled, together with the curved roof layers.

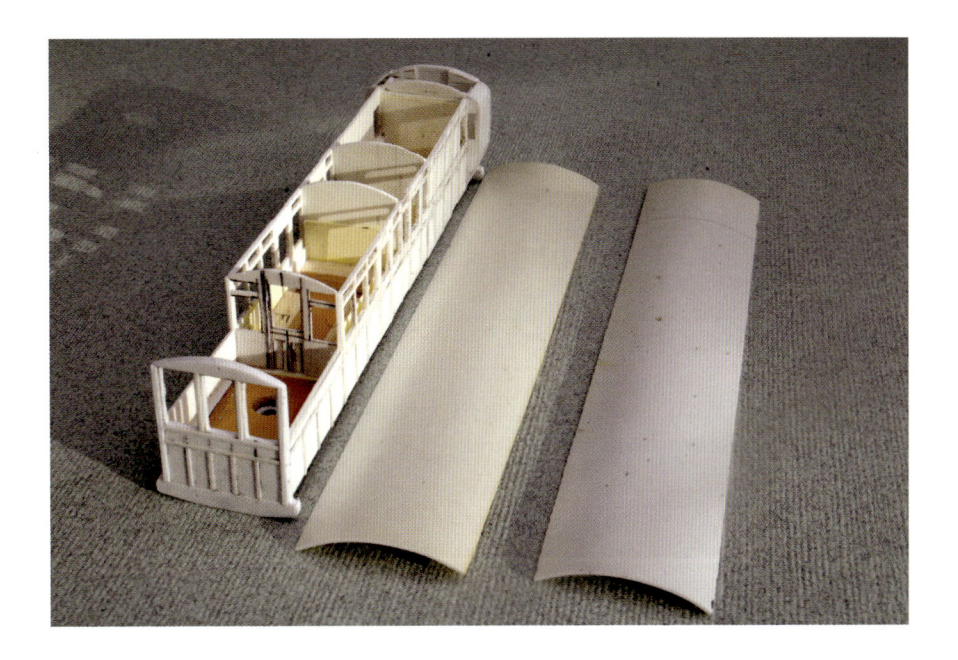

so that together they represent the moulding along the roof sides and ends. The roof is attached by a tongue under one end of the roof engaging with a plastic strip inside the observation end, and by the two handrails at the other end.

UNDERFRAME DETAILS

The underframe stays, footboards, vacuum pipes and handrails are bent and soldered from brass or nickel silver wire and brass strip.

Running trials round the curves on the layout will reveal any problems with the coach. Sometimes, areas of the wooden floor need to be carefully ground away with a small spherical cutter in a mini-drill, to ensure freedom of movement for the wheels and bogies.

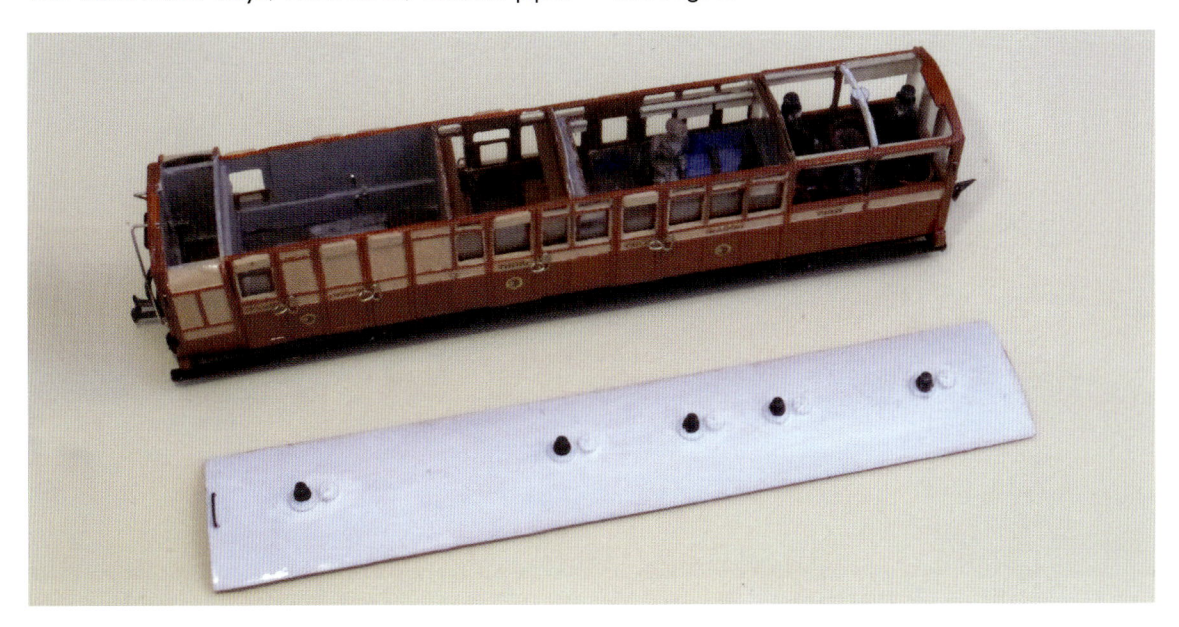

The finished coach, with its roof removed to show interior details, including Langley Victorian figures.

CHAPTER EIGHT

OPERATION, CONTROL AND SIGNALLING

PROTOTYPE OPERATION

The operation of the original line should be studied before building a prototypical model layout.

TIMETABLES

Study of public timetables can show the various services that ran on a passenger line, including the origin and destination of each service, and the crossing points of Up and Down trains on the single track that is usual on narrow gauge lines.

Some narrow gauge lines just operated trains when necessary rather than running to a set timetable, so little information is available apart from descriptions in books.

TRAIN FORMATIONS

Study of photographs can show the usual composition of trains at different times of day and different months of the year. Historically, UK trains carried a guard, who had safety responsibilities. As a result, every passenger train needs a coach with a guard's

Signals add to the atmosphere of a layout. Lyn gets the signal to pass over the level crossings on the way to Pilton.

OPERATION, CONTROL AND SIGNALLING 143

TOP: *A surviving working timetable can also indicate freight workings, light engine movements and empty carriage stock workings.*

BOTTOM: *Timetables can be visualized as a 'train graph', showing train position along the line versus the time of day. In this imaginary example, a freight train (blue) runs between scheduled passenger/mixed trains (red and green), and it may delay them if it is late.*

compartment (usually associated with a luggage area), and every freight train needs a guard's van. Different practices may exist overseas, or on industrial systems.

If offered by the railway company, all passenger trains need 1st class accommodation.

A variable passenger flow – for example with holiday traffic, market days, fairs – sometimes results in the provision of spare stock positioned at convenient locations, to increase train capacity at short notice.

When planning a layout, the possible train formations to be operated should be identified.

FREIGHT TRAINS

It is useful to understand the predominant freight traffic flow on a line. A mineral line will have a significant flow of loaded wagons from the quarry or mine to the port or transhipment siding for transfer on to main-line trains, and a corresponding flow of empty wagons back.

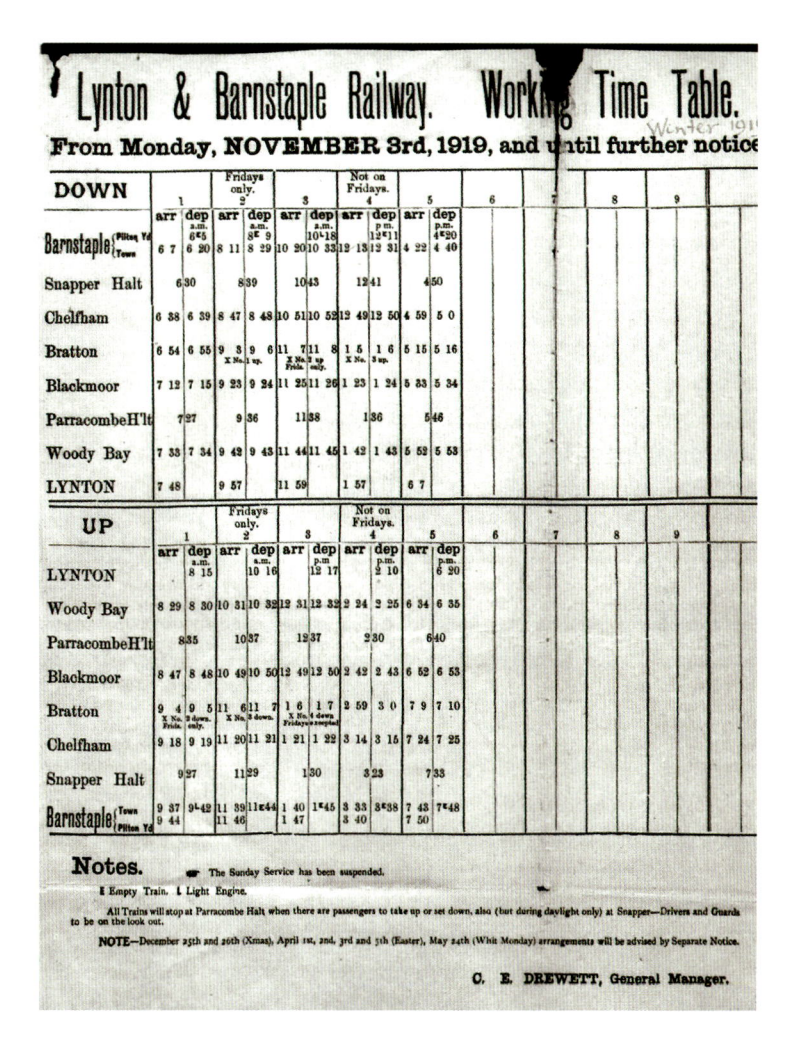

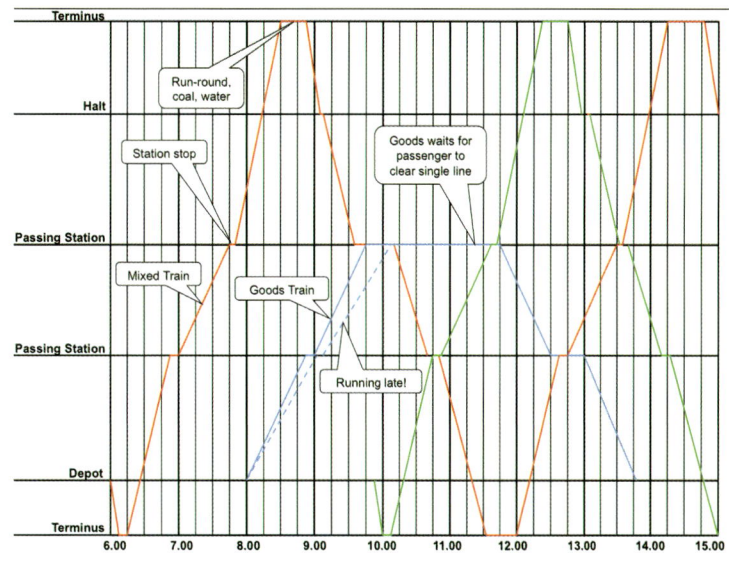

A rural branch line is more difficult to categorize. It may have been built to allow farmers to get their produce – cattle, grain, vegetables – to market in nearby towns, or to keep the rural area supplied with fuel, farm machinery and raw materials – coal, oil, building materials – from the town. Or it may well have fulfilled both purposes.

A coal merchant at a station will need wagonloads of coal from time to time. A goods shed at a station will be used to tranship vanloads of packages and perhaps open wagons carrying packing cases. Smaller packages will be carried in the luggage compartment adjacent to the guard on passenger trains, and unloaded on to trolleys on the platform during station stops.

MIXED TRAINS

Standard gauge lines generally ran separate passenger and freight services. However, on narrow gauge lines, the running of mixed trains, with both passenger coaches and freight vehicles in the same train, was more common, and adds an extra level of interest to the operation of a model. Mixed trains may have dropped off or picked up wagons at intermediate stations or sidings along the line, and this makes an interesting feature on a 009 model.

It is difficult to know how sidings were serviced by trains. It may well be that empty wagons were delivered to transfer sidings at termini by early morning services for loading or unloading during the working day, and collected empty again in the early evening. A similar pattern may have existed for wagonload deliveries to individual sidings along the line.

There are two distinct types of mixed train: partially braked trains and fully braked trains.

Partially braked trains: Lines such as the Welshpool & Llanfair had vacuum-braked passenger coaches, but freight vehicles had only hand-operated brakes. This means that freight vehicles must always be to the rear of the passenger vehicles, and that the last vehicle in the train must always be a brake van, with a guard to apply the brakes when required. It also means that trains may have to stop before steep down gradients to apply the brakes on some or all of the freight wagons, and at the bottom of the gradient to release the brakes again.

Fully braked trains: Lines such as the Lynton & Barnstaple or Leek & Manifold were provided from the outset with vacuum-braked passenger and freight stock. This meant that mixed trains could be of any formation, and required no goods brake van.

WAYS OF SHUNTING

Descriptions in books, and photographs of a line,

Shunting wagons into the siding at Woody Bay. W.J. SMALE

may indicate how shunting movements were carried out, although photographs are rare.

The shunting of mixed trains must be understood, as it affects (or is affected by) the location of sidings at each station, and the formation of mixed trains. Shunting of wagons at intermediate stations may involve using the train engine, although hand-shunting was sometimes employed (two men could push a narrow gauge wagon into or out of a siding).

The Leek & Manifold used transporter wagons to carry loaded standard gauge wagons to goods yards along the narrow gauge branch. This practice was (and is) more common in mainland Europe.

VISUALIZING THE MODEL LAYOUT

After studying these topics, a sequence of operations can be drawn up for the model, for example as a table. Columns represent each station or siding, and rows indicate the steps needed to move the trains around according to the timetable.

Armed with this table, draw out a reduced-scale plan of a proposed layout, and move scale-length pieces of paper representing engines, coaches and wagons around the layout to see how the various moves will be made, and to check available track length in sidings and loops.

Particularly when mixed trains are involved, it may be that the entire train must be shunted out of the station, and back in again, to allow freight vehicles to be shunted into sidings. This type of constraint on the layout may not be immediately apparent at the planning stage, and may require a significant length of plain track to be provided between stations, if the shunting train is not to enter the next station.

HOW BEST TO CONTROL YOUR MODEL?

Different modellers will want to operate their layouts in different ways: some will build a continuous layout, and will enjoy watching a succession of trains moving through the model landscape; others will be much more interested in shunting and making up trains.

STYLES OF OPERATION

There are three styles of operation: basic, automated and prototypical.

Basic: This style has the minimum of controls to allow the required operations, with individually operated points and signals. It is perfectly functional, and satisfies most modellers, and suits the simple track layouts usual on narrow gauge lines. The wiring involves little more than power to the rails and section switches.

Automated: Complex routes are set up according to a pre-defined programme, where trains start, run and stop without operator intervention. This style is good for large exhibition layouts, however it requires specialist electronics/software knowledge, or professional assistance, and is difficult (and potentially costly) to achieve.

Prototypical: Points and signals are operated in a realistic way (for example from lever frames). This style is satisfying for modellers with an interest in prototype railway operation, and it forms an extra attraction at exhibitions, but it is more work to build.

KEEP THINGS SIMPLE

Every modeller wants to be able to switch on a layout whenever time allows, and see trains running straight away. This is a necessity when exhibiting a layout, but it also applies at home. Reliability is therefore an important issue in layout design, and the easiest way to ensure this is to keep everything as simple as possible, thereby minimizing the number of opportunities for things to go wrong.

Thus, ideas of including fancy automated features should be considered very critically, to assess whether their benefits are outweighed by the task of maintaining them over the life of the layout.

DC AND DCC

There are two commonly used approaches for controlling 009 layouts: DC and DCC. In addition, radio control of locomotives is becoming possible.

DC

Traditional DC (direct current) operation applies variable 0–12V DC of either polarity to the running rails. The locomotives have DC motors connected directly to their power pickups, and a locomotive can only be prevented from moving by isolating the section of track where it is standing, usually by means of a switch on a control panel.

DC control is simple and well understood. However, it is not possible to run one locomotive independently of another on the same track, without isolating the track section containing one of the locos. For a line with signalled train movements, DC enables most types of operation without problems. But care is needed at the layout planning stage to ensure that sufficient separate track sections are provided to enable all the operations to be achieved.

For example, if a train is to be hauled into a station, and then reversed by a second engine that couples to the rear of the train and hauls it out of the station, an isolated track section is needed to prevent the first engine moving during this operation.

Critics of DC control would cite as a disadvantage the amount of wiring needed to energize all the isolated sections of a large layout. But DC is inherently very reliable, and fault-finding is straightforward provided the modeller keeps good records of the wiring.

CAB CONTROL

Multiple trains can be run on DC layouts to a certain extent. For many years a concept called 'cab control' has been used.

Each electrical track section can be connected to either of two controllers by a single-pole double-throw (SPDT) switch with a centre Off position. So each section can be controlled by controller A, controller B, or neither. Track sections can be reallocated instantly, as operations demand, as the section switches are commonly arranged on a 'mimic' diagram of the track layout.

By this means, one operator can 'drive' a particular train through the entire layout, rather than controlling one station and handing over control to the operator of the next station at an arbitrary boundary.

Cab control panel for a 009 layout. The grey yard area is being controlled locally (switch 'up'), the green Down loop is isolated (switch 'centre') and the blue, yellow and red sections (switches 'down') are allowing another operator to drive a train straight through the Up loop.

DCC

The detailed application of DCC (digital command and control) is not considered here, but a brief comparison is made, to allow readers to decide whether to investigate further.

DCC is based on well-established American standards. It involves feeding around +/−20 volts, digitally coded with command data, to all track sections. Each locomotive has a DCC decoder unit connected between its power pickups and motor. It detects all commands, but applies power to the locomotive only in accordance with commands addressed to it.

The advantages claimed for DCC include more reliable running due to the constant high track voltage, the ability to control lights and sound systems on each locomotive, and to control points, signals and other lineside accessories via the same system.

Proponents of DC control would say that the operator interface for DCC can be unfriendly and non-railwaylike. It requires a long sequence of key strokes on a small keypad in order to select a particular locomotive (using a number allocated to suit the DCC system, which might not necessarily correspond to the number painted on the engine), and the direction and speed to move it (relative to the front of the loco, not to the direction on the layout).

Anyone considering using DCC should seek advice from those with practical experience. Plenty of advice is available on-line, at local model shops and clubs, or through specialist books.

IS DCC SUITABLE FOR 009 MODELS?

A few 009 modellers use DCC successfully, although most continue using DC. The sort of arguments heard for and against DCC can be summarized by the following imaginary debate between two modellers:

Modeller A: I have a large collection of locos, and many of them are very small and it would be difficult to fit decoder chips. I struggle to programme the home TV recorder, so I don't want to use a similar interface for my models. I usually run my layout alone at home, and I couldn't control several moving locos at once. My layout is quite simple, and is already wired for DC. I'll carry on using DC on any future extensions.

Modeller B: I am about to start building a new model of an industrial system, with engines moving all over the place, sometimes several in one siding. I enjoy operating my layout with friends, and I want to add locomotive sound. I hate wiring. I'll use DCC.

RADIO CONTROL

In addition to DC and DCC, a recent development is to use radio control of locomotives, each of which is fitted with a rechargeable battery. This avoids the need for any wiring to the track, but is a specialized subject. Whilst common in garden railway scales, it is in its infancy for 009, and is not considered here.

OPERATOR CONTROLS

POINT OPERATION

There are many options for moving the various points on the layout:

- By hand (this relies on the points having over-centre springing to hold them firmly in position, as Peco products do)
- By rods and cranks from switches or levers at the layout edge
- By 'wire-in-tube' systems from centralized switches or a lever frame
- By solenoid point motors (sometimes fed via a capacitor discharge unit (CDU) to improve operating reliability)
- By slow-motion motors (for example Tortoise, Cobalt, and other older types)

- By servos (as used by model aircraft enthusiasts), via an analogue or digital driver unit

Points need electrical switching to connect the crossing rails positively to the appropriate stock rail, ensuring electrical continuity as trains pass over. Peco points have contacts built in, although the reliability of the electrical switching may degrade over time, as dirt and/or paint collects on the exposed contacts. Scratchbuilt points generally need a separate electrical switch, either within the point motor or operating mechanism, or by fitting a separate switch.

A relay modified with an extended armature, to operate a signal.

Peco Setrack points operated by a solenoid point motor with microswitches under it.

SIGNAL OPERATION

There are several methods for controlling semaphore signals, including:

- By rodding, wire-in-tube, solenoids or servos, just as for points. Signal servo drivers can even be programmed to imitate the 'bounce' of real signal arms on returning to 'danger'
- By levers pulling cords, the signals returning to 'danger' by weights or springs
- By relays with extended armatures

Colour light signals are less common on narrow gauge lines, but can be realized using commercial signals or by building them around small LEDs.

LEVEL CROSSING OPERATION

A gated level crossing makes an attractive feature of a model, particularly if it operates realistically for the passage of each train. Few narrow gauge lines would have remotely operated gates, most being hand-operated by the train crew or a local crossing keeper, and therefore moving sequentially.

The trackbed needed for a narrow gauge line is usually narrower than a public road, so gates that close the road when a train passes will overlap when they are swung across the railway.

Sometimes a narrow gauge line crossing a road just has gates to close off the railway track between trains, a man with a flag stopping any road traffic.

Reproducing sequential gate operation is an interesting project for a model. The possible approaches include mechanically, using a mechanism such as a Geneva drive, which rotates cranks in sequence; and electrically, using a separate point motor or servo for each gate, with electrical circuits operating them sequentially.

When designing the mechanism for level-crossing gates, the effect of faults in the drive should be considered. Trains are disrupted if the gates jam, and a sure means of moving them clear of the railway line will at least allow trains to continue running.

OPERATION, CONTROL AND SIGNALLING 149

A mechanical level-crossing mechanism drives these gates in sequence as a handle is turned.

WIRING AND CONNECTORS

Wiring diagrams are vital when designing a model layout, its control panel and the interconnecting cables. As the design is built and modified throughout its life, these diagrams must be kept up to date. Layouts often have several separable modules, so cables may be needed to make low-voltage connections to each module and/or between modules.

It is desirable to standardize on readily available ranges of industry-standard multipin connectors. Some modellers use DIN or XLR types, which offer limited numbers of pins, while others use D-type connectors, with nine-way, fifteen-way and twenty-five-way options. Even though the voltage is low, power units and control panels (which provide power to the layout) should have female connectors, interconnecting cables should be male to female, and the layout modules should have male connectors. This ensures that no connector has 'live' exposed pins,

Lever-frame and tablet-instrument connectors. DIN cables with crossed-over cores connect identical tablet instruments, XLR connectors carry low-voltage power, and D-type cables connect the units together, and the lever frame to the layout.

which could be short-circuited and cause damage. Each connector on the control panel and the layout itself should be clearly labelled, to ensure that cables are always connected correctly.

Cables should have standardized connectivity – for example Pin 1 to Pin 1, Pin 2 to Pin 2, and so on – unless the specific application requires something different (for example, identically wired units that each send and receive information from the other may need crossed-over pairs of wires). If D-type connectors are used, bought male-to-female cables can be used in most applications. Specialized cables should be clearly labelled, or be of a different type from all others.

WORKING ROUND FAILURES

It is frustrating when a failure occurs on a layout during an operating session, and especially embarrassing at an exhibition, so time should be spent at the design stage considering how trains will be operated following the different types of failure that may randomly occur. Whilst a train can always be worked past a signal stuck at danger, the failure of a critical set of points can completely disrupt train movements, just as on the full-size railway. So, in assessing the form of point control to be used, thought should be given to the following:

- If power-operated points fail to move, can they be moved by hand? Points fitted with solenoid motors probably can, whilst slow-motion motors probably cannot
- As point-operating methods usually incorporate the electrical switching, how will this be provided if a motor or a detection switch fails?

Failed connections to individual layout modules or track sections may be overcome by bridging the connection temporarily using a crocodile-clip lead. However, it may be more complex to work round faults on DCC layouts, so decoders, driving points and signals may need to be plug-connected, for ease of replacement.

A failed locomotive can easily be retired from use until repaired, and replaced with another engine.

PROJECT: OPERATION AND CONTROL OF THE RALEIGH WEIR LAYOUT

STYLE OF OPERATION

Before the opening of the line, operation of L&B contractor's trains and special trains for visitors would have been by procedures, and largely without signalling. So even if a 'prototypical' style of operation is preferred, this does not greatly influence this particular model, and a 'basic' approach to operation is adequate.

TRAIN MOVEMENTS

Several types of train movement are possible on the example layout:

- The L&B shuttle train traverses the scenic section from siding to siding, in the Up or Down direction. The fiddle yard must be completely isolated during these movements
- A contractor's train runs from fiddle yard to fiddle yard via the scenic section, in the Up or Down direction. The departure and/or arrival fiddle yard loops may be occupied by a second train. With both halves of the same loop clear, the train can run continuously around the circuit. An arrangement of staggered insulated track joints stops an entering train mid-siding if the onward route is not available
- A train approaches the worksite from the left, and waits for a contractor's train from the right to enter the siding so that it can pass
- A contractor's train is shunted within the scenic area
- Up to three contractor's locomotives may be housed in the engine shed as required

CONTROLLER

Only one train needs to move at any time, so DCC offers no advantage over DC control, and a single DC controller is sufficient. Because of the small motors, a pure analogue controller (such as a Gaugemaster Model W hand-held unit) is preferred to one with a pulse-width modulated output.

OPERATION, CONTROL AND SIGNALLING

ISOLATION SWITCHES AND POINT CONTROL

Analysis of the operational requirements identifies the need for four main track sections, as follows:

- Scenic section and shuttle siding (left)
- Scenic section, works siding and shuttle siding (right)
- Fiddle yard (left)
- Fiddle yard (right)

The over-centre sprung Peco points for the shuttle sidings and fiddle yard are moved manually, without a lever or motor. If the in-built electrical switches become unreliable over time, separate switches can be added.

The scratchbuilt siding points in the scenic section require a switch to hold the switchblades in position, and to connect the crossing electrically to the appropriate stock rail. A small slide switch is used, and is located at the front edge of the scenic baseboard.

The engine shed has two isolated track sections towards its rear, which are energized using push-buttons mounted adjacent to the siding points switch.

ELECTRICAL SCHEMATIC

The key features of the wiring arrangement are as follows:

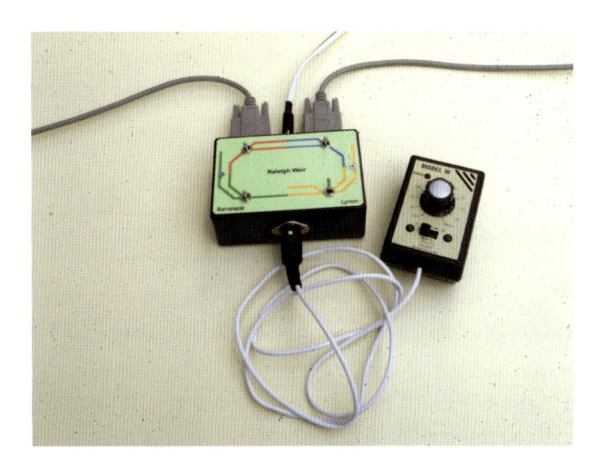

Raleigh Weir switch box with its cables and controller connected.

- Wiring is carried between the switch box and the two end baseboards by nine-way D-type jumper cables. The spare connector pins permit future power operation of the shuttle siding points, if required
- The staggered rail joints in the fiddle yard necessitate both rails being isolated between some track sections. So for standardization, double-pole switches are used for all sections, and are in a small plastic switch box, capable of being used either at the front or the rear of the layout
- The Gaugemaster Model W hand-held controller is plugged into the switch box using a DIN-type connector

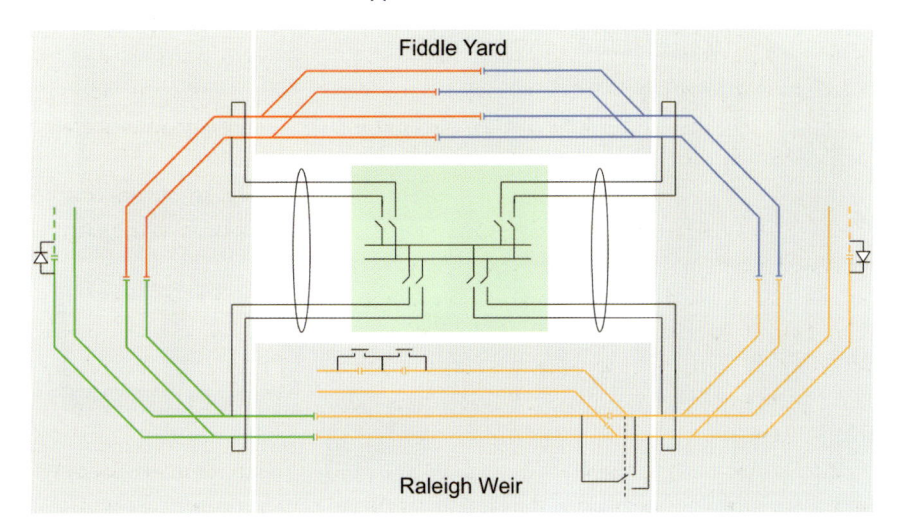

Raleigh Weir layout electrical schematic.

OPERATION, CONTROL AND SIGNALLING

- The shuttle sidings have isolated sections at their ends, each fed via a diode, so that an engine hauling a train into the siding will not hit the buffers, but can be moved out of the siding under power

SIGNALLING

The signalling on many narrow gauge lines was minimal, perhaps consisting of the following:

- Open ground frames controlling the points on the running lines at stations
- No signals, or very limited provision of signals (for example, home signals approaching stations)
- Staff (or staff-and-ticket) working of the single-line sections

Industrial systems would generally have no signalling at all, with 'trailable' points moved by hand levers for facing moves, and trains driven 'on-sight' at low speeds. A few original narrow gauge lines, and many heritage narrow gauge lines, have full signalling, similar to that on standard gauge branch lines, perhaps including:

- Ground frames in huts or lever frames in signal boxes
- Basic signals (for example, home and starter signals at each station, sometimes distant signals approaching stations)
- Electric tablet or train staff systems to allow rescheduling of passing moves on single lines

A PROTOTYPICAL APPROACH

Signals included on a layout should operate realistically, or the overall appearance of the model suffers.

From the earlier work to determine the methods of operation of the line, and a study of the signalling arrangements visible in photographs, a prototypical modeller should first understand how the prototype signalling was operated – the rôles of staff, the types of signalling equipment, and how it was used in working the traffic on the line – and second, should replicate the function of the original signalling in model form.

EXAMPLE: MODEL LYNTON & BARNSTAPLE SIGNALLING

'Knee'-type lever frames were installed in ground frame huts at smaller stations to operate the points (with so-called 'economical' facing point locks) via round tube point rodding, and to operate

1:12 scale MSE lever frame in a ground frame hut, and tablet instruments.

OPERATION, CONTROL AND SIGNALLING

Underside of the baseboard showing slow-motion point motor and signal relay.

PROJECT: LOCKING FOR AN MSE LEVER FRAME

The standard MSE lever frame kit assembles straightforwardly into a seven-lever 'knee'-type frame, with working catch handles on the cast brass levers. Kits can be combined to provide more levers.

Before assembly, the lever castings should be cleaned up, paying special attention to the handle part of the lever. Signalmen take pride in keeping the steel handles shiny – they would use a cloth to pull the levers, to avoid them being corroded by moisture and grease from the hands. To replicate this, the brass is evenly tinned with solder, and polished with wire wool before being varnished.

The locking on full-size lever frames usually prevents incorrect release of the lever catch handles, but models need to lock one lever against another directly, because of the seriously overscale operators using the frame!

lower-quadrant wooden-post semaphore home and starter signals via wires.

Authority to enter each single line section was by means of a 'tablet' issued by a connected pair of Tyer's Electric Train tablet instruments. These were located in the stationmasters' offices at each end of the section, connected by a single overhead pole line with an earth return. An omnibus telephone circuit linked all the stations on the line, and necessitated a second line on the telegraph poles.

Barnstaple Town and Pilton Yard had more conventional signal boxes, containing the lever frame, tablet instruments and telephone.

It is possible to replicate much of this signalling in model form by using the following elements:

- Overscale (roughly 1:12) lever frames from Model Signal Engineering (MSE) kits separate from the layout, with mechanical locking between levers, and switches to actuate the points and signals on the layout itself
- 1:12 scale representations of the Tyer's tablet instruments to enforce a realistic sequence of operation, but without requiring actual tablets to be carried on trains
- Motor-operated points
- Relay-operated signals

The locking tray for this nine-lever frame is made from brass sheet and 6 × 0.75mm brass strip. Each lever operates a slide moving from front to back, and several locking bars run from side to side under the lever slides.

OPERATION, CONTROL AND SIGNALLING

The locking requirements are defined in a table, and then an iterative process is used to define the optimum arrangement of locks that will provide the required functionality. Signalling websites can give guidance on the principles involved. Simply:

- Some points require other points set a particular way before being moved (and lock the other points that way)
- Clearing a signal requires that all points beyond it should be in the correct position (and prevents those points from then being moved)
- Clearing a signal requires that opposing signals should be set at danger (which then prevents those signals being cleared). It may also require signals beyond it to be clear
- Simultaneous entry of Up and Down trains into a passing loop was usually prevented by locking the two home signals against each other

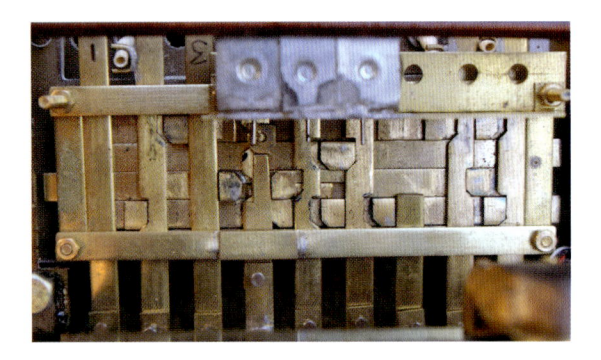

Some levers may need an electrical release (lever lock – see diagram below). For example, starter signals may only be cleared after a tablet has been issued for the single-line section.

PROJECT: REPLICA TABLET INSTRUMENTS

Tyer's tablet instruments allow the signalmen at the ends of a section to signal using bell codes, to offer or accept trains, and to cooperatively press keys to allow the signalman at the offering end to withdraw a tablet from the instrument to give to the train driver. When the train reaches the other end of the section, that signalman receives the tablet from the driver and inserts it into the instrument there, to reset the section to 'Clear'.

The 1:12 scale tablet instruments are operated like this, except that no physical tablet is issued. The instruments are made from wood, and contain switches operated by the keys and levers. The cabinet on which the model instrument stands contains a relay to release the slide when a tablet can be obtained, and a single-stroke bell. The two instruments are each connected via relays to a three-core cable linking the ends.

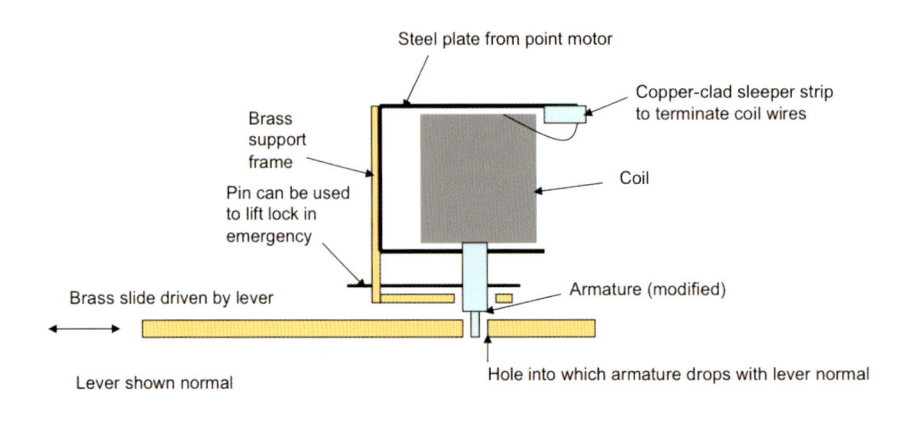

The lever frames have up to six locking bars, 'dogs' on each locking one lever against others by means of bevelled edges working against bevelled slots in the edges of the slides. The 6 × 1.5mm brass dogs are soldered to the locking bars.

A coil from a Peco solenoid point motor is fixed vertically over the relevant slide. The end of the armature is turned down and drops into a hole in the slide when the lever is normal in the frame. A release from the tablet instrument energizes the solenoid, lifting the armature to allow the signal lever to be pulled.

OPERATION, CONTROL AND SIGNALLING | 155

The Barnstaple Town signalman stands beside the Tyer's tablet instrument for the section to Pilton.
R.L. KNIGHT

Obtaining a tablet from a model Tyer's instrument.

4MM/1FT SCALE SIGNALLING ITEMS

To complement the over-scale working signalling items, the 4mm/1ft scale signalling on the layout itself is represented by the following:

- Prototypical model signals
- Models of the ground frame huts and signal boxes, including interior details
- Dummy point rodding along the side of the track from lever frames to points
- Dummy telegraph poles along the side of the track

The interior of Pilton signal box, showing the tablet instruments and the desk with the signal box register...

... and the signalman operating the lever frame.

MODEL SIGNALS

Semaphore signals, lever frames and other signalling equipment (including even the signal boxes themselves) were produced in the nineteenth century by a limited number of suppliers, each having their distinctive 'house style'. Smaller railway companies relied heavily on a preferred supplier, although some larger railways later developed their own designs. So modelling the correct signalling items helps to reinforce the authentic 'look' of a model.

Limited ranges of ready-assembled signals (of types used by the post-grouping main-line companies) intended for 4mm/1ft scale standard gauge lines are commercially available from Hornby, Dapol and P&D Marsh. Plastic kits are available from Ratio. These ranges may be suitable for freelance 009 layouts.

A wide range of specialist etched brass signal components (posts, arms, finials, lamps and other fittings) is produced by Model Signal Engineering (MSE), and the appropriate components can be selected to assemble into a model of a particular prototype.

A prototypical 009 layout should include accurate working models of the correct type of signals, from manufacturers such as Saxby, McKenzie & Holland or Stevens. Study of prototype photographs against the MSE web pages will help when choosing the components.

The appearance of a semaphore signal is determined by a number of attributes, in addition to its height and the layout of brackets (side or cross pieces) to support dolls (small posts, each carrying one or more arms). These attributes usually include the following:

- Post, doll(s) – wood, lattice, rail-built, tubular metal
- Bracket – wood, steel girder
- Arm/spectacle – upper/lower quadrant, metal/wood arm, arm shape, spectacle shape
- Finial – none, ball-and-spike, cruciform, dart
- Lamp – square, round
- Annett's shield (plate rotating with the arm, to blank the lamp from the rear) – yes/no
- Balance weight – size, shape
- Ladder, landing, balance lever – fewer variations

PROJECT: A LATTICE-POST LOWER QUADRANT SIGNAL FROM MSE PARTS

Model Signal Engineering (MSE) supply a comprehensive range of cast whitemetal and etched brass components for 4mm/1ft scale signals. By consulting their website, the most suitable components to suit the particular signal can be selected.

OPERATION, CONTROL AND SIGNALLING

The signal described here is an L&SWR lower quadrant type, for which the following components are required:

- Post — 45ft (13.7m) lattice post S0023 (includes ladder and landing)
- Bracket — N/A
- Arm and spectacle — Stevens & Co. lower quadrant parts S0011
- Finial — Stevens & Co. cruciform SC002
- Lamp — Stevens & Co. signal lamp SC001
- Annett's shield — Yes (included with arm and spectacle)
- Balance weight — LSWR/SR balance weight SC0043

The height of the post must be calculated from a photograph by counting the lattice pattern, or by using the techniques described in Chapter 3.

The MSE lattice post etch contains two main components, each consisting of two connected lattice sides. These are each bent carefully into a right angle using bending bars, and soldered together to form the post. The partly etched folded joints are also coated in solder. The post is then soldered into the base. Check that it is perpendicular.

Various detailed parts are included in MSE etches such as bearings for arms and balance levers. For a working signal, it may be better to make brass bearing plates for the front and back of the post, and use pins as pivots. The etched balance levers are a little thin for working signals, so these may be drilled and filed to shape from the scrap brass around the etches.

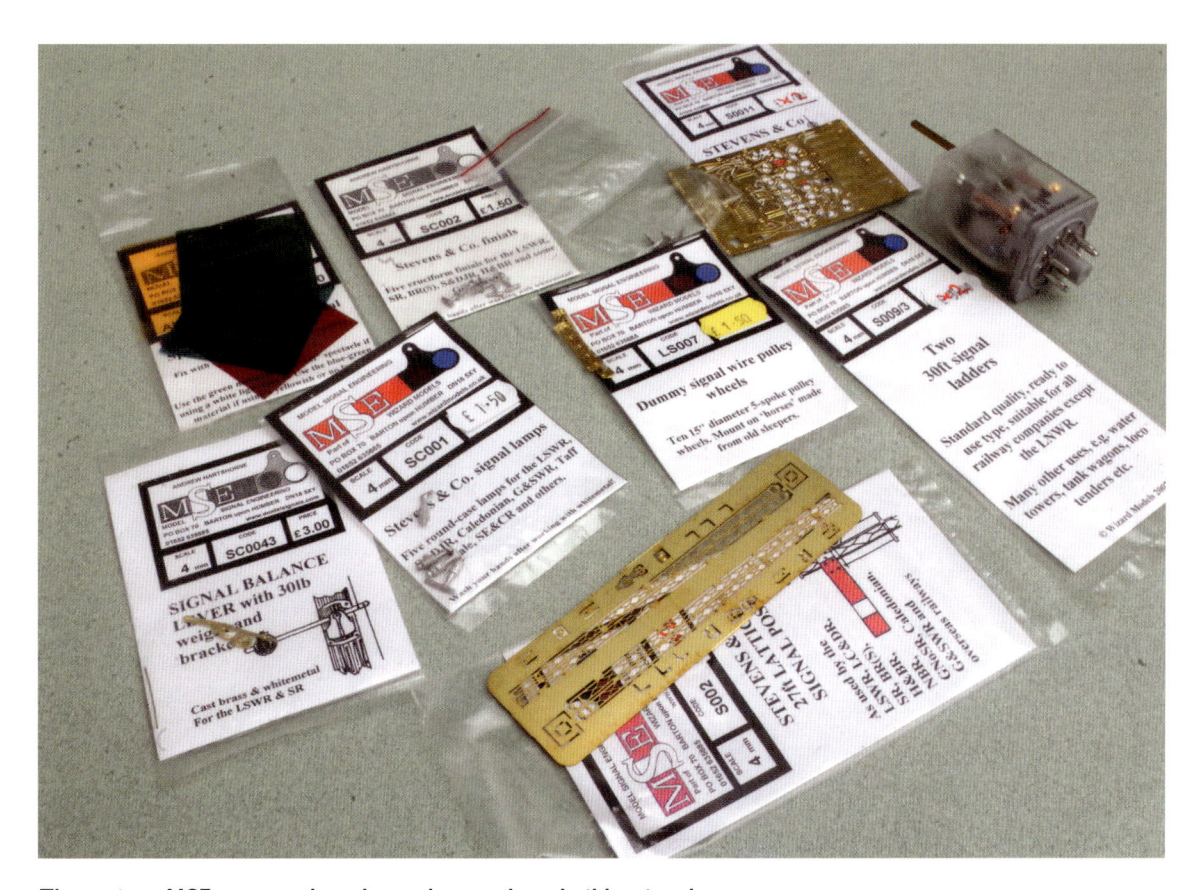

The various MSE parts gathered together ready to build a signal.

158 OPERATION, CONTROL AND SIGNALLING

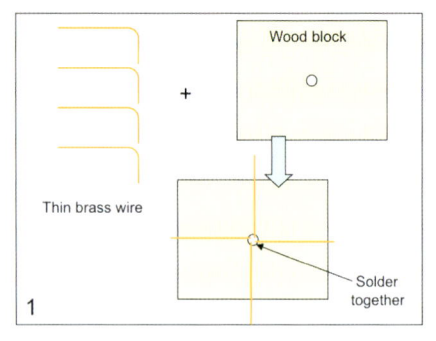

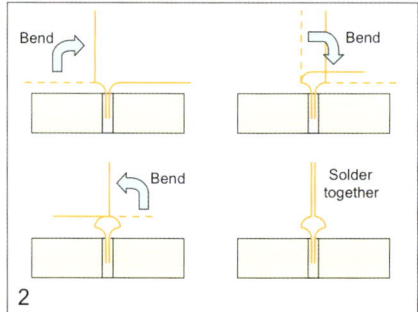

Whitemetal finials are fragile, but finials can be made from thin brass wire. Four pieces of wire are soldered into a cross shape in a wood block, the wires are bent to shape, the tops are soldered together, cut to length, and fixed into the post cap.

Making a cruciform signal finial

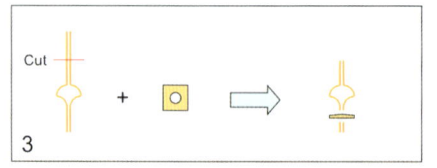

The finished lattice post signal.

DUMMY POINT RODDING

The required lengths of MSE whitemetal rodding stools (S005) are glued in place on the layout, and LMP solder is used to fix round- or square-section straight brass wire of the correct size into each slot in the top of every stool.

The most difficult part is working out the number of rods on each run, and a realistic arrangement of cranks and compensators (from the MSE rodding cranks and pulleys etch S006/1). Clear photographs of the prototype location are the best guide, but signalling websites may also give information on the rules that are applied.

Dummy point rodding between a ground frame and the crossover points it controls.

Making telegraph poles from wire coat hangers

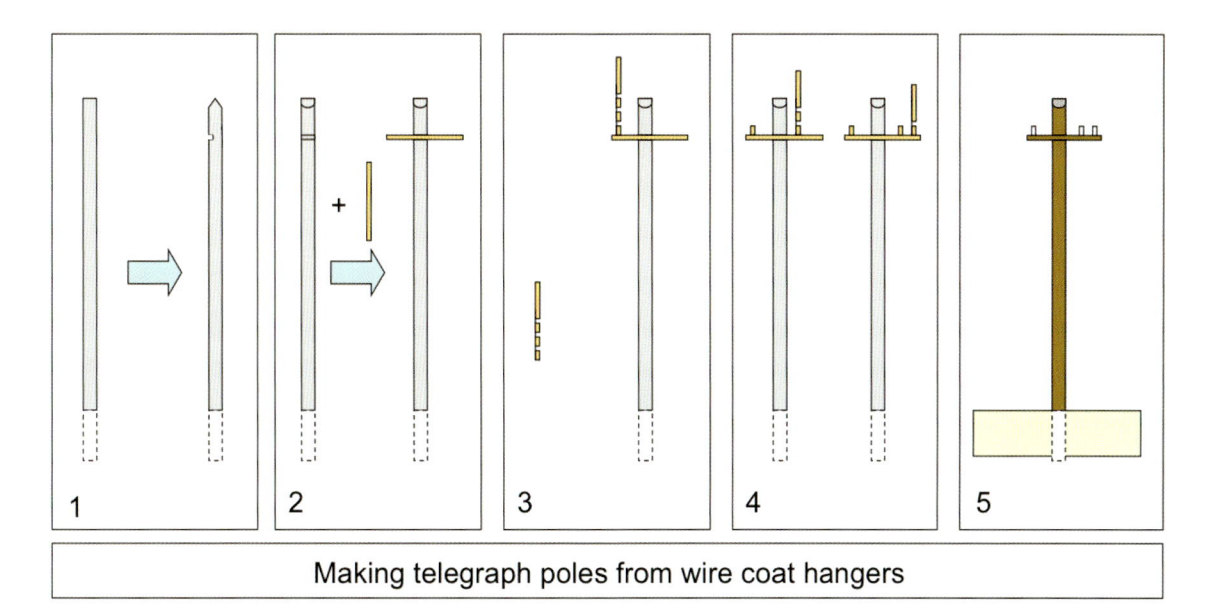

The method for making telegraph poles.

TELEGRAPH POLES

Plastic 4mm/1ft scale telegraph poles are commercially available, but they are easily broken (for instance when cleaning the rails). They also have many rows of insulators, which is unlikely for a narrow gauge line (unless the route was shared with the GPO telephone system). Two wires would be more typical, the pole near the signal box having an extra insulator, to separate the Up and Down block circuits.

Simple robust timber telegraph poles can be modelled using old wire coat-hangers (as provided by dry cleaners), or concrete posts made from square brass bar. They are made in the following sequence:

1. The post is cut to length, the top bevelled to represent the cap keeping moisture from the timber, and a slot is filed across the pole with a needle file.
2. Each crossbar is cut from 1mm square brass bar, and soldered in place in the slot.
3. 1mm lengths are *almost* severed with a piercing saw from the end of some 0.8mm diameter brass rod, and the first is soldered on to the crossbar (quickly, to avoid melting the existing soldered joint) to form an insulator, the remainder being broken off.
4. This process is repeated for each insulator required.

The pole is painted with Humbrol 98, and the insulators picked out in white paint.

The pole is glued into a hole drilled in the baseboard, with the crossbar on the 'Up' side of the pole. The spacing of poles on plain track may need to be reduced to look realistic on the compressed length of a model, but in stations the poles can be placed in the locations seen in photographs.

CHAPTER NINE

MAKING THE MOST OF A 009 LAYOUT

Having had the satisfaction of building a 009 layout and its rolling stock, it is important to continue to enjoy it over a period of years. This chapter considers some of the activities that contribute to that enjoyment.

USING THE LAYOUT

After finishing the initial construction work, time spent running trains on the layout is, of course, essential. This is also a good time to take some photographs of the results of all the work. Some advice on photography is given in the second part of Chapter 10.

The results of a photography session with the Raleigh Weir layout and its rolling stock posed in several situations are presented in the following pages. Photographs such as these provide a record of what has been achieved.

MAINTAINING RUNNING QUALITY

009 is a small scale, and can be susceptible to var-ious impediments to smooth operation. Fortunately, most of the routine issues can be resolved by carrying out a few simple tasks described below.

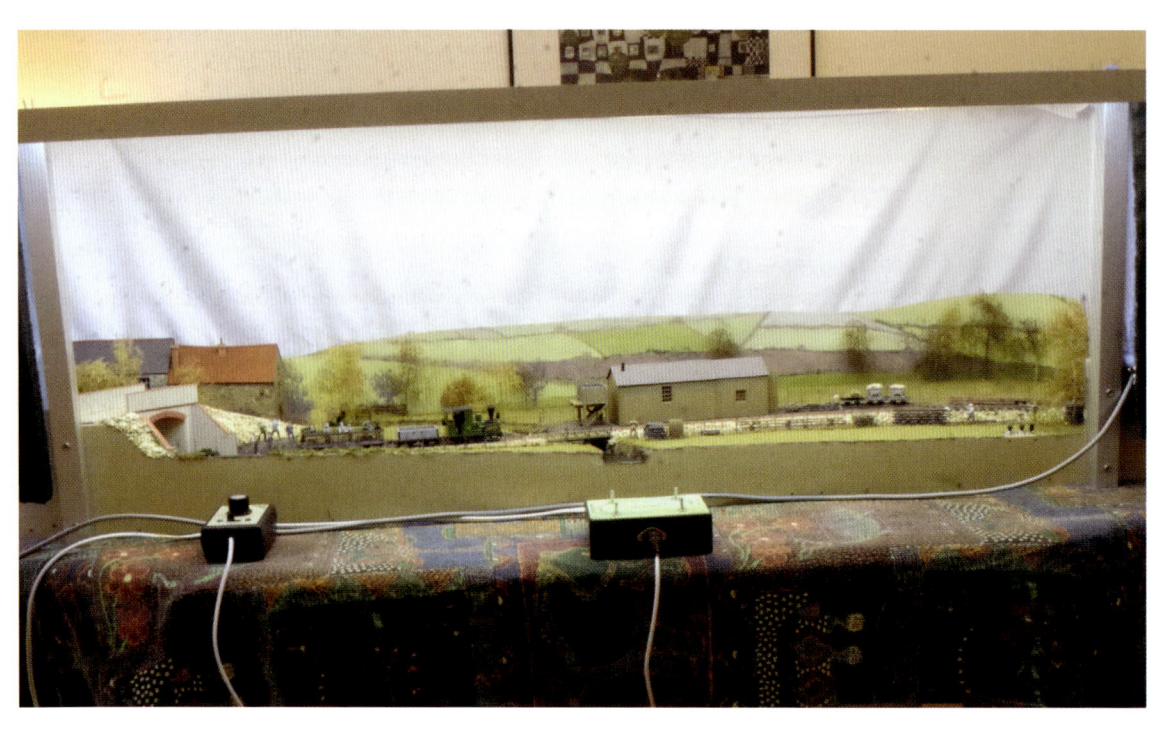

The Raleigh Weir layout is finally in use!

ABOVE: **Excelsior emerges from Bridge 6 with a train carrying local VIPs to inspect progress with the construction work in autumn 1897.**

BELOW: **Taking on coal outside Raleigh Weir shed before a day's work transporting ballast for the newly laid track back towards Barnstaple.**

ABOVE: **Ballasting in progress near Bridge 6. The transverse tippers are being used to good effect here.**

Materials in transit. This works train is carrying new sleepers and lengths of rail, as well as stone for new earthworks further up the line.

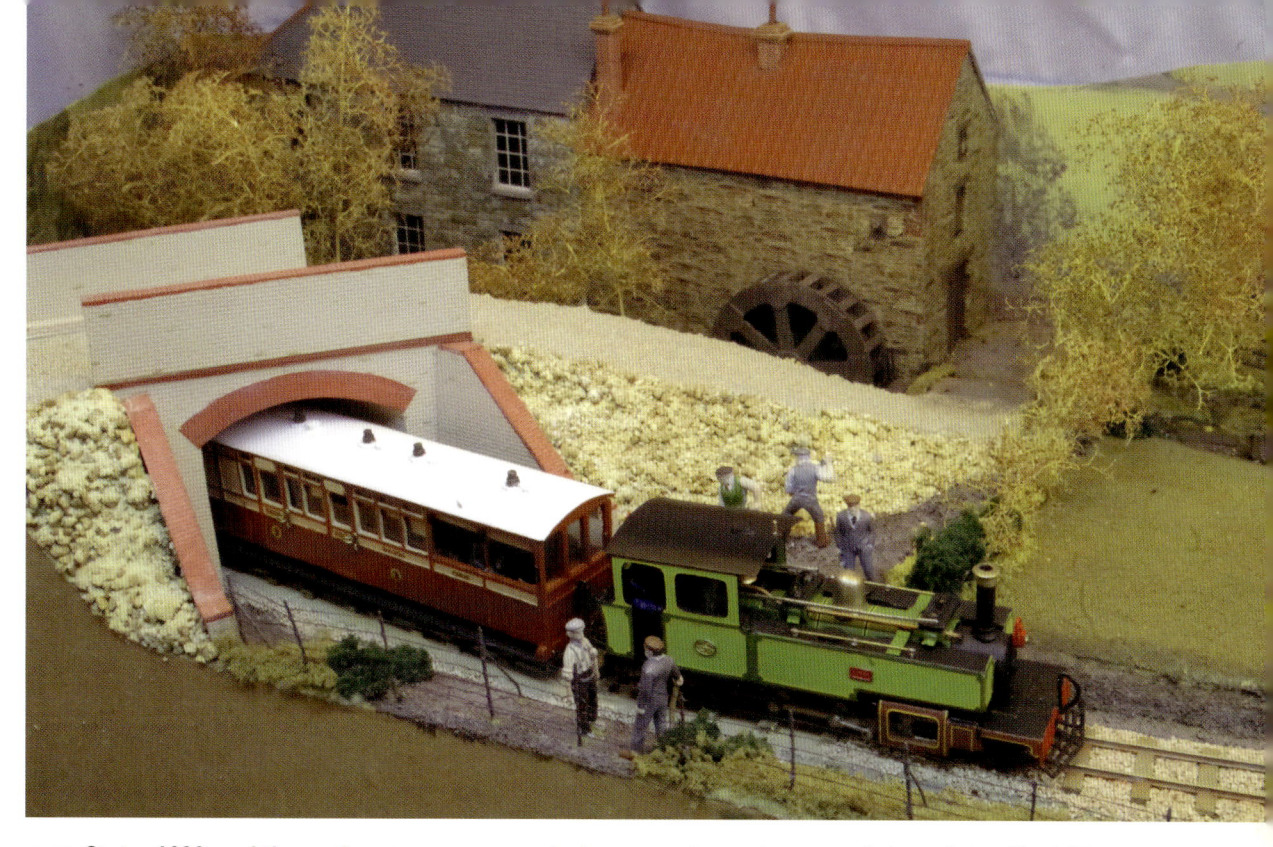

ABOVE: **Spring 1898, and the workers pause as an early demonstration train passes their worksite. The L&B locomotive pictured here is borrowed, so obtaining a loco in the attractive original livery is a priority for the layout's development.**

BELOW: **No known photograph shows the L&B's new locomotives running with the contractor's engines, but it makes an attractive scene.**

ABOVE: **Taw makes a colourful sight as it rumbles over the mill leat bridge hauling Coach 2 carrying the directors of the line. Like the foreman standing proudly by the line, we take pride in our work, and look forward to many years of use for the line.**

LEFT: **A rail-cleaning rubber in use in a narrow location on a 009 layout. Buying or making a holder with a handle could make it easier to clean along narrow gauge track without damaging signals, telegraph poles and trees at the lineside.**

RAIL CLEANING

The surface of the rails gathers dust and dirt with use, and tarnishes over longer periods between operating sessions. Both these effects impede the electrical pickup by locomotives. A periodic clean with a proprietary abrasive track-cleaning rubber is usually all that is required to keep the track in good order. Cutting a standard rubber into two or more sections may make it more suitable for 9mm gauge track.

DUSTING

The layout will, if not covered, gradually gather dust. This dims the colours of structures and scenery, although this may help them to blend to form a realistic landscape. The solution is to cover the layout between operating sessions, with old bed sheets, polythene sheeting, or similar.

Small bits of foliage from trees, bushes and ground cover also become loose and detract from the appearance, and, just like 'leaves on the line' on the full-size railway, can affect the running of trains (e.g. by preventing the closing of point blades). A battery-powered hand-held vacuum cleaner, fitted with a narrow flexible tube and nozzle, will reach into narrow spaces. A small brush dislodges dust from crevices, although holding this really requires a third hand!

LOCOMOTIVE MAINTENANCE

The locomotives are the most costly and complex element of the model, and they also need the most care and attention. When cleaning the wheels or adjusting the power pickups, a sturdy cradle lined with padded foam material is useful to hold the locomotive upside down without risk of damage.

If a locomotive begins running erratically, stopping at rail joints or points, the first thing to check is the effectiveness of its power pickups. If it fails to run well with power applied to the wheels on a particular axle, those wheels need cleaning and/or the power pickups need adjusting. Further tests – for example, applying power to diagonally opposite wheels – can reveal which of the two wheels is at fault.

It may be obvious, as the wheels turn, that their treads are dirty. Running for a short time with the brass bristles in contact with each wheelset in turn may clean them, but it may also be necessary to use a glass-fibre burnishing pencil, or in extreme cases a small screwdriver, to remove stubborn dirt. Driving wheels should be stopped at different angular positions, and the accessible section of the tread cleaned each time, until the entire tread is clean. The treads of non-driven wheels that collect power also need cleaning, and these can be slowly rotated by hand to give access to all parts.

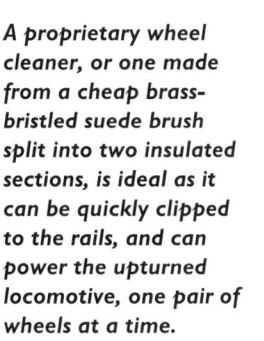

A proprietary wheel cleaner, or one made from a cheap brass-bristled suede brush split into two insulated sections, is ideal as it can be quickly clipped to the rails, and can power the upturned locomotive, one pair of wheels at a time.

Occasionally – such as after a long period of storage – a locomotive may need lubrication. After removing the body, the bearings of the motor and of the intermediate shafts and axles should each have a *tiny* drop of sewing-machine oil applied to them using a fine jeweller's screwdriver, ensuring that the oil runs into the actual bearing. Similarly, tiny amounts of oil should be applied to the bearings on coupling rods and valve gear components.

Gears may be better lubricated by applying a very small amount of Vaseline to the teeth, since the viscosity of this prevents it being immediately thrown clear as the gears rotate.

ROLLING STOCK MAINTENANCE

Rolling stock running on dirty track will gradually accumulate deposits of sticky dirt on the wheel treads. This can be carefully removed. Axle bearings may also need occasional lubrication.

A visual check will quickly reveal a wheel that is not running true on its axle, or a wheelset that has gone out of gauge. These problems can be corrected immediately by replacing the faulty wheelset with a good one, or by removing and adjusting it. This can be done by carefully applying pressure to the part. The 'back-to-back' measurement for 009 wheelsets should be 7.5mm. Problems with the small wheelsets used on 009 stock are often revealed by a particular vehicle wobbling as it runs, or bumping when passing over points.

All items of rolling stock (including locomotives) need the couplings checking from time to time. Fragile 009 couplers can become bent or damaged, which may prevent them coupling and uncoupling readily. This in turn could lead to derailments, and could cause a train to split whilst running. A coupling height gauge is used to ensure that all stock has couplings at the same height above the rail.

RELIABILITY

Derailments, or other faults occurring during operation of a model, inevitably detract from the enjoyment. Therefore operation should be monitored, and issues needing attention identified, so that a good standard of running is maintained.

FAULT LOG

During running sessions, make a note of any problems that do occur. These incidents may be as simple as a particular vehicle becoming uncoupled at a specific location, or a loco that derails or jolts over one set of points.

Even if these faults are not attended to immediately, a pattern may soon emerge, suggesting for example that there is something wrong with one particular wagon or coach, or one location on the track. The use of an on-train video camera (*see* Chapter 10) can provide very clear evidence of bad track joints.

The following could be some typical examples of faults:

- A wagon whose chassis is slightly twisted, and therefore one wheel tends to leave the rail. Stand the wagon on a flat surface (for example a mirror) to check for this
- Several derailments that occur at one track joint between baseboards, suggesting a need to realign the rails and check the level across the joint. A 6in (15cm) steel rule laid along the surface of each rail in turn will reveal bumps or dips
- A set of points that doesn't always move across fully, or a signal that doesn't always clear or return fully to danger, probably needs scenic debris clearing from its moving parts, or a small adjustment of its drive linkage. On scratchbuilt points, the soldered joint between the switchblade and the stretcher can fracture
- More than one train falters when running through a certain set of points, suggesting an issue with power continuity or switching on those points
- A scenic item has broken, or come unstuck, and needs repairing and refixing on the layout

With a list of such items, an occasional session to investigate and rectify each of the problems in turn will greatly improve the experience of running the layout.

ROUTINE REPLACEMENTS

Very few items on a 009 layout need regular replacement. However, if rail joiners are used to link tracks across baseboard joints, after a number of uses they will become slack and cease to conduct the power reliably across the joint. If this happens, they should simply be replaced with new ones, or they may be squeezed very carefully with pliers to improve their grip on the rails. On an exhibition layout, reliability will be improved by linking baseboards with separate power jumper cables.

Over long periods of time, foliage and trees become brittle, and pieces break off them. So every few years make a check of the state of trees, and carry out any remedial work (for example, sticking more foliage material to the tree armature), or decide whether to make and fit a replacement tree.

Accidental damage to vulnerable parts of the layout such as the chimneys of buildings, or small scenic items, is quite likely.

Occasional failures of more complex items must also be anticipated. An example is that point motors can become less effective with time: solenoid types sometimes stick, and the gears on slow-acting types will eventually become worn. All types can have failures of the electrical switches, which are often open changeover contacts and very vulnerable to accidental damage. It is worth keeping one or two spares of such items in stock, so that a quick replacement can be made following a failure. The wiring to slow-action point motors (for example Tortoise, Cobalt) may be terminated in plugs or harnesses, so be sure that all electrical connections are removed and replaced correctly if the motor does need to be exchanged.

In the past, the carbon brushes on DC motors wore out in time, and might have needed replacing. However, unless a locomotive is run for long periods of time (for example on a continuous layout), and quite often (several times per week), this is unlikely to be a great problem for narrow gauge models. Certainly a prototypical end-to-end narrow gauge layout will have locomotives running for a couple of minutes every now and again, and on this basis, brush wear will be minimal.

COMPONENT OBSOLESCENCE

Modellers expect their layouts to last for many years, but in today's fast-moving world, both model and industrial suppliers come and go, and products evolve ever more quickly. This means that from time to time, an issue may arise that seriously hampers our plans. A recent example that impacted 009 modellers was that production of Mashima motors stopped, and these useful items began to disappear from stockists' shelves. A kit-built or scratchbuilt locomotive can in principle be modified to use another type of motor, but this particular issue meant that there was a shortage of motors of suitable size for 009. The difficulty is that model railways are a tiny (and falling) proportion of the total market for such products, and hence have minimal influence over general industry suppliers.

There is no easy solution, and the only advice that can be given is to follow these general rules:

- Choose industry-standard electronic and electrical components (connectors, switches, relays, and so on). These types are well established because they are widely used by many industries, and are offered for sale by several suppliers. It is therefore likely that they will remain available for many years
- Identify any single-source item on which the model is totally reliant, and buy some spares whilst they are available. In the worst case scenario, once an item is no longer available you may have to design and scratchbuild a replacement
- If a ready-to-run model or kit aligns with your plans for a future model, buy it when it first becomes available. Many products are made in small batches by a company or an individual working on his or her own, and repeat batches will only be produced if demand justifies it (and if the supplier continues in business). An item bought in this way will usually be saleable later if it turns out not to be required, and in fact if the

item is no longer commercially available, it may even be sold at a profit!
- Come to terms with the fact that you may sometimes have to scratchbuild an item that you had previously planned to buy off the shelf

DEVELOPMENT PLAN

When running a layout over a period of time, the need for operational or scenic improvements gradually becomes apparent. It is useful to jot these down and think about them for a while, before deciding to tackle them when time permits.

The following are examples of possible improvements:

- A particular tree spoils a good view (and good photographs) of trains running at a certain location, and could usefully be relocated to improve visibility
- The need for an additional track section isolating switch becomes apparent as the layout is used, and patterns of operation are developed. For example, storing several DC-controlled engines in a siding will be difficult unless separate electrical sections are provided
- For freelance layouts, ideas may come to mind for additional features – sidings, platforms, loading bays and so on – that would make operation more rewarding. Prototypical modellers do not have this possibility open to them, but may

The author's portable Chelfham diorama is convertible between the 1910s and the 1930s. Here it is seen in Edwardian guise with trains in pre-grouping livery…

... and here twenty years later. The buildings, platform fences, signs, lamps, telegraph poles and even one tree are exchanged, the resulting appearance suiting rolling stock in Southern Railway livery.

- discover additional information about the location that requires the model to be corrected
- It may become clear that there is insufficient room to shunt the longest train in a particular station
- An idea for an extension to the layout, or a new item of rolling stock, may come to mind
- For a prototypical modeller, an interest in different periods of a line's existence might lead to changing the layout, or one station, to represent a different era

PROJECT – A DEVELOPMENT PLAN FOR THE RALEIGH WEIR LAYOUT

Having constructed the Raleigh Weir layout, several additions are still needed, and these form the basis of a development plan for the layout:

1. Build the contractor's two saddle-tank locomotives, *Slave* and *Kilmarnock*, possibly by scratch-building bodies to fit further Minitrains chassis. These projects will be similar in complexity to the construction of *Excelsior* described in Chapter 6.

2. Acquire an L&B Manning Wardle in original condition and livery – this is needed to haul prototypical trains with Coach No. 2. Three approaches can be considered:

    - Wait (for how long?) until Heljan produce r-t-r models with the original style of cab and the early L&B livery. This appears to require a new cab casting, a new cab front moulding and a modified firebox/bunker moulding
    - Scratchbuild a Backwoods kit with the original cab. However, this involves a lot of work…
    - Replace the cab on an existing Heljan loco with an original-style cab built using parts left over from a Backwoods etched brass kit

3. Periodically maintain the Sea Foam winter

foliage, which is rather brittle, and prone to accidental damage.
4. Carry out further detailing work on the construction areas – however much 'clutter' has been incorporated, there is always room for more.

MAKING CHANGES

Changes may need to be made to the model, such as:

- The type of small improvements identified during day-to-day operation, as described above; these can often be done quickly, and without major planning
- The need to re-lay an unsatisfactory set of points, to improve running. When a task such as this is tackled, the new work must either be carefully matched to the old (the colour of the ballast, for example), or it may be attractive to make a feature of the change, such as posing figures around the new trackwork, reflecting that actual railways do have to renew track periodically
- A general refurbishment of an older layout section, to bring it up to a higher standard and/or to refresh scenery. When doing this, it is a good idea to alter the small scenic details, such as people or road vehicles, so that new photographic possibilities are provided
- Major surgery to baseboards, or the creation of new layout modules, due to the relocation of the layout to a different room, or even to a different house following a house move

The addition of a photographic backscene, adjusted to blend with the scenery on a very narrow baseboard, transformed the author's model of Caffyns Halt.

MAKING THE MOST OF A 009 LAYOUT

SECURITY AND STORAGE

SECURITY OF ROLLING STOCK

The most valuable part of a model railway is usually the collection of locomotives and rolling stock, whether they are bought items or scratchbuilt over many hours. They are also the most portable part of the model.

It is a sensible precaution to pack valuable locomotives, and perhaps also irreplaceable items of rolling stock, away out of sight when the layout is not used for a long period. This reduces the risk of accidental damage, and also of any loss resulting from burglary.

Putting each individual item back into its manufacturer's packaging after every operating session is impractical, so it is easier if a proper system of stock storage boxes is used – and boxes are needed for scratchbuilt items anyway. The solution is to buy or make plastic or wooden boxes, of a size to suit 009 stock.

Stock storage boxes are also essential when taking models to friends' layouts, or when exhibiting a layout.

This box was from a cheap watercolour painting set. Catches hold it closed, and linkable carrying handles provide an extra level of security in transit. When the source of these boxes dried up, further ones were made from stripwood and MDF. The boxes are numbered, and marked to show which way up they should be opened.

The interior is divided by MDF shelves into several longitudinal sections, and all inside surfaces are lined with thin foam plastic sheet (the packaging received with purchases of white goods, or sold as underlay for laminate flooring). Blocks of thicker foam are wedged between shelves, to keep items separate.

SECURITY OF THE LAYOUT

There will be times when a layout cannot be set up for operation, for example before, during and after a house move, or during domestic building or redecorating work. At such times it will pay off to consider at the planning stage of a layout how it will be stored. It is undesirable (and impractical) to have to store large amounts of empty space, so a compact arrangement of the stored layout is important.

Folding layouts may protect themselves when folded, if carefully designed. Otherwise, pairs of baseboards of the same size, each with a rigid backscene, may be screwed or bolted together to form a closed box, with extra protection only needed for the ends with track joints.

For a one-off baseboard, a piece of plywood screwed to the front will provide good protection for the track, buildings and scenery, especially if the layout module is then put in a large plastic bag, or wrapped in polythene sheet.

END OF LIFE

Like anything else, a model railway layout will begin to develop problems over long periods of time (several decades), particularly if many structural changes have been made to it, and there may come a time when its problems seem insuperable. However, that need not be the end of a cherished layout.

The train to Lynton departs from Woody Bay station behind Baldwin 2-4-2T *Lyn* on the author's 009 model. This station has had more than one scenic upgrade and many extra details added during its long life.

It is perfectly possible to build new baseboards, lay new track, and transfer the buildings and structures to the reincarnated layout, benefiting from all the experience gained with the previous version. That is an approach that may appeal to a prototypical modeller, who has invested a lot of time and effort in research and building rolling stock and structures for a particular prototype.

A freelance modeller, on the other hand, may welcome the opportunity to start afresh with a different type of model, once a layout becomes old.

Complete 009 layouts, being relatively compact, are sometimes offered for sale, although the prices obtained will in no way reflect the amount of effort involved in building them. But a good-quality layout may be attractive to another modeller, and the original builder can get satisfaction from knowing that his or her efforts are now giving pleasure to others.

OBTAINING AND GIVING HELP

One of the pleasures of 009 modelling is that, being something of a niche scale, it is populated by a small and generally friendly community of people. That is not to say that everyone agrees about everything, as their interests range over a wide field – but all are willing to offer advice if asked, and equally to ask for help themselves when needed.

009 modellers are fortunate in having a dedicated society catering for their interests – The 009 Society (www.009society.com). This publishes a monthly magazine, 009 News, and organizes local gatherings and area group meetings for members. It also has an on-line forum where it is easy to ask a question, and usually receive a few responses, either offering advice directly, or suggesting someone who might be able to help.

Attending 009 Society gatherings – usually small, informal, one-day exhibitions in local church halls or schools – is a very good way to meet other 009 modellers. Anyone who brings along a locomotive or some rolling stock will probably be invited to run it on one of the layouts present.

In addition to the mainstream model railway press, there are also specialist narrow gauge magazines, including *Narrow Gauge World* (which includes a modelling section in each issue), *Voie Étroite* (a French narrow gauge magazine which is also published in English), and *Narrow Gauge & Industrial Railway Modelling Review* (which features some superb models that are sure to inspire others).

One way to make friends among the 009 community is to post reports on your latest models on a forum such as the 009 forum. To create interest, it is desirable to include photographs, and the next chapter outlines some of the techniques for successfully photographing individual 009 models and complete layouts.

A further step in sharing experiences with others is to write a short article for a magazine, and submit it, along with photographs. Not all submissions will necessarily be chosen, but it is worth trying. Some modellers describe their progress (and setbacks) in an on-line blog, and well-known layouts may have web pages devoted to them.

The ultimate experience with a model layout is to exhibit it at a model railway show. This subject is covered in the following chapter.

CHAPTER TEN

EXHIBITING AND PHOTOGRAPHING A 009 LAYOUT

EXHIBITING A 009 LAYOUT

Taking a layout to an exhibition is not an activity that everyone will decide to do, but it is worth considering. A great advantage of modelling in 009 scale is that a visually and operationally interesting portable layout is eminently possible. The baseboard(s) can be transported on the back seat of the family car, and will stand on a trestle table at the venue, making exhibiting as easy as it can be.

The best way to try exhibiting is to offer to bring a layout to a local show. These are often one-day events, in a local church hall or school. The bigger two-day shows usually plan a long time ahead, and book layouts that have featured in magazines, or have been seen at other shows locally in the recent past.

Before committing to exhibiting a layout, you need to work out the likely cost, and who will pay. A big show at a far-away venue will pay some expenses for an invited layout, but at a small local show you will generally be expected to meet your own costs. These might include:

- Improvements to the layout, such as lighting
- Portable appliance testing (PAT) for any mains-powered equipment to be used. This can be carried out quickly by good electrical retailers, but the cost can be significant if several devices are involved. PAT labels have a validity period shown on them, and the organizers of larger shows require these labels to be currently valid
- Transport costs: 009 is at an advantage over standard gauge and larger scales, as many layouts can be fitted in the family car, and hiring a van may not be necessary. However, the fuel cost must be assessed
- Overnight accommodation: the bigger shows will often book rooms (usually on the basis of shared twin rooms in a budget hotel), but may not pay for evening meals, as they will probably have provided exhibitors with lunch each day
- Costs for helpers: additional operators may incur additional transport and overnight costs

DECIDING HOW TO PRESENT THE LAYOUT

Before seeking an invitation to a show, some thought should be given as to how best to present the model. There are various aspects of this, such as layout configuration, operator position and presentation.

Layout Configuration

Which sections of a layout are to be exhibited? For example, a layout at home might consist of two stations linked by some plain track scenic modules. Are all these modules to be taken to the show, or would one terminus and a fiddle yard be as interesting for visitors and more manageable for the operators?

Operator Position

Some layouts at shows are operated from behind the backscene, either with operators visible or, occasionally, by completely hidden operators. The latter (often big club layouts) seem rather impersonal, and it can be near impossible to find someone to answer questions about the model. 009 layouts, being smaller, usually have a visible operator who will willingly discuss aspects of the model with visitors to the show.

Other layouts have an operator seated at the front corner of the layout, and therefore able to explain

EXHIBITING AND PHOTOGRAPHING A 009 LAYOUT   175

Fallgate on the Ashover Light Railway. Brian Love's model (now owned by Stephen Little and Matthew Barrett) is operated from the rear, allowing discussion between visitors and the exhibitors. The layout fascia and lighting pelmet display information for visitors.
PETER AINLEY

BELOW: *The author's Barnstaple Town is one section of a home layout, temporarily used with a fiddle yard for a 009 Society one-day exhibition. It is operated from the front using the lever frames and hand-held controller. The lighting reuses reconfigurable parts made for a previous show.*

to visitors what is going on, and to answer questions. This arrangement makes it possible to exhibit a domestic layout, which will usually be designed for operation from the front and may include control panels, signalling lever frames and suchlike, which cannot easily be relocated for use at a show.

Presentation

Some additional presentation features are desirable for exhibitions. For prototypical layouts, a brief history of the original line, with some photographs, will enhance the experience for visitors. They may enjoy comparing the historic photographs with the equivalent locations on the model. In addition, some publicity material for the society dedicated to preserving the line may usefully be included.

Builders of freelance lines often invent a history to explain the features of the model, and this can be presented alongside the layout itself. A clear distinction should be made between fact and fiction, to avoid confusing visitors.

Some exhibitors arrange a small quiz or I-Spy competition for visiting families with children – for example: how many dogs can you find? What is the name of the village shop? Can you spot a man asleep on a bench? A few layout builders allow children who have shown an interest to 'pull the lever to clear the signal, so that the train can go', or even to drive a train, under supervision.

This diorama of Chelfham station and viaduct was designed for exhibition, and here is seen as part of the L&B Trust stand at a large local exhibition, with publicity material and merchandise about the L&B displayed alongside the 009 layout.

Quirky items hold the visitors' interest. This horse tram would entertain children, who would delight in pointing out that the horse runs on wheels!

SEEKING AN INVITATION

In order to gain an invitation to a show, describe the layout in a document that is suitable to 'sell' it to show organizers. You might include the following information:

- A layout plan drawn on the computer, such as would be published in a magazine article
- A few photographs of the layout
- A short description, mentioning the period portrayed by the model, the type of traffic, and the way the layout will be presented to show visitors – for example operator position, built-in lighting, loco sound, displays about the prototype
- Clearly state the number of operators you will need at the show. Operating at a busy show is quite hard work, and regular relaxation breaks are essential. Organizers expect trains to be running continuously throughout the day (typically 10.00 to 17.00), so even for a small layout a spare person is required to enable others to take regular breaks
- Details of any previous appearances of the layout (or the builder's earlier layouts) at shows, and of any magazine articles published
- A dimensioned plan of the whole area needed to accommodate the layout, showing the shape of the layout itself, and the operator position(s) where operator access is required (for example front, rear, and access from front to rear at one end)
- The layout height – not more than 1m (3ft) above the floor is preferable, in order to be

visible to children and those in wheelchairs and on mobility scooters
- A list of items required from the organizers; for example, 009 layouts are often placed on tables (folding tables in halls are commonly 1.8 × 0.6 or 0.75m (6ft × 2ft or 2ft 6in) in size, sometimes a little larger)

Consulting the websites of local model railway clubs can reveal the planned dates of future exhibitions, and will give contact details for the exhibition manager. Larger shows are planned two or even three years ahead, but a smaller show may be able to accommodate a small layout at its next event.

PLANNING

If invited to attend a show, good preparation is needed to make sure that nothing essential is forgotten. It is therefore a good idea to assemble the following:

A drawing of mains power distribution arrangements, and a list of mains cables and extension leads needed. You may be expected to provide a plug-in residual current device (RCD) for your connection to the venue's mains power, to ensure that no electrical fault in your equipment can affect the power supplies within the building.

A drawing of all low-voltage cabling, power units, control panels, and so on. Plug-coupled cables and jumpers are preferable for speed of assembly and reliability.

A plan of work to be undertaken in preparation for the show. For example:

- Layout improvements (such as repair of any damaged items, correction of any inaccuracies revealed since original construction, additional detailing)
- Layout maintenance (checking of cables, track joints)
- Layout presentation (lighting, signage)

A checklist of items to take to the show:

- Layout modules (packed for protection in transit)
- Supports (unless table tops are to be used). Standard venue tables, at around 0.75m (2ft 6in) high, can be a little low for optimum viewing by visitors, particularly if in-built lighting presumes a particular viewing angle. A solution is to make and include some substantial wooden blocks, to raise the layout above the table top, bringing it to (say) 0.9m (3ft) in height
- Lighting, if not already designed as part of the layout itself. Lighting should illuminate the layout area, without shining directly into the eyes of visitors or other exhibitors (for example behind the layout). Striplights or LED tape lights are better than spotlight bulbs, as they create more even illumination, and softer shadows
- Table covering, frontal curtains, and any curtains or screens needed to shield 'hidden' areas of the layout from view. Curtains are often required to stop around 15cm (6in) above the ground for fire prevention, and may need to be treated with flame-retardant spray
- Any movable accessories (buildings, road vehicles) that must be packed separately
- Controllers, control panels, power supplies and cables
- Rolling stock (teams of exhibitors have been known to arrive at a distant show, only to find that everyone thought someone else was bringing the rolling stock!)
- Spares (rail joiners, cables, light bulbs, fluorescent tubes)
- Tool kit for assembly and dismantling of the layout, including a selection of packing pieces and wedges, to level up the layout on an uneven floor. A couple of small woodworking clamps should be included, to hold things together in an emergency
- Tool kit for maintaining the layout during operation, including re-railers, track-cleaning rubbers, uncoupling hooks, as well as small hand tools such as pliers, screwdrivers, craft knife, tweezers and glue. A multimeter and some

crocodile-clip leads may prove useful in the event of an electrical fault

The checklist should identify which items will be packed in which box, and all the boxes should be clearly labelled.

REHEARSAL

The planned layout configuration should be set up at home some time before the show, to enable it to be operated as though at the show. Helpers should be instructed in the methods of operation, and in the little quirks of the layout that only you know about. If appropriate, the preferred sequence of operation should be clearly defined, so that operators get into a routine that will be easy to follow under exhibition pressure.

Update the checklist (described above) throughout this process, to ensure it is as complete as possible.

Ideally, dismantle the layout after this rehearsal, collecting together all the items you have used in the rehearsal into their labelled boxes. The night before a show is not the time to be worrying about what is missing!

AT THE SHOW

A bigger show on Saturday and Sunday will usually have a period for set-up of layouts on the Friday afternoon/evening. For a complex layout it is good to complete the assembly to the stage where a train has run round the layout before you depart on the Friday, even if some details are still to be completed the following morning. However, a self-contained

Packed up and ready to go! The author's Chelfham diorama and fiddle yards are in the large box, the lever frame and tablet instruments are in the smaller wooden box, the bags contain the curtains, power units, control panel, removable buildings, signs and so on, and the tools are in the tool box. We just need to remember the rolling stock boxes…

Many visitors at exhibitions enjoy studying a convincing 'cameo' within a layout. The publication of a previously unknown photograph of Lynton goods yard allowed this scene to be recreated.

009 layout may be simple enough to be set up on the Saturday morning, and the smaller one-day narrow gauge shows may expect exhibitors to set up early on the day itself.

Organizers usually ask that layouts are fully set up by (say) 09.30, ready for a 10.00 opening. In any event, some contingency time for fault-finding should be allowed, in case nothing moves the first time it is switched on.

Certain times of day can be very busy at shows, and it is a good idea to ensure that operators get a break every hour or so, to get a cup of tea or coffee, to walk around, and to view other layouts.

PHOTOGRAPHY OF 009 MODELS

Many modellers spend a lot of time building a layout, and then never photograph their achievements. This section shows some of the possibilities that photography can offer. With digital photography, results can be inspected immediately, and shots may be repeated until satisfactory results are obtained. Digital post-processing of the images may help non-specialists to achieve good results.

PHOTOGRAPHY AS A TOOL IN MODELLING

Close-up photographs of models are notorious for revealing blemishes and 'non-prototypical' or 'out-of-scale' details. This effect can be turned to the modeller's advantage when detailing a model or a layout. Also, by taking pictures at each step of detailing, the effect can be critically assessed, and the standard of work can be improved where necessary. For this purpose, the technical quality of the pictures is of secondary importance to convenience,

Model layouts inevitably omit most of the 'plain track' between stations, so it is a good idea to photograph trains in such locations as are modelled. Here, **Lew** *hauls a train up the 1-in-50 gradient approaching Woody Bay station.*

as pictures of partially completed models will be of little interest once construction has progressed to the next stage (unless their construction is to be described for a magazine article or book).

A compact 'point-and-click' digital camera or a smartphone can be inserted among the structures on a layout, and can give a useful eye-level view of the scene without worrying about camera settings and lighting. These devices generally have quite wide-angle lenses, which are an advantage since they give a good depth of field. Using such devices, the layout can be seen from angles not possible during normal viewing, and can therefore provide an extra level of satisfaction with the results of the builder's hard work.

A particular use of photography is to check the lighting of a layout and its backscene. The eye tends to correct imbalances in illumination levels, but the camera does not, so a quick shot will reveal whether the backscene is too bright compared to the scenic part of the layout, and will also show whether the foreground of the scene is adequately lit – always a difficult aspect of a model.

PHOTOGRAPHY OF THE FINISHED LAYOUT

It can be very satisfying to obtain a set of good-quality pictures of a 'finished' layout, and such photographs are essential if submitting an article to a magazine, or offering the layout for an exhibition.

Publishers will usually seek photographs of at least 300dpi resolution. This means that the minimum size of image that will do full justice to a model is around 3,000 × 2,000 pixels. Almost any digital camera used at maximum resolution will produce more than adequate images, even allowing

Although of poor quality compared to a posed image, this sort of shot taken on a phone whilst working allows detailing (in this case the wire fence) to be checked from various angles.

for some cropping later. However, be sure always to save JPEG files at high resolution, and to avoid resizing images (for example, when attaching them to an email).

The key points for such photography are summarized below.

Cleanliness

Dust on the layout and on rolling stock spoils photographs, so be careful to clean everything visible within the shot. All rolling stock should be brushed over with a soft brush after setting up on the layout. A particular problem can be fragments of foliage becoming detached from trees and hedgerows and giving the effect of tumbleweed on the track.

Composition

Great care is needed in setting up each photograph, including double-checking that all wheels of rolling stock are on the rails, and all couplings connected. When taking a series of shots, move the train slightly under power between shots so that driving cranks and valve gear are seen in different positions.

Trains need to be positioned so that they are visible to the camera, and that crucial parts are not obscured by trees or telegraph poles (certain scenic details may need to be repositioned slightly to facilitate this). Avoid strong verticals such as telegraph poles at the extreme edges of the scene, as the resulting shots may cause these to appear distorted or leaning.

This photograph makes an interesting composition, but a shot from such an angle can reveal that the background is a flat backscene. PETER AINLEY

184 EXHIBITING AND PHOTOGRAPHING A 009 LAYOUT

Bear in mind that the backscene is inevitably best viewed from a limited range of angles, and may not look effective if viewed along its length from one end.

Lighting

Good lighting is needed for successful photography. If the layout has built-in lighting, this should be used; otherwise, bright overcast skies outdoors give good illumination without strong shadows. Photography in bright sunshine is more difficult.

Indoors, two or more adjustable lights with bright daylight bulbs – such as the anglepoise type – can be positioned to provide a good balance of lighting on the model. A large sheet of white paper placed behind the light can be helpful.

When shots require long exposures, an additional lamp can be waved over the model during the exposure, to soften the shadows.

Camera

A camera that is to be used for serious model photography requires two specific features.

Firstly, it should have a mode that permits the user to define manually the lens aperture (A or AV mode). The smallest possible aperture – for example f29 rather than f4 – is needed for close-up photography, to achieve the best possible depth of field in the shot. Secondly, it should be possible to select manual focus, overriding the autofocus facility. A digital SLR camera is ideal in this respect, though some other cameras may also be suitable.

An example of an effective 'cameo' shot of a detail on a 009 layout. There is little railway interest, but it forms an important part of a portfolio.

Tripod

Use of small apertures means that exposure times are long (up to a second), so a rigid tripod is essential. A further technique to avoid movement of the camera is to use the self-timer feature, to avoid the risk of shaking the camera whilst pressing the shutter.

Focus Stacking

The dramatic professional photographs looking along the track seen in model-railway magazines are produced using so-called 'focus-stacking software'. A series of identically composed pictures is taken with the focus carefully adjusted between successive shots, and the whole series of photographs is combined by the software to create an image that includes the parts of each individual image in sharpest focus. This is a specialized technique, although free software is available for those who wish to experiment with it.

With care, however, perfectly good photographs can be obtained without the use of such techniques, provided that the limitations of depth of focus are borne in mind. For example, the impact of a photograph may be enhanced by reducing the depth of focus to slightly blur the backscene on a layout.

Post-Processing

Importing images to a computer or tablet allows post-processing to be used to improve the results. It is a matter of personal preference, but ideally this should be kept to a minimum. The basics are to optimize the brightness, contrast and colour balance of the scene as necessary, and to consider whether mid-tones need to be lightened slightly (for example, to show up the details on dark areas such as locomotive underframes). Beyond this, extraneous non-railway features unavoidably captured at the edges of shots can be cropped, or bucket-filled with white, and practical features, such as joins between baseboards and backscenes, can be carefully edited out.

Some skilled photographers add smoke and steam effects digitally, but opinions vary as to whether this enhances a photograph or not.

Portfolio

A set of photographs of a layout should include a good mix of scenes, including an overview of a whole area, and close-up 'cameo' shots of small scenes in the model (such as railway and purely scenic). The study of magazine articles will give some ideas.

PHOTOGRAPHS OF 009 LOCOMOTIVES AND ROLLING STOCK

Rolling stock can be set up on a short length of track against a light-coloured cartridge-paper background. This helps to achieve the uncluttered effect seen in studio photographs.

However, the techniques described above can equally well be used to take photographs of individual items of rolling stock – for example, a recently completed locomotive or coach – in operation on the layout, and this may show off the model to better advantage.

VIDEOS OF 009 LAYOUTS

Digital cameras allow interesting video clips to be obtained of 009 layouts. It is simplest to use a camera with an internal memory card (for example SD or micro-SD), as this allows the resulting shots to be imported, viewed and edited on a computer. Video editing software enables a video of the whole line to be assembled from a number of movie clips taken at different locations, perhaps interspersed with some still photographs.

Examples of 009 layouts filmed successfully in this way can be found on YouTube.

Trackside Video

A small video camera or a smartphone can be carefully positioned at the trackside, and used to film passing trains. In addition to the considerations mentioned earlier for still photography, it is clearly necessary to strive for smooth operation of the trains when a video is taken. Working features of the layout such as signals, level crossings and turntables help create an interesting video record of the layout.

Phones and small video cameras (for example, GoPro or Polaroid Cube) often have quite wide-angle lenses, making it difficult to exclude unwanted peripheral clutter from video shots. For example, layout lighting may be seen above the layout, or the operator may appear in shot whilst running the trains.

On-Train Video

A camera small enough to fit under bridges on a 009 layout can be used to create an unusual (if not particularly high quality) record of a layout. As an example, a cheap USB-stick camera can be mounted on a support that fits into an open wagon, and propelled around the layout at a realistic speed by a smooth-running locomotive.

The best approach is to use a camera with a narrow field of view, even though this may necessitate taking separate shots on curves with the camera rotated slightly inwards. The narrower viewing angle minimizes the intrusion of extraneous clutter into the shots. Tests will show the optimum angle for mounting such a camera, but pointing slightly down towards the track usually seems to work best.

A 009 wagon fitted with a narrow field of view USB-stick camera on a swivelling mount.

A video from an on-train camera gives an unusual perspective on a layout, but reveals unnoticed imperfections (loose foliage material needs cleaning from the track here). It is hard to avoid non-railway elements in the field of view (such as the rafters above this loft layout).

APPENDIX

SUPPLIERS OF 009 PRODUCTS

Many of the suppliers referred to by name in this book, along with some other sources for 009 modellers, are listed in this appendix. The suppliers are categorized into large manufacturers (whose products are usually sold via stockists), smaller specialized suppliers who may sell direct or via stockists, and stockists of 009 products from other manufacturers.

The list is not exhaustive, and alternative suppliers and stockists can also be found by searching on-line. New specialists are entering the market all the time (especially in the field of 3D printing), and of course some small suppliers may cease trading due to retirement or ill health.

LARGE MANUFACTURERS OF 009 ITEMS

Products usually sold via stockists

Bachmann (Europe): r-t-r 009 steam locomotives and rolling stock, narrow gauge buildings. Also Liliput H0e diesel locomotives. Also Grafar N gauge r-t-r locomotives and rolling stock, useful as a source of chassis for 009 models. http://www.bachmann.co.uk

Bachmann (USA): r-t-r 009 locomotives and rolling stock as part of a 'Thomas and Friends'

Exe shunting at Lynton station. The locomotive and all the rolling stock in this scene are ready-to-run.

188 SUPPLIERS OF 009 PRODUCTS

range, imported into the UK by specialist dealers (see below).
www.bachmanntrains.com

Heljan: r-t-r 009 steam locomotives.
www.heljan.dk

Kato: Wide range of N gauge products, including powered chassis and bogies that are popular with 009 modellers. Sold via stockists such as Gaugemaster in the UK.
www.katomodels.com/index_e.shtml

Minitrains: r-t-r H0e and 009 steam and diesel locomotives, rolling stock, track systems, controllers.
www.minitrains.eu

Peco: r-t-r 009 coaches and wagons, locomotive body kits, track systems, couplers. Also N gauge wagons whose chassis are widely used for 009 models.
www.peco-uk.com

Roco: r-t-r H0e steam, diesel and electric locomotives, rolling stock, track systems, controllers, couplers.
www.roco.cc/en/home/index.html

Woodland Scenics: Scenic materials. Has a useful YouTube channel of instructional videos about using their products.
www.woodlandscenics.woodlandscenics.com

SPECIALIST MANUFACTURERS OF 009 ITEMS

Products sold direct, or via stockists

009 Society: Sells a small range of 009 rolling stock kits to members, and to non-members via society sales stands at exhibitions. Also offers a 'members' sales' service to dispose of unwanted models to other members.
www.009society.com

A1 Models: Sold via stockists such as Dundas Models.
No website.

ARB Modelcraft: Rolling stock and signal kits.
www.arbmodelcraft.com

CWRailways: 3D-printed locomotive bodies, rolling stock and accessories. Also offers a 3D-print service for customers' own designs.
www.cwrailways.com

Dundas Models: Locomotive body and rolling stock kits. Also a major stockist for other 009 product ranges.
www.dundasmodels.co.uk

Five79: Products sold via Dundas Models.
No website.

Fourdees: r-t-r 3D-printed + etched brass locomotives.
www.fourdees.co.uk

Gem: Products now sold via stockists.
No website.

Golden Arrow: Locomotive body kits, and historical rolling stock kits.
www.goldenarrow.me.uk

Gramodels: Rolling stock kits, sold via stockists.
No website.

Greenwich: Couplings, widely used by 009 modellers.
www.gdngrs.com

Jelly Models: r-t-r H0e locomotives, locomotive and rolling stock kits, track.
www.jellymodels.com

Langley Miniatures: Locomotive body and rolling stock kits, accessories.
www.langley-models.co.uk

SUPPLIERS OF 009 PRODUCTS

The 009 Society sales stand is always popular at shows, and often a bargain may be obtained... MICK THORNTON

Meridian: Locomotive body and rolling stock kits, couplings. Now sold via stockists.
www.meridianmodels.co.uk

Narrow Planet: Locomotive and rolling stock kits, components and accessories from a variety of individual designers. Offers bespoke design and production service for 3D-printed 009 items and for etched brass nameplates.
www.narrowplanet.myshopify.com

N Brass Locos: Locomotive and rolling stock kits, plates and accessories.
www.nbrasslocos.co.uk

N-Drive Productions: 009-powered chassis, rolling stock kits.
www.n-driveproductions.com

Nigel Lawton: Locomotive and rolling stock kits, powered chassis, motors and accessories. Stockist for ranges from some other small suppliers.
www.nigellawton009.com

No Nonsense Kits: Railcar body kits, sold via stockists.
No website.

Old Time Workshop: Transfers, sold via stockists.
No website.

SUPPLIERS OF 009 PRODUCTS

Rodney Stenning: Locomotive body kits sold via Dundas Models.
No website.

Roxey: Locomotive body kits, motors.
www.roxeymouldings.co.uk

R T Models: Locomotive and rolling stock kits, components, couplers.
www.rtmodels.co.uk

Shapeways: Many individual designers market their 009/H0e designs via Shapeways 3D-print bureau. Some may accept commissions to produce bespoke designs.
www.shapeways.com and search for '009' and the specific category or item.

There are too many designers to list; these are examples known to, or used by, the author:

Model Engine Works: Locomotive bodies, rolling stock, accessories.
https://www.shapeways.com/shops/model-engine-works

Robex: Prototypical locomotive bodies, rolling stock, accessories.
https://www.shapeways.com/shops/robex

TB Models: Freelance locomotive bodies, rolling stock, accessories.
www.shapeways.com/shops/tebee

W D Models: WDLR wagon kits, military figures, accessories.
www.wdmodels.com

Paul Windle: Couplers, sold via stockists.
No website.

Worsley Works: Brass etches for diesel loco bodies and a wide range of coaches.
www.worsleyworks.co.uk

STOCKISTS

Dundas Models: Their own range of 009 locomotive and rolling stock kits. Also stockists for most of the large and smaller suppliers listed above, and supplier of N gauge chassis to suit kit-built and 3D-printed locomotive bodies.
www.dundasmodels.co.uk

Most of the big stockists advertising in the model-railway magazines sell 009 items from the large manufacturers, but not necessarily products from the smaller ones.

MATERIALS FOR 009 MODELLERS

C&L Finescale: Nickel silver rail and track components, solder and flux.
www.finescale.org.uk

Direct Train Spares: LED lighting components and power supplies, electrical components.
http://www.directtrainspares-burnley.co.uk/

Eileen's Emporium: Brass and nickel silver sections and sheet, tools.
www.eileensemporium.com

Markits: Wheels, motors and other components for building locomotives.
www.markits.com

Model Signal Engineering: Signal and lever frame kits, signal components.
www.modelsignals.com

009 SUPPLIERS NO LONGER TRADING

Items often seen for sale in on-line auction sites

Backwoods Miniatures: Etched brass locomotive and rolling stock kits.
http://www.backwoodsminiatures.com

INDEX

3D-printed models 85, 86, 96–98

Axe 102–103

backscenes 71–72
ballast 66
baseboards 58–60
  joints 58–59
  lightweight 59–60
  track across joints 59
bogies
  coach 128, 136–137
  wagon 129

changes, making 170
chassis, locomotive
  inside-framed 74, 99, 103
  outside-framed 75–76
  ready-to-run 87, 97, 99, 103
  scratchbuilt 91–94, 124–126
  split-axle 79–80, 117
coaches
  assembly 137–138
  bogies and running gear 128, 136–137
  detailing a Peco coach 128–129
  door handles 139–140
  ends and seats 136–137
  floor 135–136
  guard's duckets 137
  interior detail 129, 138
  panelling 134–135
  roof 140–141
  scratchbuilding 132–141
  sides 132–135
  underframe details 141
  windows 138–139
control
  cab control 146
  DC 146
  DCC 146–147
  radio control 147

coupling rods 92, 93, 125
curve radius, minimum 43, 77, 89, 113, 114, 123, 125
cylinders 92–93, 116, 125

Dennis 98–100
development plan 168
difference between 009 and 00 modelling 26–27
drawings 33–34
  from photographs 54–57
driving cranks 81, 93
dusting 165

electrical wiring 66
end of life 172
engineering practice 28–35
etched brass kits 88–91
Excelsior 104–111
Exe
  body 120–124
  chassis 124–126
exhibiting a 009 layout
  at the show 179–180
  operator position 174–176
  planning 178–179
  presentation 176
  rehearsal 179
  seeking an invitation 177–178

fencing, lineside 72
fiddle yards 48–49
freelance modelling 17–18

gauge, *see* scale and gauge
gears 77–79, 125
Glyn 100–102
ground contours 70–71
  higher ground 71
ground frame

Hancock, Philip 16
Heddon Hall 96–98

Hoyland, Jim 15

kinematic envelope 44–45
kits
  locomotive 87–91
  rolling stock 127

layout configurations 46–50
  cameo 47
  fiddle yards 48–50
  micro 48
layouts
  available space and viewing position 45–46
  development plan 168–170
  freelance 39–41
  modularity 46
  operator position 46
  planning 50–53
  prototype–inspired 37–39
  prototypical 36–37, 41–43
level crossing, *see* operation
lever frame, *see* signalling
lighting 73
livery
  lining 119
  painting 111, 118, 97–98, 138
  ready-to-run 87
locomotives
  curving ability 77
  drive train 79, 89, 113, 125
  gear ratio 77–78
  modelling issues 75–83
  motors 78, 89
  scratchbuilding bodies 94–95
  scratchbuilding chassis 91–94, 124–126
  valve gear 125–126
  weight 95
Lyn 112–120

maintaining running quality
  dusting 165

INDEX

fault log 166
locomotive maintenance 165–166
rail cleaning 165
rolling stock maintenance 166
Mander, David 16
manufacturers of 009 items 187–190

narrow gauge railway, types of
construction projects 25
military 24–25
mineral/freight 23
mixed traffic 23
private industrial 23–24
tourist and heritage 25
UK, continental, colonial 19–23

obtaining and giving help 173
operation, model
cab control 146
DC and DCC 146–147
level crossing operation 148
point operation 147–148, 151
radio control 147
signal operation 148
styles of operation 145, 150
train movements 150
operation, prototype
freight trains 143–144
mixed trains 144
shunting, ways of 144–145
timetables 142–143
train formations 142–143

people 72
photography
as a tool in modelling 180–181
of locomotives and rolling stock 185
of the finished layout 181–185
videos of 009 layouts 185–186
points – see track and points

power pickup
insulated-wheel 80–81
split-axle 79–80, 117
prototype-inspired modelling 37–39
prototypical modelling 36–37

quartering driving cranks 93

rail, scale size 61
ready-to-run locomotives
3D-printed 85
compromises 86
details 86
livery 87
making changes 84–85
manufacturing methods 83
ready-to-run chassis 87
ready-to-run rolling stock 127
reliability 166
replacements, routine 167
researching a prototype 41–43, 68, 109
rolling stock
kits 127
modified ready-to-run 127–131
ready-to-run 127
scratchbuilding 127–128, 132–141

scale and gauge 9–15
09 14
H0e 14–15
H0f 14
origins of 009 scale 15–17
signalling, model
4mm/1ft scale signalling items 155–159
locking for an MSE lever frame 153–154
point rodding, dummy 158
signal box 155–156
signals, model 156–158
telegraph poles 159
sketch
body 33, 101, 103, 106

chassis 33, 123, 125
component 33, 121
skills required for 009 modelling
soldering 31–35
low melting point 34–35
space model
layout 51, 53
locomotive 33
structure 66
security and storage 171–172
stockists of 009 items 190
structure gauge 44–45
structures
engine shed and water tank 68
overbridge 66–67
Raleigh tucking mill 68–69
underbridge 67–68

tablet instruments 154
tools 29–30
track and points
building points 64–66
fixed geometry track 61–62
flexible track 61
scale track 61
scratchbuilding track 62–64
train length, maximum 43–44
trees 71

valve gear 81–82, 125

wagons 127, 129–131
bogie 129–130
four-wheeled 130–131
loads 131
weight, locomotive 81, 95
wheels
coach 128
driving 76
leading and trailing 82–83, 89
whitemetal kits 34–35, 88
glue or solder? 34–35
wiring and connectors 148–150

work, places to 28–29
workshop rules 30–31